Inhuman Nature

Theory, Culture & Society

Theory, Culture & Society caters for the resurgence of interest in culture within contemporary social science and the humanities. Building on the heritage of classical social theory, the book series examines ways in which this tradition has been reshaped by a new generation of theorists. It also publishes theoretically informed analyses of everyday life, popular culture, and new intellectual movements.

EDITOR: Mike Featherstone, *Nottingham Trent University*

SERIES EDITORIAL BOARD
Roy Boyne, *University of Durham*
Mike Featherstone, *Nottingham Trent University*
Nicholas Gane, *University of York*
Scott Lash, *Goldsmiths College, University of London*
Roland Robertson, *University of Aberdeen*
Couze Venn, *Nottingham Trent University*

THE TCS CENTRE
The *Theory, Culture & Society* book series, the journals *Theory, Culture & Society* and *Body & Society*, and related conference, seminar and postgraduate programmes operate from the TCS Centre at Nottingham Trent University. For further details of the TCS Centre's activities please contact:

The TCS Centre
School of Arts and Humanities
Nottingham Trent University
Clifton Lane, Nottingham, NG11 8NS, UK
e-mail: tcs@ntu.ac.uk
web: http://sagepub.net/tcs/

Recent volumes include:

Ordinary People and the Media
Graeme Turner

Peer to Peer and the Music Industry
Matthew David

The Media City
Scott McQuire

The Sociology of Intellectual Life
Steve Fuller

Race, Sport and Politics
Ben Carrington

Inhuman Nature

Sociable Life on a Dynamic Planet

Nigel Clark

Los Angeles | London | New Delhi
Singapore | Washington DC

697776327

SAGE Publications Ltd
1 Oliver's Yard
55 City Road
London EC1Y 1SP

SAGE Publications Inc.
2455 Teller Road
Thousand Oaks, California 91320

SAGE Publications India Pvt Ltd
B 1/I 1 Mohan Cooperative Industrial Area
Mathura Road, Post Bag 7
New Delhi 110 044

SAGE Publications Asia-Pacific Pte Ltd
33 Pekin Street #02–01
Far East Square
Singapore 048763

Library of Congress Control Number: 2010927635

British Library Cataloguing in Publication data

A catalogue record for this book is available from
the British Library

ISBN 978-0-7619-5724-9
ISBN 978-0-7619-5725-6 (pbk)

Typeset by C&M Digitals (P) Ltd, Chennai, India
Printed by the MPG Books Group, Bodmin and King's Lynn
Printed on paper from sustainable resources

'Drawing on an impressive array of philosophical, social, and natural science sources Nigel Clark's magnificent *Inhuman Nature* provides a compelling account of the respects in which modern ways of living are perpetually exposed to unpredictable natural processes and transformations and the manner in which communities have responded with care and hospitality to the desperate plight of others.'
Barry Smart, Professor of Sociology, Portmouth University, UK

'*Inhuman Nature: Sociable Life on a Dynamic Planet* is a watershed for social theory. Nigel Clark's engaging book brings together earth systems science, philosophy, and history to challenge the longstanding impasse created through the philosophical separation of humans from the world. This book does not simply 'take nature into account': fires, floods, volcanoes, climate change, and hurricanes take centre-stage in this thorough re-writing of the organic and inorganic. *Inhuman Nature* asks the most important questions of our time, and is a must-read for anyone who takes nature and our future on this planet seriously.'
Myra Hird, Professor of Sociology, Queen's University, Canada

'This is possibly one of the most important books you are ever likely to read, particularly if you have been duped into thinking 'nature' and 'planet earth' are merely benevolent forces at the mercy of an insane, disordered humanity. According to Clark this just-so story illustrates our twin bad habits of focussing almost exclusively on human powers (exaggerating them wildly) and developing a blindness to the agency and powers of non-humans. This book reveals what the world is like when we come to our senses, literally. You wont look back (the view is better).'
Adrian Franklin, Professor of Sociology, University of Tasmania, Australia

This book is dedicated – with much love and across too many miles – to my parents, Elaine and Derek Clark.

Contents

Acknowledgements

This book began in a different disciplinary home, in another hemisphere, in what is now officially a bygone geological epoch. It started out as a plea for the social sciences to take environmental issues to heart. Only gradually, haltingly, did it become a call for social thought to engage more deeply with the dynamics of the earth itself – an appeal not to allow the problem of our own impact on nature to overshadow the question of what nature can do of its own accord. A number of worldly events contributed, often brutally, to this change of direction. As did a great many conversations, more gently and generously – too many, I'm afraid, to get the gratitude they deserve. My thanks to those whose insights, promptings and invitations nudged me along the way, in no particular order: Myra Hird, Steve Hinchliffe, Doreen Massey, Mustafa Dikeç, Kathryn Yusoff, Nick Bingham, Joe Smith, Clive Barnett, Rosalyn Diprose, Nick Stevenson, Arun Saldanha, Sarah Whatmore, Bruce Braun, Tariq Jazeel, Beth Greenhough, Bron Szerszynski, John Urry, Mike Featherstone, Phil Macnaghten, Divya Tolia-Kelly, Dave Humphreys, Steve Pile, George Revill, Paul Harrison, Angela Last, Uli Beisel, Caitlin DeSilvey, Jenny Robinson, Michael Pryke, Lynn Margulis, Dorion Sagan, Graham Harman, Mark Brandon, Susanne Sargeant, Mike Petterson, Adrian Franklin, Barry Smart, Vicki Kirby, Wallace Heim, Olafur Eliasson Simon Rees, Anthony Krivan, Vicki Kerr, Heather Worth, Claudia Bell, and John Lyall. And for many things, thought provoking and enlivening, Yasmin Gunaratnam and Zac Gunaratnam-Bailey. Thanks to Katherine Haw and Jai Seaman at Sage for guiding me and my somewhat dishevelled manuscript through the various phases of the editorial process, and to Chris Rojek for his encouragement over more years and iterations than he probably cares to recall.

Sections of Chapter 3 have been adapted from `Living through the Tsunami: Vulnerability and Generosity on a Volatile Earth' (2007) *Geoforum*, 38 (6) pp. 1127–39, and parts of Chapter 5 from `Volatile Worlds, Vulnerable Bodies: Confronting Abrupt Climate Change' (2010) *Theory, Culture and Society*, 27 (2–3) pp. 31–53. Smaller fragments were aired in *Space and Culture* (Chapter 6), *The International Journal of Urban and Regional Research* (Chapters 7 and 8) and *Parallax* (Chapter 6).

Introduction

There still remains a difficulty in the combination of freedom with the mechanism of nature in a being belonging to the world of sense: a difficulty which, even after all the foregoing is admitted, threatens freedom with complete destruction. (Kant, 1967 [1788]: 194)

I don't understand why doubters claim and believers deride the idea that it isn't man made. If global warming _isn't_caused by man, doesn't that mean we're even more fucked? (Ivan, post on Boing-boing.net, 4 March 2008)

Ivan's question, everyone's problem

A strange thing happened on the way to the apocalypse. Just as we were beginning to get our heads around the idea that our species is responsible for transforming nature in its entirety, another shock came our way. A truth perhaps even more 'inconvenient' than the one about global climate and the rest of the natural world becoming a human product.

To assess the extent of 'our' transformations of global and local environments, and in order to have a sense of how physical systems might respond to these incursions, we need to have a rough idea of what the earth would be doing in the absence of any anthropogenic influence. This is what has been asked of scientists in regard to the issue of human-induced climate change. There are many ways to assemble a record of past climate, with some of the clearest evidence coming from boring into the sedimented ice of Greenland and other polar regions. Earth scientists have known for a long time about the rhythmic movement in and out of glacial epochs and its significance for environmental conditions across the earth. But in the two-mile deep, 110,000-year-long, ice archive they came across something unexpected.

By analysing the layers of ice, researchers can tell how cold Greenland was in any year. They can gauge the composition of the earth's atmosphere, how much rain fell, wind patterns and the intensity of storms, levels of volcanicity, and even the global extent of wetlands (Alley, 2000: 4). The story the ice told was not the anticipated one of a succession of long slow clamberings in and out of ice ages, not the grinding, inching change we usually associate with the word 'glacial'. What the ice cores showed were the signatures of sudden transformation (see Broecker, 1987; Alley et al., 2003). Each long wave movement in and out of an ice age turned out to be rent by multitudes of rapid warmings and coolings, vicious see-sawings that saw the temperature of Greenland transformed by around 15 degrees Fahrenheit in a decade, and global weather tipped into a completely different state in as little as a few years.

As glaciologist Richard Alley reflects: 'for most of the last 100,000 years, a crazily jumping climate has been the rule, not the exception' (2000: 120). If scientists have it right, this tells us that the reason why global climate is susceptible to being changed by human 'forcings' is because it is inherently unstable: 'The real point is that not only is climate change natural, but it's also easy to set in motion' (Matthew Huber cited in Purdue University, 2006). This shouldn't be taken to imply, as Ivan's post might suggest, that what's happening to the earth's temperature at present can be put down to extrahuman causes. There is now overwhelming evidence that once natural variation has been accounted for, only human impact can explain observed trends in global climate. But in other respects, Ivan's logic is sound. What he is pointing to, with admirable candour, is the broader issue raised by the emergent understanding of climatic volatility. Whatever 'we' do, ice cores and other proxies of past climate profess to us, our planet is capable of taking us by surprise. With or without the destabilizing surcharge of human activities, the conditions most of us take for granted could be taken away, quite suddenly, and with very little warning (Clark, 2010a).

On a crowded, densely settled and heavily worked planet, that's about as inconvenient as it could be. For all their initial surprise, the unfolding trajectories of abrupt and oscillating climate change are in accord with what scientists are learning about a whole range of natural processes. Intricate physical systems have dynamics of their own, and this often includes absorbing pressures or changes of input up to a point then lurching, quickly and unstoppably, into a new state. This in turn folds into a bigger story about the way our planet operates that has been taking shape over the course of five or six decades of intensive research in the earth and life sciences. The vision that has been emerging, through a succession of discoveries, controversies and convergences, is one in which instability and upheaval, rhythmical movement and dramatic changes of state are ordinary aspects of the earth's own history.

In this way, the realization that there are patterns of variance at almost every scale at which we view climate resonates with evidence from most other physical systems on earth and even beyond our planet. If terms like 'capricious' and 'crazily jumping' are suitable evocations of climate, so too are they starting to sound like apt descriptors of the earth as a whole. All of which suggests that the experience of 'living without guarantee' that social theorists talk about as the condition of the latest phase of our modernity might go a lot further and deeper than most of us have assumed (see Bauman, 1991: 257; see also Smart, 1999: 16).

Return to earth

Over two centuries ago, Immanuel Kant looked closely at the scientific accounts of the terrestrial and celestial processes that were then on offer. What he saw both thrilled and terrified him. Gathering evidence suggested that the earth, like other planets, periodically went through 'revolutions' (Kant, 1993 [1938]). On our home planet, these upheavals appeared to have extinguished earlier forms of life, and this implied that paroxysms still to come might similarly obliterate current inhabitants. This was a moment when the full implications of the Copernican revolution were sinking in, and the whole idea of deep, geological time was taking root. Kant recognized that the temporal and spatial dominion of our species was disturbingly inconsequential when viewed in the context of the earth's eventful history or the vastness of interplanetary space. 'A being belonging to the world of sense', a creature with the capacity to absorb and process the phenomenal productions of physical reality, was at the same time one which was at risk of being overwhelmed by the exertions of the earth and cosmos. Humankind, the only known efflorescence of thought, or proper freedom, was thus vulnerable to being swept away – which would leave the universe utterly devoid of any way of making sense of itself.

In response to this literally unthinkable predicament, Kant set about developing ways of bolstering the human subject, so it might draw strength from its confrontation with the powers that threatened its annihilation. For most of the intervening centuries, Western philosophical and social thought has pretty much accepted Kant's injunctions to steer clear of what the turbulent forces of the universe could do on their own account, and fix our attention on our own interface with the world around us. Eschewing the threats and allures of deep time or interstellar space – or any other domain where elemental forces thrash it out among themselves – we have busied ourselves with the best and the worst that our own species has to offer. Philosophical thought, social and cultural thought, *critical* thought has kept its focus firmly on the various achievements and potentialities of human agency, both in terms of our capacity to engage with each other and to articulate with the physical world around us. By and large, we have left the rest up to physical science to sort out, even as we've maintained our suspicions about their apparent success in doing so.

But once again the raw physicality of the world is rising up the agenda. Once more, the inherent forcefulness of the earth and cosmos, nature's capacity to be a great deal more or a lot less than what we would ask of it, is weighing upon us. 'Long ignored by the humanities, and traditionally seen by society as simply the supplier of raw materials for the industrial machine', philosopher–geologist Robert Frodeman observes, 'the Earth sciences today are moving to the center of public consciousness and conversation' (2000: viii).

The findings of the geosciences are escalating in importance, according to Frodeman, primarily because of the irruption of concern over the ways in which human demands are pressing against the physical limits of the earth and threatening to transform the major systems and subsystems upon which we rely (2000: ix). As Michel Serres suggests, in one of the first full-length philosophical engagements with the modern environmental crisis, our understanding of earth processes is being radically shaken up by way of our dawning recognition that we ourselves have become a force of geological magnitude. Whereas the human species was once distributed across our planet's surface in small pockets and minor assemblies, 'lightweight in body and bone', we now gather in vast conglomerations: 'colossal banks of humanity as powerful as oceans, deserts, or icecaps, themselves stockpiles of ice, heat, dryness, or water' (1995: 17).

The awareness that humankind has grown into a preeminent force in planetary nature – and all the associated questions about how to deal with this situation – is undoubtedly one of the most momentous events our species has ever had to cope with. And we should not make light of the effort it has taken to get it up there on the agendas of social thought and practice. But I want to wager that what the earth sciences have been telling us lately about the way the physical world operates of its own accord, alongside or in spite of our hefty surcharge, is no less significant. And that it makes little sense to agonize over our own contributions to earth processes without as full an understanding as we can get of the dynamics and potentialities that are constitutive of material reality in and of itself.

This book is about coming to terms with a planet that constantly rumbles, folds, cracks, erupts, irrupts. It's about living with earth and cosmic processes that have gone on since long before our species made its appearance, look likely to go on long after us, and continue to happen all around us. It explores some of the issues that arise out of the condition of being sensuous, sociable beings in a universe that nourishes and supports us, but is forever capable of withdrawing this sustaining presence. And it begins to ask how better we might live – with other things and with each other – in the context of a deep, elemental underpinning that is at once a source of profound insecurity.

It is not a guidebook, however. There is already a thriving literature which presents various threats to human life in their full nihilating intensity, only to draw back, take stock and put forward eminently sensible suggestions for living more sustainably and securely. But a good case has already been made that it is our very attempts to step back from the world, gather our resources together, and then advance into projects of improvement and securitization that have got us into some of our more fearful predicaments in the first place (see Beck, 1992). And in some senses, this is what we have been doing ever since Kant first offered his counsel.

Instead of beginning with what we believe to be our powers and capabilities, I set out from the position of our susceptibility to the earth's eventfulness, from our all-too-human exposure to forces that exceed our capacity to control or even make full sense of them. I want to work with and through our vulnerabilities, rather than trying to find a way around them. As fleshy, sensuous creatures, we have always been exposed to the energy and the inertia, the flow and the congealing, the mobilization and the halting of the earth. It is constitutive of our humanness, I argue, that we are inherently liable to being thrown off course by the eventualities of our planet. But just as the earth can perturb and excite us, so too are we receptive to the incitements of others who have been shaken up in some way by the inconstancy of the ground they depend upon. A volatile world can impinge upon our selves directly, or it can present its demands and allures by way of others who turn to us in times of need. This too, I suggest, is part of our constitutive openness to a forceful cosmos.

Worlds beyond us

One of the major developments in social thought over recent decades has been the growing acceptance that what we have called 'the social' is a much more heterogeneous blend than we may have previously imagined: the idea that society is composed not only of human beings but of an array of other-than-human things. As actor-network theorist Bruno Latour would have it: 'Things are everywhere mixed with people; they always have been' (2003: 37). Because these multitudes of things do not simply do our bidding, but have agency or forcefulness of their own, we need to be judicious in the way we incorporate and rearrange them. Problems like ozone holes, global warming and pathogen outbreaks, by this logic, ought to be viewed as the unsurprising outcome of not taking enough care in the way we assemble our worlds.

To help us think about how we might organize our transactions with diverse objects and elements more carefully, Latour (1993) has proposed a 'parliament of things'. His 'parliament' is an imaginary forum for bringing together processes of political representation – people voicing their interests about what kind of world they would like to live in, and processes of scientific representation – the act of speaking for or about nonhumans. In Latour's proposed re-constitution of people and things, we will all ideally have the opportunity not only to confer about the sort of social order or cultural life we desire, but about the kind of other-than-human objects we wish to acknowledge, join forces with, or exclude from our lives. In this way, it is no longer simply a matter of how we engage with a world already given to us that is up for grabs, but the whole question of how to make or assemble the realities we will be dwelling in.

There's a nice twist on this 'constitutive' approach to society and nature in the introduction to the recent *Making Things Public* exhibition. Here, Latour speaks of the thousand-year-old 'Althing', in Iceland – reputedly the world's first parliament: 'the ancient "thing-men" – what we would call "congressmen" or MPs – had the amazing idea of meeting in a desolate and sublime site that happens to sit smack in the middle of the fault line that marks the meeting place of the Atlantic and European tectonic plates ...' (2005: 23). Latour tells this story to drive home the point that political questions are also questions of nature: to remind us that how we put social and physical things together requires rigorous and sustained attention.

Today, when Haiti's Government Palace has been reduced to rubble along with much of the rest of Port-au-Prince, the logic of siting parliaments – or any other human edifice – on active tectonic plate junctures has a bleaker undertone. In their midst, forces that are sublime from a distance or in the abstract tend to be utterly shattering. A major upheaval of the earth, survivors tell us, not only takes the ground out from beneath your feet, but unravels the very fabric that holds things together and allows us to make sense of the world. There is a moment towards the end of the *Natural Contract* where Michel Serres recounts his personal experience of an earthquake in a way which evokes this sudden coming apart of reality:

> All of a sudden the ground shakes off its gear: walls tremble, ready to collapse, roofs buckle, people fall, communications are interrupted, noise keeps you from hearing each other, the thin technological film tears, squealing and snapping like metal or crystal; the world finally comes to me, resembles me, all in distress. A thousand useless ties come undone ... (1995: 124)

The fearsome capacity of the earth to undo our sustaining connections and footings, in this way, serves to remind us that all is not equal in the world of mixing and mobilizing things. Like Haiti's seat of government, the ancient Icelandic parliament is much more vulnerable to the geo-tectonic movements beneath its foundations than tectonic plates would be to any motions passed in the parliament. In other words, there is an asymmetry here: the impression that deep-seated forces of the earth can leave on social worlds is out of all proportion to the power of social actors to legislate over the lithosphere.

It is not only seismic upheaval which draws us into realities that seem to be beyond the reach of 'negotiation'. Climate change takes us on a similar journey. As soon as we move past the slender horizon of human-induced global heating and confront the issue of climate change as an integral and ongoing aspect of our planet's variability, we are drawn into regions where there is only the nonhuman. Where everything is most definitely *not* mixed with people.

A lot of pressing contemporary issues which at first seem to reside comfortably in the realm of human–nonhuman interaction soon take us to these other zones. Whether we are dealing with the cyclicality of cyclones, the rhythms of wildfire, the emergence of novel pathogens, the availability of mineral or energy resources, or the fate of biological diversity, we find ourselves parting company with any significant human presence. Follow the threads that weave in or out of these matters of concern, trace their lines of causality or ripples of consequence and they lead us back to epochs before humans emerged, take us deep into micro-ecologies too tiny and too multitudinous to even imagine, drag us down to the molten and lifeless interior of the earth, whip us up into the stratosphere and out into the solar system.

In fact, if we take seriously the injunction of some recent critical approaches to track all the relevant material linkages that converge on the field that interests us, then it's difficult to conceive of any issues that will not sooner or later hive off into regions of existence utterly alien to the human.

It is vital that we continue to inquire into those aspects of nature that are sensitive to our impingements and compositions. But almost everyone knows this. It is no longer controversial. Central to this book is the insistence that social scientists and humanities scholars need to push through this zone of inter-mixity of human and nonhumans and press on into regions *where we are absent*. What was once the defining interest of the physical sciences – dominions devoid of human imprint – is now opening up as a topic of importance for all of us. Increasingly, crucial decisions about how to live on, live well, or deal with loss of life on this planet are dependent on notions of how things work in the universe, irrespective of our influence.

Fidelities

The idea that there is political significance and intrigue to be found in decisively extra-human domains has been rumbling away in the social sciences and humanities for some time, especially in extrapolations from certain strands of French post-structural thought and in the feminist concern with biological embodiment. It has recently received a timely shove from a new brand of philosophical realism that refers to itself as 'speculative'[1] (see page xxii). A cohort of philosophers who have grown impatient with the legacy of Kant's restrictive concern with human access to the world have been re-opening the question of what the rest of reality gets up to in the absence of a mediating human subject. Rigorously rebuking many of the sanctions that held philosophical or social thought back from any consideration of 'things in themselves', these theorists are encouraging us to liaise with 'the most colourful details of the earth' in ways that exceed the warrants of much critical thought and practice (Harman, 2002: 237).

While there are pleasures to be found in this new intimacy with the 'world-in-itself', it also smoothes the way for social thinkers to engage more directly with the findings of the physical sciences, including their more perturbing discoveries. With the easing of the requirement to endlessly circle back through the co-relation of thought and world, we find ourselves increasingly free to join natural scientists in their contemplations of a 'universe … packed with fateful revolutions: the emergence of the heavier elements from hydrogen; the birth of solar systems; the breakup of Pangaea into multiple continents; the emergence of multicellular life …', as philosopher Graham Harman envisions (2005: 243).

It is, of course, crucial for social scientists to maintain a critical attitude towards the premises, practices and products of the physical sciences. We know this well enough by now that it need not be rehearsed at every meeting or reading. But critique is no longer enough. And it never was. Science is one of the most important ways we have of gaining an understanding not only about the ways our activities interweave with the rest of the world's doings and happenings – but about what the world does in our absence. By collapsing the world's own functions and operations into a side-effect of our access to the world or our inscriptions on the world, we have too often convinced ourselves that the realm of autonomous goings-on is a non-existent or dubious category. And besides blinkering us from many wondrous events, that's a very dangerous thing to do.

The sort of issues, problems and risks that I've been talking about and will be saying a lot more about demand ontological commitment as well as political commitment. They ask of us that when we are done with our critique, or while we are performing our critical manoeuvres, we add our weight to specific models or visions of how the world actually works. This is more or less what Stephen White (2000) refers to as 'sustaining affirmation' and Alain Badiou (2005) terms 'fidelity'. If critical social, cultural and philosophical thinkers shelter behind the issue of 'access' to reality, with all its admittedly intriguing epistemological complexities and political vexations, then the question of what sort of planet and cosmos we inhabit and what kinds of imperatives arise out of this inhabitation will continue to be under-examined.

But I am also insisting that we cannot simply assume that all of reality is up for re-negotiation. Some moves to hitch ontology to politics seem to want so much two-way traffic between these terms that the entire universe ends up looking as though it is amenable to the collective deliberations and contestations of human actors. Conceding all of extra-human material reality to the physical sciences may be an option that critical social thinkers are no longer content with. But assuming all of existence now comfortably resides within the domain of the 'negotiable', the 'co-enacted' and the 'could-be-done-otherwise' is just as unsatisfactory. And perhaps just as dangerous.

The 'colossal banks of humanity' that have assembled themselves over recent centuries, and at an accelerating rate over recent decades, have not been around long enough to sample anything like the full range of variability that their environments have to offer (Davis, 1998: Ch. 1; Clark, 2003a; Kaika, 2005). Indeed, there is no 'full range', for there are always new, untried possibilities in any region, or physical system – including the earth in its entirety (see De Landa, 1992, 1997). We do not yet know, cannot know, precisely what human-induced climate change has in store for us. Or what the ordinary, ongoing rhythms and movements of the earth will deliver us into. But it is fairly clear that most of our current living arrangements, our patterns of settlement and provisioning, have not evolved with enough attention to natural variability and volatility. And that puts billions of us – all of us, in fact, in a globalized world – in a very precarious position.

For sociologist Ulrich Beck, the motivating force in what he termed 'risk society' could be encapsulated in the phrase 'I am scared' (1989: 95; see also Clark, 1997). But that was some time ago. What should we now make of a situation in which it is the scientific experts who are scared – and who desperately wish that publics could be even more worried than they already are? There is nothing new about scientists with worldly concerns, but clearly, climate change and related issues are drawing scientific 'witnesses' into unfamiliar ethical–political quandaries and affective intensities (see Frodeman, 2000: vii–x). 'On the record, they use very conservative scientific language; they speak in terms of estimates and trends and probabilities', reports journalist Ross Gelbspan of his encounters with climate scientists. 'Off the record, they told me this stuff is scary as hell' (2006: unpag.).

This is why we need fidelity to the stories that physical scientists tell us. For these and a host of other reasons, those of us who study 'the social' and 'the human' are finding ourselves, as never before, 'called to science', to use a formulation from cultural theorists Adrian Mackenzie and Andrew Murphie (2008: 89). And with this summons comes a new pressure for the social sciences and humanities to engage substantively with scientific findings – to move through critique towards dialogue and collaboration (Mackenzie and Murphie, 2008: 89). As well as being interested in what scientists actually do, we need to be interested in what scientists are interested in: our critical rituals must lead on to decisions, allegiances and, especially, to commitments.

This book draws upon both scientific and philosophical evidence about the ways in which mostly other-than-human elements and events compose the worlds we inhabit. In fact, my argument depends utterly on the 'substantive' findings of the earth sciences and on the recent philosophical re-activation of the question of 'things-in-themselves'. Though fascinated by questions about what nonhumans get up to when we are not around, my focus is – conventionally enough – with the way that our own species catches the fallout of this extra-human universe.

My pressing concern is about how we might get by, and get on with each other, in the full knowledge that most of material reality is not ours to make over. So while we certainly need to hammer away at the ethical and political implications of those aspects of physical existence conducive to recomposition, we must also account for forces, events and objects that can't be done differently or done away with – or things that will be otherwise whatever *we* chose to do. These too are political questions. But they are also questions about the limits of what usually counts as politics, about the limits of any kind of human action, doing or making.

Planet of strangers

An earth or a cosmos which human beings rely upon for the basal conditions of their existence is also one which can withdraw its vital support. This is Ivan's point, put more politely. It is my rationale for hitching the issue of earthly volatility to that of bodily vulnerability.

The idea that much of our humanness might lie in our sensuous and somatic susceptibility to a violating exteriority has been on the agenda of philosophy and social thought for some time (see Turner, 2006: Ch. 1). As a way of taking issue with modernity's championing of sovereign, self-asserting subjects, the stress on the precariousness of embodied life serves as a reminder that there are things that happen to us which we can't anticipate or avoid, events that wrench us from the course of our daily existence. 'Beneath the surface of ordinary life – the surface of productive, functioning, busy lives – there lurks an abyss', writes ethical philosopher John Caputo. 'Beneath the surface of healthy agent bodies the abyss of flesh stirs, an abyss of vulnerability that can swallow every joy' (1993: 235).

The thematization of human frailty and perviousness has taken place predominantly in response to tragedies of our own manufacture. Indeed, some have argued explicitly that the forces of the earth, now demystified by their scientific deciphering, are totally overshadowed by the inherently unfathomable horrors we inflict upon each other. And yet, even when we know earthly upheavals to be ordinary agents of geomorphology, their impingement on the soft tissue and impressionable psyche of the human organism can be as unforgiving as any socio-political atrocity.

Those who have been caught in an earthquake, seen a wall of water surging towards them, felt the air they breathe turn to flame, can feel as thoroughly abandoned as anyone whose social supports have been dismantled or turned against them. They speak of the shock of being forsaken by an earth or an ocean or a sky whose sustaining presence they once trusted, and bear witness to the difficulty of re-embracing a world that has betrayed a basic faith. 'Before the Tsunami the sea was my friend, my livelihood, the backdrop to my life' recounts Arjunan, a fisher from Tharangambadi village in Tamil Nadu. 'Now if there is even a slight storm I become afraid that the same thing might happen again' (cited in Kwatra, 2005: 10).

While there may be no permanent respite from the pressures of a fitful and fluctuating world, there is more to the issue of our fleshly exposure than the potential for harm. To be vulnerable to otherness, theorists of embodiment insist, is not just to be open to being unmade, but to being remade into something other than what we are. It is to be liable to diversion, to being propelled in new and unforeseeable directions. As cultural theorist Pheng Cheah would have it, '(i)t is precisely this internal vulnerability of any present being to alterity – its pregnancy with the movement of altering – that allows something to alter, change, or transform itself in time, or to be changed, transformed, or altered by another ...' (1999: 191).

Like any other organism, we humans have become what we are over time, through countless generations of tussling with environmental challenges and opportunities. In this way, most of the physiological, cerebral and social capacities we take to be our own come to us from others who have gone before us. Or as philosopher Judith Butler puts it, 'the very bodies for which we struggle are not quite ever our own' (2004: 26). But our susceptibility to the effects of natural variance is not limited to those events which we or our ancestors have directly experienced. It can come to us by way of others whose links with ourselves are less direct. Recent disasters like the Indian Ocean Tsunami, Hurricane Katrina or the Haiti Earthquake serve as reminders that ordinary people can be moved by the plight of strangers, even when far afield. The visible inequalities and injustices that positioned certain bodies in the path of these catastrophes should not obscure the fact that these events also inspired outpourings of generosity. To be an open body, in this way, is also to be able to sense the need of others, to be touched, moved, swayed by the plight of strangers.

The 'strangers' who populate this book are not simply those who come from someplace else, but the ones who have been made strange by events – those who have been estranged from their world, their own former selves as much as from fellow humans. Nothing dictates that the victims of natural disaster or environmental extremity will meet with sympathetic responses, just as nothing predetermines that a 'fateful revolution' of the earth or cosmos will necessary find human targets in its path. But I want to make the case that the asymmetry of the human relationship to the rest of nature resonates in the asymmetrical relationship of self and other.

Just as the earth and all its constitutive physical systems have a tendency to veer away from the regularity of a strict orbit – with unpredictable effects, so too are human beings susceptible to being wrenched out of their usual circuits by an encounter with an other – in unforeseeable ways. As natural forces act upon us with no expectation of a return movement, so too is there a possibility of an offering or welcome to one who has been laid low by the forces of the world that does not wait upon a reciprocal gesture.

Today, on top of the already fraught matter of all those who are pushed and pulled across the globe by turbulent social forces, comes the problem of how to deal with the vast populations who are likely to be displaced by human-induced climate change. But even as the question of justice for the uneven causation and disproportionate consequences of global heating presents itself in all its diabolic complexity, it is already cut across by the raw fact of deterritorializations which belong to the earth itself. Our planet is not going to stand still while we do our sums and stage our tribunals. This juncture zone, where the inherent excess of the earth crunches into a social imperative for equity and moderation is the point where many of the issues raised in this book converge.

There is nothing close to a way out of these dilemmas in the chapters that follow. But there is a kind of faith that there already exists a vast reservoir of experience – inscribed in communities, bodies, landscapes, stories, objects – about how to make it across the inconstancies that belong to the earth itself. And an equally hopeful sense that there are, taking place at any moment, a great many acts of care and support for those who have been struck by forces beyond their tolerance. An intimation that, along with all the dispute and contestation so prized by critical thinkers, there are also deep, ordinary and extraordinary dispositions of generosity to others coursing through everyday social life.

Note

1 'Speculative realism' was an early place-holder term for this philosophical current. Other terms in play include 'object-oriented ontology' and 'speculative materialism'.

1

The Earth in Physical and Social Thought

Introduction: homeland insecurity

My country is about to be torn apart. I don't mean that metaphorically, in the sense of a social conflict or crisis of national identity. I mean it literally. The land where I grew up is formed at the juncture of the Pacific and Indo-Australian tectonic plates, two great crustal slabs that continue to graunch together with what is, in geological terms, unusual haste. This collision along the 'Alpine Fault' has thrown up a range of mountains which form the backbone of the largest island. Geologists estimate that these alps have been uplifted by 20,000 metres over the last 12 million years, and only the accompanying speed of erosion has kept their peaks just below 4,000 metres. The two plates are currently locked, but when the tension between them reaches a certain level a significant readjustment will occur in the form of a major seismic event. The longer the delay, the bigger the earthquake is likely to be. And it will occur 'with no recognizable warning'. As geohazard experts anticipate:

> There will be death and injuries, especially in the Alps and West Coast. Rescue services and medical services will be overwhelmed, and remain so for weeks in places ... Shaking damage and land instability will disrupt surface transport for months, tourists will be trapped, and distribution of vital supplies ... will be limited. Hydro stations will shut down immediately and may be slow to restart, power reticulation will be damaged ... Landslides into lakes and fiords may cause tsunami, as may the collapse of river deltas in lakes or the sea ... No services will be as normal. (Davies and McSaveney, cited in Booker, 2006)

The consensus amongst scientists is that a 'readjustment event' occurs about every 250 to 280 years, with the last major rupture on the fault line occurring in 1717 – an earthquake likely to have measured at least 8 on the Richter scale. In the words of geologist Tim Davies, this means that '(t)he most likely time [for the quake] is now. The next most likely time for it to happen is tomorrow' (cited in Booker, 2006).

I live on the other side of the planet now, in a country which is, geologically speaking, relatively quiescent. But here on the rim of the North Atlantic there are also dangers. For some years, geologists have been monitoring the volcano Cumbre Vieja, on the island of La Palma in the Canaries. A series of fractures opened up on its flanks during a bout of combined eruption and seismicity in 1949. As a result, a mass of rock is now unstable and threatens to slide four metres or so into the ocean (McGuire, 2005: 12). A slump of this sort is part of the normal life cycle of any island volcano, though it may occur only once in 100,000 years. When the landslide does occur on Cumbre Vieja, and it is a matter of when not if, it will be over in a minute or two. But it will generate a surge almost a kilometre high, waves that will still be many tens of meters high by the time they strike the islands of the Caribbean, the coast of north-west Africa, Brazil, the eastern seaboard of the USA and Western Europe (McGuire, 2005: 19).

It has been suggested that the offending rock face could be quarried away to reduce its impact. As volcanologist Bill McGuire has roughly calculated, even if the material was amenable to being shovelled out, and could be done so at the rate of a 10 cubic metre truckload every minute of the day, it would take somewhere between 10 and 35 million years to safely excavate the potential slip (2005: 132). Despite the mass of the unstable rock, La Palma is not a large island, and in terms of the earth's history, this would be, in McGuire's terms, 'a relatively minor geological event' (2005: 15). Unlike the rupture of Aotearoa New Zealand's Alpine Fault where periodicities are relatively well understood, there is much more uncertainty about the timing of this event. The cliffs of Cumbre Vieja may well hold fast for tens of thousands of years.

We hardly need speculations to remind us of the consequences of the earth mobilizing itself, of the collisions of its own temporalities and spatialities with the times and spaces of human life. From the Indian Ocean Tsunami to Pakistan's recent earthquake, from Haiti to Chile, media audiences across much of the world have witnessed the aftermath, and sometimes the very unfolding, of naturally triggered catastrophes that have cost hundreds of thousands of lives. There is nothing new about the precipitating forces, but there is no precedent to the degree of exposure we now have to the suffering of others. The same vectors and networks that allow us to see the faces of distant people caught up in world-shattering events also enable us to offer sympathy and assistance, if we choose. But these forms of connectivity and flow also implicate us in the lives of those who are physically far away in more mundane but no less momentous ways. Why some of us have resources to give, why others are more vulnerable to earth processes than we may be, has a great deal to do with forces of social, economic, cultural and technological globalization that bring us together and hold us apart in new and complex ways.

Just as global interconnectedness has emerged as an integral topic in social science research over the last few decades, so too has planet-scaled integration and interactivity been a unifying theme in the earth sciences for more than 50 years. While social scientists have been demonstrating how human activities in one locality have repercussions for other places near and far, earth scientists have been showing how physical phenomena that manifest themselves in one part of the world are implicated with processes operating across the planet, beneath its surface, even beyond its circumference. Whatever disciplinary divisions endure in the corridors of learning, research and policy-making, nearly everybody these days agrees that it makes good sense to look at the dynamics of the social and physical worlds together. But it's much harder to reach agreement about how best to do this, where to start, what weighting to give the respective forces and processes, how to bring very different elements into the same storyline. It's difficult enough for social scientists, humanities scholars or earth scientists to come to a consensus amongst themselves, let alone to reach across meta-disciplinary divides – and a whole world of jostling interests and values – to attain some shared planetary vision.

This chapter looks at the diverse imperatives towards thinking 'globally' in contemporary Western thought. In broad strokes, I sketch out some of the possibilities for and impediments to thinking about our planet in an integrated way. I begin by looking at how a select group of philosophers and social theorists laid out the challenge of thinking through and about the earth, and then address the different ways that the social sciences and earth sciences have approached the issue of globality, before returning to some relevant themes in recent philosophy. And then I come back, once more, to considering what is at stake in sorting out our collective relationship to the dynamic planet which remains our only home.

The equivocation of the earth

Some two decades ago, in an early philosophical engagement with human environmental impact on 'a physical system millions of years old', Michel Serres highlighted the need to confront these issues at the same spatio-temporal scale as they are playing out. '(W)e must decide about the greatest object of scientific knowledge and practice, the Planet Earth', he proposed (1995: 30). Still further back, on the cusp of the emergence of modern environmental concerns, social theorist and philosopher Henri Lefebvre surveyed the cultural milieu of his time, conceding that images of nature had been excessively reproduced and the very concept of nature trivialized. 'And yet', he mused, 'the notion of nature has not been exhausted. It is still buoyant. It still has a few metaphilosophical or philosophical surprises in store for us' (1995 [1962]: 132). Lefebvre noted that ways of thinking about 'matter', 'things' and 'objects' allow the issue of nature to be articulated in clearer, less confused ways, but in the process lose something of the richness and complication that lends the concept of nature its continuing relevance. Recognizing all the ideological risks of a unified vision of a world or universe, Lefebvre nonetheless advised the materialist critiques then on offer not to dispense with the challenging questions arising out of the interplay between nature as a ground and as an object. As he counselled: 'there is one fact which this critique must be careful not to overlook: we have before us, here and now, a whole. It is both the condition for production and the product of action itself, the place for mankind and the object of its pleasure: the earth' (1995: 133).

As Lefebvre's comments notify us, the earth did not have to await any awareness of material despoliation in order to emerge as a theme of theoretical analysis and speculation. Already, in the earlier twentieth century, prior to the crystallization of discourses of global environmental crisis, the earth was construed as problematic – as 'under threat' in an experiential or phenomenological sense. Western philosophy has a history of inquiring about 'the ground': which is to say that it engages with foundations or originating forces, including the generative and supportive conditions of an intelligent being. Over the course of the last century, philosophers increasingly turned their attention to worldly changes that have affected our experience of the ground, focusing especially on techno-cultural transformations that seem to disturb our sense of stability and anchoredness.

In his first major published essay, Jacques Derrida (1989 [1962]) zeroes in on the question of what to make of the earth in our time. The work is an extended introduction to phenomenologist Edmund Husserl's *Origins of Geometry*, and it offers a still resonant point of entry to the issue of why the earth is troublesome for social and philosophical thought, even without the surcharge of ecological crisis.

Derrida looks at how the modern experience of the earth pulls in two irreconcilable directions. Following Husserl, he notes how the Copernican and Newtonian view of the 'geometrical' earth – as one amongst a system of similarly spherical, orbiting bodies – constitutes the planet as an object; graspable, accessible to thought. This is the earth that anyone schooled in elementary astronomy knows to be revolving around the sun: the third rock from the sun – celestial neighbour of Mercury and Venus. And yet, as Husserl famously responded to the standard scientific interpretation: 'The original ark, earth, does not move' (cited in Himanka, 2005: 621). By which he meant not that Copernican science had it wrong, but that our primary experience of the earth is as a supportive and sustaining ground – as the resting point from which we register the movement and thingness of all other things. The earth cannot simply serve as one astronomical body – one object – amongst others, as it is the very condition of our encountering of everything else. For Husserl, as Derrida explains: 'the earth … is the *exemplary* element (being more naturally objective, more permanent, more solid, more rigid, and so forth, than all other *elements*; and in a broader sense it comprises them)' (1989: 81, author's italics).

In a move which prefigures much of his subsequent work, Derrida dismisses neither Husserl's return to an earth radically at rest, nor the scientific objectification of the planet. Suggesting that they are neither totally exclusive nor fully reconcilable, he shows how both dispositions work to destabilize or contaminate the other:

> the possibility of a geometry strictly complements the impossibility of what could be called a '*geo-logy*', the objective science of the Earth itself … The Earth is, in effect, both short of and beyond every body-object – in particular the Copernican earth, as the ground, as the here of its relative appearing. But the Earth exceeds every body-object as its infinite horizon, for it is never exhausted by the work of objectification that proceeds within it. (1989: 83, 85)

To put it another way, just as the most 'grounded', nature-loving modern knows that our planet is spinning relentlessly around the sun, so too does the career astrophysicist wake up trusting that their house or their observatory will sit as it did the day before, anchored to the ground, beneath a familiar sky. No conversance with the scientific facts can ever entirely displace this visceral trust in earth, sky, life and water, and no amount of tree-hugging or nature poetry can fully efface the mental image of circling spheres. Each of these experiences is a part of modern life and understanding, and each insinuates itself in the other, Derrida is saying.

But whilst Derrida accepts that the 'world objectivation' of the physical sciences cannot completely override the basic kinaesthetic experience of having our feet planted on the earth, he breaks with Husserl over the question of how we access or experience this terra firma. Husserl believes that the objective scientific interpretation is novel and superficial, and detracts from our core human experience of groundedness. Thus, we ought to burrow beneath science's crass new factuality, and peel off its layers of artifice and abstraction in order to unearth a substrate stable enough to provide ontological certainty, in the hope that this primordial experience might gather us together and reunite us over all our differences. Whereas for Derrida, in the gesture that made his name, there can be no pure presence of the solid, enduring earth. There will be no 'unity of all humanity … correlative to the unity of the world' (1989: 84, footnote 87). Instead, the true nature of the ground beneath us or the sky above us is never finally revealed. They withdraw from us, retain the secrets of their own emergence, continuity and destination: '… preculturally *pure Nature* is always buried' (1989: 81).

In another few years, Martin Heidegger (1976) will have caught sight of photographs of our planet snapped by astronauts – and condemned them as the final blow in the uprooting of humanity; the conclusive technological undoing of the capacity of the earth to provide a supportive and gathering ground (Turnbull, 2006: 126). But so too will the environmental crisis have added its seemingly irreversible charge to the problematization of the human experience of the earth. The problem from here on in, as John Caputo puts it, is that 'we have not only disenchanted the forest but deforested it too' (1993: 34). Worse than being reduced to an object or a 'standing reserve', our planet becomes a threatened object, a depleting reserve. And this palpable undoing of the earth by our own hands sets it equivocating in new, unprecedented ways.

The point that Derrida and subsequent post-structural critics made about Husserl, Heidegger and similarly melancholic musings over the loss of the ground was that what was really at stake was the loss of philosophy's ability to shore up its own foundations. And in particular, the waning authority, not so much of the earth, but of specific cultural and national territorializations of the earth to provide this anchoring.

But there's something else to keep in mind. At the historical moment when Derrida was engaging with Husserl, claims that the earth was 'permanent', 'solid' or 'rigid' had a meaning that was about to be compromised. A 'metaphilosophical surprise' was in store, and it did not have to wait on any indictment of human activity. In just a few years' time, accumulating scientific evidence would confirm the theory of plate tectonics – the key to conceiving of the earth as a single, integrated and dynamic physical system. We might see this as the Copernican turn coming home. In a similar way that the astronomical sciences had once informed us that we inhabit an orbiting spherical body, the earth sciences – from the late 1960s onwards – would tell us a coherent and more-or-less consensual story about the inherent tendencies of the earth's crust to shift and buckle, about the normality of periodic upheaval and the ordinary instability of the ground beneath our feet.

The earth science story about an intrinsically restless planet is not opposed to the human-induced environmental degradation story. At least it shouldn't be. For it is the pronouncements of physical science that enable us to understand how and why human forcings change the earth's weather, water, soil or life. However, with regard to the ontological, experiential and political dimensions of inhabiting the planet, these discourses can pull in very different directions. In both senses, the radical rest of the earth – Husserl's 'original ark' – is in for an upset. But an inescapably volatile earth and a planet 'we' ourselves have made unstable do not have the same implications for how we think about human agency. And what to make of human agency remains a definitive concern of the social sciences.

Lost planet? Social thought and global nature

Social scientists and cultural theorists have their own deep-seated disciplinary motivations for disavowing the idea of an originary and anchoring earth. They have long assumed, often justifiably, that accounts of human behaviour which make recourse to naturalistic causes diminish the purchase of social or cultural explanations and thereby undermine the potential for human agents to take responsibility for shaping their own worlds. This congenital antipathy to attributing causal efficacy to nature goes a long way towards explaining social and cultural inquiry's initially slow reaction to the environmental predicament of the latter twentieth century. In order to engage with the materiality or physical dimensions of the 'ecological crisis', it was first necessary to find ways of articulating human-induced destruction or perturbation which did not appear to valorize the bio-physicality under threat.

This was achieved both by constantly circling back on the issue of the cultural investment in particular constructions of nature and by making the claim that, in its very materiality, nature had ceased to be available for direct communion or foundational experience. 'In this actual world there is ... not much point in counterposing or restating the great abstractions of Man and Nature', wrote cultural theorist Raymond Williams. 'We have mixed our labour with the earth, our forces with its forces too deeply to be able to draw back and separate either out' (1980: 83). Or as geographer Neil Smith asserted, surveying the cumulative effects of ever-expanding forces of production: 'No God-given stone is left unturned, no original relation with nature unaltered, no living thing unaffected' (1984: xiv).

The claim made by Williams, Smith and others that what used to be known as 'nature' is now so thoroughly modified by socio-technical processes that it can no longer provide an external platform from which to pronounce on the state of human sociality has had an irresistible appeal to subsequent critical social thinkers. It at once treats the environmental predicament with deadly seriousness, and shrewdly turns this predicament around so that it bolsters rather than undermines the resistance of social and cultural thought to the natural referent. But it's worth noting that this is not the same thing as saying, along with the early Derrida, that 'preculturally *pure Nature* is always buried' – for it is much more than a matter of nature not being *experientially* or *cognitively* inaccessible in any direct, unmediated way. It's about this nature being physically transformed *out of existence*.

The idea of the 'end of nature', in its various guises, paved the way to drawing environmental problems and technological hazards into the heart of social theories of globalization. When globalization established itself as a key concept in the social sciences in the closing decades of the twentieth century, it was construed almost entirely as a social process, albeit one with a range of environmental or other biophysical consequences. Critical social thinkers were at pains to avoid all association of the 'global' in globalism, globality or globalization with nature, so as to head off any suggestion that the particular forms of world-encompassing order then on the ascendant were a 'natural' outgrowth of a human expansionary drive or an inevitable outcome of our 'planetary' domicile (see Law and Hetherington, 1999).

But the rise of environmental or technological problems that appeared inherently transboundary in their make-up, together with a more general ecological predicament that seemed paradigmatically 'global' in its manifestations, demanded something more than a blunt denaturalization of globalization. Even before the ascendance of climate change as the overarching threat to the 'global environment', issues were shaping up in ways that demanded social analysts to take account of properties and potentialities of 'actors' other than the human. Earlier manifestations of the end-of-nature argument began to appear overly monolithic in their narration of nature's eclipse, and variations on the theme turned towards the propensity for generative and unpredictable behaviour that characterized non-humans as much as it did their human counterparts. Although distinct in other ways, Ulrich Beck's 'risk theory' (1992, 1995, 1999) and Bruno Latour's 'actor-network theory' (1993, 1999a) both drew attention to the inherent reluctance of other-than-human elements to hew to the grids and groves we humans lay out for them, and proposed that this was a key as to why environmental or technological problems are so complex.

For a new generation of critical social and cultural thinkers engaging with nature–society questions, then, three interrelated themes have come to the fore. First, in the contemporary world, human agents are probing ever more deeply and intricately into the workings of nature, and recruiting more and more extra-human elements into our machineries and circuitries. And we are doing so with undue haste and inadequate care. Second, the nonhumans which play a constitutive role in these arrangements do not necessarily stick to the agendas we set them, and thus exacerbate the overall state of precariousness and unpredictability. And third, the whole process of enrolling ever more diverse entities in ever more extensive networks – and all its attendant risks – is increasingly global in scope.

In this way, what were formerly addressed separately under the headings 'nature' and 'society' are both revealed to be heterogeneous compositions – forged out of complex, shifting permutations of human and physical ingredients. Importantly, this means that it is not only 'society' that might be organized differently, as politically progressive thinkers have long imagined, but 'nature' also. If the natural and the social have become so inextricably bound together that they now comprise a single 'hybrid environment', then the transformation of society and the transformation of nature are effectively one and the same process. Given the claim that there is no longer any uncompromised 'external' nature, then logically there is no aspect of physical existence which is not potentially open to being reworked in some way. As geographer Eric Swyngedouw puts it: 'The key political question is one that centers on the question of what kind of natures we wish to inhabit, what kinds of natures we wish to preserve, to make, or, if need be, to wipe off the surface of the planet ... and on how to get there' (2007: 23).

No one is suggesting that 'nature' – or rather the multiple, hybridized nature-cultures that now serve as our realities – will ever submit to total control, for it is routinely acknowledged that arrangements of such complexity are incapable of having an order or logic imposed upon them. But the assumption that all of reality is now in some sense 'negotiable', even if it is not always spelt out as such, is a remarkable one. And it needs to be carefully scrutinized. I will be addressing this more closely in the next chapter, but for now I want to rough out what's at stake in the idea of 'global natures', and especially what it might mean for thinking about the earth as an entity or as a ground.

If we think back to the challenge of bringing the question of nature and its destabilization into discourses of globalization, it is apparent that there is a dilemma here. Critical thinkers perceived a need to engage with physical processes and nonhuman entities at the scale of the globe, and yet did not want to re-invest in a concept of nature which might restrict the possibility of globalization being open to alternatives. This challenge seems to have been met by way of imagining 'global natures' or hybrid nature-cultures that have rich and active lives of their own, yet are effectively untethered from the 'earth', 'the biosphere' or any other pre-existing geophysical entity. By concentrating on the concrete processes by which physical or nonhuman entities are uploaded into novel globe-spanning constellations, the new critical nature theorists keep their focus firmly fixed on forms of globality that are orchestrated by human associational and techno-cultural capabilities, while leaving leeway for the non-human to assert or insert itself. As geographer Bruce Braun helpfully sums up:

> For many writers the key concern has been making these geographies (of 'global' nature) visible and understanding the practices and processes that compose them, from technological innovations, transnational trade agreements and the local-global practices of environmental groups, to the lively materiality of the non-human 'stuff' of nature, which brings its own spatial forms and logics to the story. (2006: 644)

Or as Latour puts it, rather more bluntly, when talking about the globality of nature: '*global* is largely, like the globe itself, an invention of science' (2004a: 451).

Natures, then, in the language of contemporary critical social and cultural thought, are 'multiple' and 'situated'. They can be put together or composed in many ways, and the components out of which they are assembled, for all that they may issue from particular situations or contexts, are increasingly likely to be mobilized over long distances. What we need to keep our eye on here is the repeated insistence that there is no outside to the new hybridized environments: thus no functionally intact nature enduring beyond, beneath, amidst or after this assimilation. The claim about the end of nature's exteriority and the story of an all-subsuming rise of new technologically mediated global nature-cultures make for an extremely potent combination. It is a fusion, I want to argue, which discourages any political or ontological investment in a geo-physical materiality with an autonomy and integrity of its own.

Effectively, the new hybrid social–physical topologies are presented as self-supporting. They are shown to be composed, step by step, link by link, out of every conceivable component, but they do not appear to require a substrate. They have no ground, in other words. Unless, that is, we go so far as to consider humanly instigated networks as the underpinning or foundation of nature.

In this way, whether intentionally or as a more subtle performative effect, the bold new commitment to global natures is resulting in a marked reluctance to confront the question of the earth as an autonomous entity – or as the ground out of which humans and other beings emerge. Indeed, the earth as an object of interest at all seems to be largely precluded, at the very time when just about every other conceivable object, from door knobs to space shuttles, is on the agenda.

As we will see when we turn to the recent history of the earth sciences and to developments in continental philosophy, there is more than one way (unsurprisingly) to conceive of the multiplicity and situatedness of nature. Before leaving social and cultural thought, I want to return to Raymond Williams, who is so often cited for his contribution to the end of a certain way of conceiving of nature. A few pages on from his canonical adieu to the 'great abstraction' of Nature, Williams called upon his audience '(t)o re-emphasize, as a fundamental materialism, the inherent physical conditions – a specific universe, a specific planet, a specific evolution, specific physical lives – from which all labour and all consciousness must take their origins' (1980: 108). This is the end of nature not simply by way of its ascendance into new networks or assemblages, but as the prelude for a profound and substantive return to the earth.

Earth science and planetary dynamics

To follow an account of recent thinking about nature in social thought with a parallel precis of the earth sciences is to tell a tale of two globalizations. Roughly contiguous in the timing and scoping of their concern with the global; resonant in their shared use of tropes of connectivity, complexity, multiplicity and uncertainty; convergent in their anguish over human impact on terrestrial environments – social-scientific and geo-scientific globality look at first glance to have been made for each other. And yet, I want to argue, they are near antithetical in their broader implications, and are being held apart by this largely unspoken dissonance at the very moment when their rapprochement is most urgently needed.

As numerous overviews concur, the last 50 or 60 years of research in the earth sciences has fitfully but cumulatively transformed the scientific understanding of our planet (Davis, 1996; Wood, 2004). Step by step, project by project, debate by debate, a whole range of processes and components that were previously addressed in sub-disciplinary or regional specialisms have been assembled into a new conception of the earth as an integrated and dynamic system.

The key to the emergent global vision of contemporary geoscience, most commentators agree, was the confirmation of the theory of plate tectonics in the late 1960s (Davis, 1996; Westbroek, 1992: 53). The crucial event – a fortuitous offshoot of projects prompted by cold war rivalries – was the discovery that the ocean floors were bisected by extensive mountain chains (see Menard, 1986). These submarine ranges turned out to be the sites at which crust-forming magma pumped out of the planet's interior. Subsequent research established that liquid rock welled up at these deep-ocean spreading centres, that it hardened and moved outwards, eventually rising into continental landmasses whose ultimate fate was to be forced underground once again by the pressure of new crustal formation (Colling et al., 1997: 114–15; Smil, 2003: 116–21).

In this way, a story took shape in which the earth's crust was in constant motion: the new global tectonics providing a unifying schema through which all regional geological processes could be viewed as manifestations of a unified and continuous cycling of the planet's entire lithosphere. This was a transition that implied a radical reassessment of earthquakes, volcanoes and other geophysical upheavals. No longer envisaged as exceptions to a normal state of quiescence, such events came to be accepted as ordinary and inevitable expressions of the earth's unceasing crustal dynamics.

The acceptance of the theory of plate tectonics was followed by a cascade of further discoveries and amalgamations. Building on the conceptual suturing of the basic componentry of hydrosphere, lithosphere and atmosphere, research in the 1970s and 1980s homed in on the interactions between the most important chemical constituents of the outer earth. The emergent meta-discipline of geochemistry forged itself around explorations of the principle reservoirs of carbon dioxide and free oxygen, sulphur and carbon, and the silicate minerals contained in the basalts, granites and other rocks that emanated from the deep earth (Westbroek, 1992: Ch. 4; Smil, 2003: Ch. 5). Once again, the focus was unequivocally global, as geoscientists tracked the channelling of key elements back and forth through their atmospheric, lithospheric and hydrospheric sinks. Along with these planet-scaled couplings, researchers also mapped out a range of complex reticulated exchanges that enmeshed each of the main cycles into a single encompassing 'geo-chemical' system (Westbroek, 1992: 93; Wood, 2004: 90).

In consort with the new geophysics, this globalist chemistry would come to serve as the mainstay of the modelling of climate at a global level. There were other major components of the outer earth that also called for full consideration. Growing interest in Antarctica, during and after the International Geophysical Year of 1957–8, gradually drew *ice* – or rather, the 'cryosphere' – into full conversation with the other dominions of the whole earth system (Pyne, 1988; Macdougall, 2004). Ice ages had long been considered epochal events in the shaping of the earth's surface features and in the periodic rebooting of biological succession, but the new glaciology, plumped with polar paleoclimatic data, helped to redefine ice sheets as 'interesting, dynamic systems, full of feedback mechanisms' (Pyne, 1988: 287). Glacial episodes came to be construed as key players in the planet's overall self-regulation, the new grasp of their machinations helping to draw the earth more closely into the domain of astrophysical movements and rhythms (Pyne, 1988: 287).

While great slabs of rock or ice have effectively become more mobile and active, life has come to be seen increasingly as a weighty and momentous force in the moulding of the earth. For a number of reasons, biological life arrived late at the new planetary synthesis. Even where the will was there, the entangled flows and trajectories of living matter have proven more of a challenge to large-scale quantification and mapping than physico-chemical elements (Westbroek, 1992: 65). Perhaps also, alongside the hurdle of inherited boundaries between life and earth sciences, biology's own long-standing privileging of more conspicuous multi-cellular organisms at the expense of the much older, metabolically wider-ranging and far more prolific microbial kingdom has held back a fuller appreciation of 'life as a geological force' (Westbroek, 1992; Margulis, 2001).

In the 1920s, the Russian mineralogist Vladimir Vernadsky (1998 [1926]) had already developed the idea that biological life – or what he preferred to term 'living matter' – played a central role both in mobilizing the mineral elements of the earth's crust and in determining the composition of the atmosphere. Popularizing the term 'biosphere', he not only proposed that all living things meshed into a unified and dynamic planetary force, but also stressed the extent to which the enveloping sphere of terrestrial life was an expression of the earth's openness to the energies of the solar system (Smil, 2003: Ch. 1). The resurgence of interest in life as a prevalent element in the generation and maintenance of the planetary system half a century later was also sparked by the consideration of earth in relation to the wider solar system. It was in the light of work with NASA on the probability of finding living things on the earth's neighbouring planets that geochemist James Lovelock (1987), independently of Vernadsky, arrived at his own theory about the integral role of biological life itself in sustaining the earth as an environment fit for living things.

While Lovelock's depiction of the earth system as a sort of superorganism has ruffled scientific sensibilities, there is broader support for his argument about the capacity of the biosphere to function homeostatically in response to perturbations of the earth – including significant changes in the solar flux (see Smil, 2003: 230–1). What became known as the 'Gaia hypothesis' has been greatly fortified by microbiologist Lynn Margulis's evidence about the unique role of the microbial life in establishing the biosphere and her arguments about their continued prominence in mediating major earth processes (Margulis, 1998: Ch. 8; Hird, 2009: Ch. 6).

Despite the continuing contentiousness of Gaia theory, the idea that living organisms and their global environment form a tightly coupled system has encouraged interdisciplinary researchers to take account of the biosphere as a major geochemical reservoir and to consider the global cycling of life alongside that of rock, water and air (Smil, 2003: 231; see also Schneider and Boston, 1991; Bengtsson and Hammer, 2001). Together with other ongoing issues (such as the significance of the planet's energetic and material openness to the cosmos), questions around the role of life's co-implication with other earth-shaping forces are indicative that the integrative approach to the earth is still evolving. Even so, the last 50 or 60 years of earth science offer plentiful evidence that a major shift has already occurred in the way scientists conceive of our 'specific planet'. As physical geographer Dennis Wood sums up, prior to this succession of developments, the standard view was that:

> Things ... *touched*. They sort of pushed each other around. But there was none of the sense of interpenetration, of multiple causation, of feedback, of mutual interdependencies, of ... *the structural coupling* that is the essential characteristic of our situation as we understand it today. (2004: 69–70, author's italics)

It is the geosciences' escalating ontological commitment to the globality of their objects of inquiry that has enabled the comprehension of the earth's climate dynamics to reach its current level, including the awakening to the possibility of abrupt changes in climatic regimes at the planetary scale. After some debate, many earth scientists have come round to the idea that human forcing of climate is now substantial – and substantiated – enough to mark an epochal shift out of the Holocene and into the 'Anthropocene' (Crutzen, 2002; Davis, 2008). But if such a pronouncement is taken by critical social scientists to be supportive of their case for an ultimate 'end of nature', in the earth sciences it is more likely to be read as an affirmation that our species belongs among other biological and geophysical forces.

Similarly, there is an apparent convergence between a nascent social scientific uptake of complexity theory and a more established natural scientific turn towards understanding the behaviour of physical systems by way of complex, nonlinear dynamics generalizable over a range of different contexts or fields. Sociologist John Urry (2003, 2005) and fellow transdisciplinary-minded social theorists may well be onto a promising line of inquiry when they point to a potential convergence between the social and natural sciences as a way of grappling with the dynamical properties of a densely and heterogeneously interconnected globe – one in which physical and social elements are inextricably bound together.

But this is where we need to be sensitive to the differences in the way that globality is currently being imagined in critical social thought and in the earth sciences. Social science discourses on complex, hybridized nature-cultures, I have argued, wager on the co-constitutive relations of the social and the physical – and discourage thinking in terms of natural systems in which the human imprint is negligible or non-existent. No less than the social sciences, the earth sciences invest in a version of relationality, one in which observable realities are understood in terms of inextricable entanglements, mutual interdependencies and co-constitutive relations. They too have a strong sense of 'multiplicity', especially with regard to the recognition that complex earth systems and sub-systems are capable of moving between alternative states (none of which is afforded preferential treatment over others) as well as having the capacity to generate entirely novel forms of organization. And they also go to great lengths to 'situate' the earth in its current manifestation – both in terms of its own eventful history and in the broader context of an evolving cosmos.

Aside from the relatively restricted spatio-temporal span in which humans make their presence felt, however, the complex global 'co-enactments' of interest to earth scientists occur without input from our species. Not only is it absolutely crucial to any understanding of earth processes that major rhythms, cycles and singular trajectories reach far back beyond any human presence, but it is also routine to track causal processes well beneath the inhabited surface of the earth and beyond the planet into the solar system or further.

For all that they intersect or overlap at significant junctures, then, the deep temporal and extended spatial sensibilities characteristic of earth science 'globality' pull in very different directions from the enthrallment with co-present entities that currently prevails in pro-gressive social and cultural thought – in ways which I will be further exploring in the following chapter.

Much of the recent reassessment of nature in critical social science and cultural theory takes inspiration from post-war continental phi-losophy. In this regard, the assaults on totality, closure, universality and foundationalism which are perceived to be definitive gestures of post-structural philosophies have been especially pertinent. With this in mind, I return to the question of the earth in some influential currents of recent philosophical thought, picking up where Derrida's critique of Husserl left off. What kinds of globality, I ask, do the live-lier currents of philosophy deal in – and how do their takes on the earth articulate with those of the social and earth sciences?

Continental philosophy and the ungrounding of the ground

The shift towards taking heterogeneous 'materialities' seriously in the social sciences is in many ways a reaction against the prioritizing of cultural, discursive and linguistic themes in some recent fields of social and cultural inquiry. This so-called 'cultural turn' – with its characteristic thematizing of the indeterminacy of meaning, identity and representation – itself drew inspiration from an interest in systems of language and communication in 1950s and 1960s continental philosophy: a concern that played an important part in the shaping of post-structuralism (see Johnson, 1993: 1–3). I want to set out from this conjuncture – not only because of what it tells us about later engagement with physical processes in philosophy, but for what it reveals about the strange (and unfortunate) destiny of the thematic of 'writing' or 'sign play' over the course of its uptake into social and cultural thought.

For a number of key French philosophers, it was the achievements of post-war biology – especially the deciphering of the genetic code – which inspired a reconceptualization of language, and later 'writing', into a much more-than-human capacity. Quite suddenly, it became possible to conceive of the play of difference and sameness, of chance and necessity, of coding and indetermination, as generic operations – as common structural dynamics that drew the knowledgeable, communicative human subject into the infinitely more encompassing current of biological life (Johnson, 1993: Ch. 5; see also Monod, 1971). As it also implicated life in what has usually been taken to be our own unique and defining capabilities. Or as philosopher Georges Canguilhem expressed it: 'Life has always done – without writing, long before writing even existed – what humans have sought to do with engraving, writing and printing, namely, to transmit messages' (1994: 317).

This interdisciplinary encounter went far beyond socio-historical or epistemological reflection on science: it saw the sciences as bearers of truths with profound ontological significance. 'Interpreted in a certain way', Canguilhem went on to reflect, 'contemporary biology is somehow a philosophy of life' (1994: 319). It also went beyond the life sciences, to take in developments in information theory and cybernetics: fields which were witnessing a turn away from concerns with homeostasis and equilibrium toward an understanding of the way noise, interference and the emergence of novelty co-existed with tendencies for conservation (see Hayles, 1999: Ch. 6). Commenting on François Jacob's presentation of the new biology, Michel Serres sought to grasp the broader import of this resonation of themes between otherwise disparate fields: 'Like the other sciences', he wrote of molecular biology, 'it points towards a general philosophy of marked elements' (cited in Johnson, 1993: 3).

This search for a philosophical understanding of the play of difference and repetition that goes well beyond human symbolic systems – or any anthropologistic register – links the work of Michel Serres, Gilbert Simondon, Georges Canguilhem and Gilles Deleuze (see Gualandi, 2009). Though it is more controversial, there is ample evidence that it is also pivotal to Derrida's conception of writing 'in the general sense' (see Johnson, 1993). As Derrida puts it himself, albeit more cautiously than some of his compatriots: 'I prefer always to speak of the iterability of the *mark* beyond all human speech acts. Barring any inconsistency, ineptness, or insufficiently rigorous formalization on my part, my statements on this subject should be valid beyond the marks and society called "human"' (1988: 134, author's italics; see also 1984: 2).

What the move towards a 'general philosophy of marked elements' demonstrated was that philosophical inquiry could unhinge itself from the human subject without losing its passion for action or transformation (see Rabinow, 1994: 21). At least for a moment, philosophy had cast off its anthropocentrism for a materialist critique which denounced any privileged place for reflection on *human* knowing or doing. As Alberto Gualandi vouches: 'The French philosophers of the sixties attempted something … audacious. According to them, man and his thought would be but finite forms among others, all engendered on the basis of an obscure and infinite ground that one might call Being or Nature' (2009: 502).

While it is well known that these thinkers were fiercely resistant to the metaphysics of presence – the assumption that there once was a pure, stable and plenitudinous nature to which we ought to try and return – this is not the same thing as rejecting the function of the ground. As Alain Badiou would later put it, in conversation with the thought of Deleuze: 'One should not be too quick to believe that one has finished with the ground'. Before going on to add that the rethinking of the ground, for all that it is 'rendered complex by the conditions of our epoch', remains a necessary and pressing task in the contemporary world (2000: 45, 55, 46). And as Gualandi's comments remind us, we shouldn't rush into thinking we are done with nature as the ground of human thought or action: which also means questioning the very idea of 'denaturation' as an inherently progressive or critical manoeuvre (Nancy, 2007: 87; see also Cheah, 1996).

What those rather remarkable 'philosophies of marked elements' were doing was wrenching away Husserl's sense of a permanent or rigid ground, and replacing it with one that was unstable, mutable, transformative. As Derrida would later put it, there is no ultimately solid bedrock to connect with, only a further play of elements, and another, and another: 'bottomless, endless connections and … the indefinitely articulated regress of the beginning' (1981: 333–4). This is still a ground – it remains a source, a subtending, a reservoir of possibilities for later developments. It just doesn't provide any anchoring, any certainty, any promise of unity. Quite the inverse, a ground that is characterized by an unending 'textural' interplay of elements functions as an impetus for further differentiation and change for all those beings or entities that rest upon it. It gives rise to the very play of difference and sameness that more conventional social or philosophical inquiry routinely attributes to language and other cultural systems.

To be sure, it was biology, to a far greater extent than the geo-sciences, which provided the initial push towards a more mobile and exuberant ground. In the writings of Michel Serres (1995, 2001), however, the noise and indeterminacy of the biological is comple-mented by a much more encompassing sense of elemental dyna-mism: one which takes in the rhythms and entwinings of earth and sea and air. But it's the work of Gilles Deleuze and Felix Guattari that has come to be most strongly associated with the idea that the earth itself is the primordial and exemplary form of the unstable ground.

As early as *Difference and Repetition* (1994 [1962]), Deleuze was grappling with the philosophical implications of the nascent study of nonlinear and chaotic systems. Here, he speaks specifically of physi-cal systems 'bifurcating' – that is, passing through critical points into alternative states – and more abstractly of a generative chaos from which the earth and cosmos emerge (1994: 147, 199; see also De Landa, 1992; Bonta and Protevi, 2004: 6–7).

In their first collaborative work, *Anti Oedipus* (1983 [1977]), Deleuze and Guattari begin to think of the earth as a full, indivisible and generative entity: a pulsing body of productive forces. From the outset, theirs is a very different story from that favoured by social scientists engaging with ecological issues. Where social researchers repeatedly proceed from the observation that environmental prob-lems overflow national boundaries, Deleuze and Guattari make their ontological priorities clear by insisting that first there is an earthly body composed of energetic and material flows, and only later does there arise a human impulse to deal with this inherent dynamism by inscribing marks on the surface of earth (1983: 139–44). In *What is Philosophy?* they develop this sense of the earth as the primary source of life-altering provocations into a fully fledged 'geophiloso-phy'. We inhabit a planet, Deleuze and Guattari argue, that is liable to spontaneously reorganize its elemental strata and flows into novel configurations: 'an earth (which) constantly carries out a movement of deterritorialization on the spot' (1994: 85).

All material bodies, they propose, have this potential to disaggregate and recompose their constituent parts into a different state of being. But just as Husserl's earth gathered in and bound together all the other elements, so too for Deleuze and Guattari does the earth play an 'exemplary' role: 'The earth is not one element among others but rather brings together all the elements within a single embrace …' (1994: 85; see also Turnbull, 2006: 135). In contrast to Husserl's 'immovable ark', however, their earth is far too volatile to ever function as an anchoring ground. Its integrative role is merely an interval before the earth shakes off its composure and reactivates its constitutive elements '… using one or another of them to deterritorialize territory' (1994: 85). Effectively, what Deleuze and Guattari's earth bundles together are all the terrestrial capacities for upheaval and metamorphosis. Their earth is a *metastratum* of inherently excessive forces and energies, in which even the most apparently stable or stratified formations will sooner or later unsettle themselves (1987: 40). Or, if we look at these strata through a long enough lens, we will find that they were morphing and flowing all along. For, as Deleuze had earlier noted, 'the hardest rocks become soft and fluid matter on the geological scale of millions of years' (1994: 2).

Whatever their other differences, Deleuze and Guattari share with Derrida a strategy of constantly seeking openings between a chosen focus of inquiry and whatever context or field lies beyond it – and beyond that and so on. In Derrida's case, for all his ostensible commitment to the 'indefinitely articulated regress of the beginning', promising gestures beyond the human rarely eventuate into sustained forays into extra-cultural zones (Protevi, 2001: 9). Though it must be added that more maverick interpreters have productively extended his characteristic tactics and manoeuvres deep into the recesses of the organic and the inorganic (see, for example, Kirby, 1997, 2001; Craw and Heads, 1988; Wilson, 1998), Deleuze and Guattari, famously, have no hesitation in leaping from one domain or strata to another. If the earth is the preeminent reservoir of the material–energetic resources in the immediate vicinity of the human species, our planet in turn opens out to a no-less excessive and perturbing cosmos. And in this way, any human or other terrestrial life form not only channels the forces packed into our home planet, but ultimately taps into the 'Whole of the universe' (Deleuze, 1990: 77). Thus, in the Deleuzoguattarian oeuvre, philosophical immanence implies anything but a globality with no exterior. It means that 'the potentialities of any given actuality are the cosmos as a whole' (Williams, 1997: 236; see also Clark, 2005a).

There is another strand to post-war French philosophy that posits a turbulent and generative earth that is ex-orbitant in its openness to the cosmos. In a thesis that influenced Derrida, Baudrillard, Foucault and other key post-structural thinkers, George Bataille (1991 [1967], 1993 [1976]) argued that all our 'restricted' economies – economic systems in the conventional sense that only account for what can be calculated and exchanged – need to be reconsidered in the light of their interchange with the more exclusive or 'general' economies that are their context. Bataille insisted that the only way to understand the predicament of the human and all its achievements and challenges was to think in terms of 'an economy on the scale of the universe' (cited in Stoekl, 2007: xiv). By this he meant that we need to understand our economic, cultural and political existence not only in relation to the spatial limits imposed by our inhabitation of a finite, spherical planet, but also in regard to the excess of solar energy which the earth receives – and the pressure towards growth and expansion implied by this abundance (Bataille, 1986 [1957]: 94, 1991: 23).

Bataille took inspiration from Friedrich Nietzsche's depiction of the sun as a source of endless energetic gifts to the earth for which it demanded nothing in return: taking this primordial stellar act of pure generosity as indicative that abundance comes before scarcity, and that unilateral offerings or openings precede relationships built upon the expectation of a return (Bataille, 1991: 28). But it's noteworthy that this affirmation of radical asymmetry had another, very different inspiration. Though he has been taken to task for the way his celebration of excess and lack of self-restraint promotes the aestheticization of all modern values (see Habermas, 1983: 14), this line of critique misses the crucial significance of the conversation with physical science in Bataille's work. As signalled by references in his magnum opus, *The Accursed Share*, Bataille was an early and receptive reader of Vernadsky, whose theorems on the operation of the biosphere, as I noted above, anticipated many of the subsequent turns taken by earth science (see Bataille, 1991: 29).

Vernadsky's insistence that '(t)he biosphere is at least as much a *creation of the sun* as a result of terrestrial processes' (Vernadsky, 1998 [1926]: 44, author's italics) resonates in Bataille's argument that all the economies we construct for ourselves are open to the wider environment, to the earth itself, and must ultimately 'measure up to the universe' (1991: 11). It's intriguing to speculate that

Vernadsky's model of a solar-charged biosphere – surely one of the most prescient scientific ideas of the last century – has left its glowing residue, via the writings of Bataille, in the core of post-structural philosophy. Bataille's 'accounting' for the role of solar energy in human and other terrestrial life was at the crux of his argument – taken up as a staple of post-structural and postmodern thought – that the systems we compose for ourselves can neither be closed at their beginning nor at their end – and are thus destined to be perpetually energized and animated by their outside.

But Bataille went further than this, proposing that our reliance on a monstrously excessive energy – the fact that our social existence is fuelled from a source far beyond our control or containment – ensures that we are inescapably exposed to the most violent, perturbing forces of the cosmos. As Nick Land gleefully proclaims of Bataille's crucial insight: this 'energetic trajectory … is the molten terrain of a dark communion, binding him to everything that has ever convulsed upon the Earth' (1992: 32).

Taking cues from Serres, or Deleuze/Guattari, or Bataille about conceiving of the ground as inherently shifting and precarious, may help see off an earlier enthrallment with permanent moorings, but it need not spell the end of the phenomenological concern with the experiential dimensions of earthliness. Now that the 'objective' earth of the physical sciences is as much the shuddering terrain directly under foot as it is an 'abstract' astronomical body, the irreducible tension between Husserl's earth radically at rest and the intangible mobility of an orbiting sphere ought to have lost much of its bite. While the empirical or cognitive account of the planet's complex dynamics does not directly disclose the bodily, sensuous and affective dimensions of inhabiting an endemically unstable earth, it nonetheless points more toward a necessary (indeed urgent) complementarity than it does to a terminal incommensurability.

Indeed, one of the most important implications of evolving earth science discourses may be their imperative to bring the theme of the abyssally playful ground into closer proximity with that of the constitutive openness and receptivity of the phenomenal body.

Conclusion: down to earth

Meditating on the 'inconstancy of the world' shortly after the devastating Lisbon Earthquake of 1755, the young Immanuel Kant concluded: 'Man was not born to build everlasting cottages upon this stage of vanity' (1994 [1756]: 29). It was not until over two centuries later that the earth sciences could offer a certain and coherent explanation for the world's more momentous 'inconstancies'. Revealing the entire surface of the earth to be in grinding, juddering motion, the geoscience story suggests that what are catastrophes for soft, fleshy creatures like us are for the earth merely minor and mundane readjustments.

The convulsions of nature that so perturbed Kant and fellow Enlightenment thinkers subsequently drifted far out of philosophical focus. So far, in fact, that whole schools would embrace the solidity of the earth beneath our feet – and assume that this abiding base offered 'thought' (a synecdoche for all human endeavour) its best or only foundation. While such a sense of earthly certitude has been frequently and thoroughly problematized, it has been troubled most often on account of the way that certain kinds of human experience – especially those associated with techno-cultural change – mediate between 'us' and the earth we stand upon. Even in the midst of the revolutionary discoveries of latter twentieth-century earth science, there has only infrequently been any real consideration about what the planet's own complex dynamics might mean for rethinking the 'ground'.

In a creative outburst of French theory in the 1960s, an opportunity opened up for drawing the emergent understanding of the dynamism of the earth into the core of Western thought. Inspired especially by the new understanding of the indeterminate coding that animated biological life, a cohort of thinkers began to explore the idea that nature itself was an unstable, unlimited and incessantly generative ground for human becoming. And yet, while a feeling for the 'vitality' of the organic has intermittently resounded through subsequent philosophical and social inquiry, a full acknowledgement of the differential force of elemental processes more generally has yet to really take hold.

Deleuze and Guattari's geophilosophy, Serres' rhythmically pulsing planet, and Bataille's energetic geophysics have each in their own way gestured towards an expansive sense of the earth and cosmos as the volatile ground of human and other creaturely life. Only recently, however, have these openings begun to be taken up in a sustained and serious way, and arguably we still await a full encounter between the best that philosophy has to offer on the topic of the ungrounding ground and the many provocations of earth science (see Frodeman, 2000: viii–ix). While there have been several decades of productive articulations with the life sciences, especially in feminist theorizing of the body, explicit engagements with a nonliving materiality remain rare. As a few philosophers have lately noted, in most of the encounters with elemental matter to date, it has paradoxically been the 'liveliness' of the inorganic that has been highlighted, at the expense of properties that are more specific to the mineral or chemical structures that make up most of the known universe.

Resuscitating what he sees as exceptional more-than-organic themes in the work of the eighteenth-to-nineteenth-century nature philosopher Friedrich Schelling, Iain Hamilton Grant contends that modern philosophical thought has rarely proceeded further than animality (2006: 9, 18). In not daring to leave the 'ontological cul-de-sac of organism', he argues, it has failed to give adequate attention to the unstable ground – the 'brute matter' from which life emerges (2006: 81; see also 2010). Or as Graham Harman, in conversation with Grant, has put it: 'Life-philosophy is an alibi for refusing to deal with the inorganic ... it's a way to stay close to the human while claiming that you're going deeper than that somehow' (Harman, 2007: 382).

This recalls an earlier point made by Jean-François Lyotard in reference to use of the concept of 'Life' to cover generic processes of 'desire' or 'complexification': his contention that 'resort to this term seems still far too derivative of human experience, too anthropomorphic' (1991: 45). But both Grant and Harman seem to be going further than this, for they are also wishing to disabuse philosophy of any expectation that 'merely crude matter' *should* complexify, *should* give rise to life, *should* have any such 'higher' effects in order to qualify for our consideration (Grant, 2007: 360; Harman, 2007: 382). If we demand of matter that it acts as though it has vitality, then we overlook or downgrade the possibility of it simply persisting in a rock-like or mineral condition. And that means that we foreclose on the challenge of thinking through or about a domain of existence that is devoid of any trace of thought, feeling, will, or any other quality we habitually recognize in ourselves. To take a lead from Harman, 'rather than anthropomorphizing the inanimate realm', we need to start 'morphing the human realm into a variant of the inanimate' (2009: 212).

Such speculations are rife with potential for a new kind of engagement with earth science, a conversation that could pick where the old 'philosophies of marked elements' left off – only this time moving well beyond the enthrallment with the continuity between biology and human expressive capacities. If philosophy, as the introduction to a recent collection put it, is 'to come back "down to Earth", it is an

Earth which we no longer fully recognise, and which continues to offer numerous challenges – by turns urgent, melancholy, and twisted – to the thought it has given birth to' (Mackay, 2010: 19).

As the philosophical return to earth gathers momentum, it remains to be seen whether social thought will be joining the adventure. Looking beyond the current fixation on the connective capacities and motilities of our own species, human geographer Doreen Massey confronts the ancient manoeuvring of life and rock. And concludes that this is 'a planet that has ever been a global mobility' (2005b: 98, 138; see also 2006). But in the realms of critical social and cultural thought, this is still a rare admission (but see Hinchliffe, 2003). Even after a good decade and a half of concerted reaction to the so-called 'cultural turn', even after years of promoting an active and agential 'materiality', the best that most of us can offer is a concession that not all of the realities we inhabit are made by humans alone. Granted, attention to the way that humans and nonhumans mutually confederate each other continues to make a crucial contribution to the understanding of a certain category of socio-technical problem, of which more in the next chapter. But these are not the only threats or hazards or inducements that weigh upon human life.

Like many of his compatriots in the social sciences, Ulrich Beck continues to insist that 'Nature ... has ceased to exist', that 'nature "in itself" cannot form an analytic point of reference' (2009: 83). And yet, just a few pages earlier he expounds:

> the year 2005 reminded us once again, with the tsunami catastrophe, the destruction of New Orleans by Hurricane Katrina, and the devastation of extensive regions of South America and Pakistan, of how limited the claim to control of modern societies remains in the face of natural forces. (2009: 50)

But why exactly is it, we must wonder, that even after half a century of insistent tutoring by the earth sciences, our 'modern societies' still need to be reminded of their exposure to 'natural forces'? Could it be that critical social thought's own tenacious disavowal of any grounding function of nature is itself as much a part of the problem as it is a solution? Can any approach that rebukes the exteriority or independence of nature, any theorem that restricts globality to an effect of human orchestration really get to grips with the full potentiality of the earth and cosmos – or the extent of human vulnerability to this eventfulness?

In the following chapter, I zoom in on those modes of engaging with natural or material agency that currently predominate in critical social scientific thought and practice. Keeping firmly in mind that 'life' is only one variant of the forcefulness or agency of the world, I set out from the particular concern with life's exuberance and mobility that is currently galvanizing social theorists working the society–nature juncture. I consider both the strengths and limitations of recent approaches to understanding the processes by which the worlds we live in get made, and weigh up the alternatives that are now on offer. And in this way, I come back to the renewed philosophical interest in an earth which does its own thing, whatever surcharge we add to its mobilizations – or to its obduracy.

2

Ways to Make a World:
From Relational Materiality to Radical Asymmetry

Introduction: excesses of life

'Life is open to the universe and to itself', as biologist Lynn Margulis and science writer Dorian Sagan pithily put it (1995: 199). One of the many forces that life is open and responsive to are the threats to its physical environments that are caused by that part of life itself which is the human species. That 'we' are transforming local ecosystems and impacting on terrestrial processes in ways that are deleterious to numerous other life forms has been one of the major environmental concerns of recent decades. Life may well be a geological force, but humans too function as earth processes, contributing to changes that alter the overall conditions of biological life on the planet.

But many of the 'environmental' problems that researchers and practitioners now find themselves confronting pull in very different directions from the concern with the vulnerability of biological life in the face of advancing human agency. There are pressing issues in which what is most alarming is life's very exuberance; its unregenerate capacity to multiply, transform and mobilize itself; its proclivity to turn up in forms we didn't anticipate, at sites we don't want it, in numbers we can't deal with. This happens with some quite big and 'charismatic' fauna, such as mountain lions or coyotes which find new niches in urban areas. It's more often the case with a range of less conspicuous creatures across many phyla that hitch rides on human conveyances or skip their allotted plots in order to pullulate in places that are ecologically unprepared for them (Clark, 1999, 2002). But most of all, it's a matter of microscopic organisms, of seething, unseen multitudes which are capable of pursuing devastating paths through human dominions, including entities so brutally simple in their constitution that we are not even decided as to whether or not they qualify as 'alive' (Clark, 2000, 2007a).

Escalating fear over the threats posed by unregenerate biological life, especially pathogenic micro-organisms, has recently resulted in a burgeoning of interest – both pragmatic and academic – with the question of 'biosecuritization'. Our species, like all other relatively large and lumbering life forms, has always been susceptible to the bodily incursions of much more minuscule beings. We have also slowly, painfully, imperfectly, learned to live with many of these troublesome organisms. But there is a growing sense that in a world of intensifying global interconnectivity, we are multiplying vectors and niches for our microscopic nemeses far faster that we can physiologically or culturally adapt to their exertions. A whole range of outbreaks and threats, including HIV AIDS, avian flu, SARS and mad cow disease – feature combinations of life's own procreative capacities with the novel opportunities provided by our own sociomaterial infrastructures, prompting desperate measures to try and curtail the very flourishing that we are inadvertently promoting (Dillon, 2007; Hinchliffe and Bingham, 2008a).

In many respects, the whole predicament of unwanted irruptions of biological life is turning out to be an ideal testing ground for the new generation of critical theoretical–empirical approaches that parcel humans and nonhumans into the same problematics. The complex topologies of intractable and infectious life, with its unpredictable patterns of emergence and its inextricable insinuation in everyday human material existence, presents a problem of immeasurable proportions. No existing discipline is geared up to engage with situations that encompass the transformative capabilities of micro and macro-biological life, expanding global transport and communication infrastructures, advancing techno-scientific capacities for manipulating living things, changing patterns of urbanization, shifting public understanding and wavering affective states, proliferating institutional arrangements for policing biosecurity, and so on. A clutch of still relatively novel 'relational' ontologies and research agendas oriented towards the interaction of heterogeneous objects has risen to this challenge, generating some of the most exciting, creative and urgently needed 'social' (read 'more-than-social') theory of recent years.

My intention here is neither to celebrate nor critique this still rapidly evolving body of work, but to take a step back, and address it in a broader context. The recent efflorescence of literature on biosecurity is a useful starting point, but it's not my main focus here. I take this work more as a kind of portal into the issue of 'life's openness to the universe and to itself', and the more general question of the part life and other physical processes play in the realities we inhabit. Picking up on a theme from the previous chapter, I'm interested in life as a force on earth, as an ingredient in the making and remaking of our planet. And, especially, in what life's lengthy and momentous achievements to date mean to 'us' as late-coming life forms and social beings. While deeply sympathetic to the research and theory which is now attending to the demands of the present – to the pressing issues that are the emergent properties of our current inter-national, inter-species, and inter-object relations – I want to stretch things even further, and to consider what life has done long before we were around to intercede in its adventures.

One of the themes that has begun to assert itself in what we might short-handedly call the 'relational materialist' approach to biosecuritization issues is the degree of human susceptibility to a vitality we cannot presently or perhaps ever hope to contain. As Steve Hinchliffe and Nick Bingham sum up:

> The potent mixings and interplays within and between people, places, animals, forms, chemicals, embargos, cells, and so on are more than likely to be generative, to produce new conformations ... given this heterogeneity and incompleteness, biosecurity may be as much about surrendering control as it is about jurisdiction over the bios. (2008b: 227)

This acknowledgement of a ceiling on our ability to order or regulate our transactions with the living is timely and important. If it underscores a crucial need to reorganize or recompose our relations with other things, I want to suggest, it also points up this project's excess or remainder – gesturing towards the very limits of collective human action. These limits – why they exist and what to make of them – are my concern here.

On the issue of our entanglement with other life forms and elemental processes, Bruno Latour asks 'What would a human be without elephants, plants, lions, cereals, oceans, ozone or plankton?' (1998: 231). His answer is not a lot, or even nothing at all. From a social science perspective, we should not underestimate just how radical this question is. But what if we were to turn the question around and ask what plankton (and other microorganisms) or plants or oceans would be without human beings? What does it mean that our answer might be – ought to be – very different from the one we have just given? And what might this discrepancy mean to Hinchliffe and Bingham's proposition about the limits of our interventions, about 'realities' beyond our jurisdiction?

In this chapter, I take a closer look at how the study of 'relational materialities' seeks to account for the heterogeneous composition of the worlds we inhabit, and explore the affinities of these approaches with Deleuze and Guattari's philosophical engagement with the way disparate materials come into association. While attentive to the advantages of the 'ontological levelling' that permits us to take the agency of things, objects and materials seriously, I ask what happens when some categories of things rely on other kinds of things in ways which are not reciprocated. How might we think through situations where whole bundles or collections of objects – we might say 'worlds' – function as the originary site and the indispensible underpinning of other aggregates of objects? What does it mean to say that life, or the earth, or nature, or the universe are not just constellations of material and energy with which humans forge connections, but realities upon which we are *utterly dependent* – in ways that are out of all proportion to life, nature, the earth or the universe's dependence on us? Turning from the characteristic concern of relational materialities research with the mutual entanglement between nature and human life to the question of a radical asymmetry between the natural and the social, I look at what this implies for human agency, for our capacity to construct, enact, perform, compose, assemble, or otherwise renegotiate the realities in which our lives pass.

Relational ontologies and the agency of objects

Variations on the theme of nature coming to a physical and conceptual terminal point, as we saw in Chapter 1, emerged as a staple of critical social scientific engagement with technological and environmental problems. But in the very process of laying nature to rest, much of this work served to imbue inhuman elements and entities with a renewed vigour – if not always intentionally. Ulrich Beck's (1992) risk society thesis is a case in point. In keeping with his artificialization-of-nature scenario, Beck shows how new and unprecedented interventions into matter and life precipitate deadly systemic breakdowns. Ostensibly, it is incautious human agents who engineer the conditions under which dangerous elements are likely to be accidently released into the world. But the backstory tells of a disconcerting *willingness* on the part of these absconders to break loose, disperse and pursue their own agendas. As in analogous tales of ecological or technological misadventure, what the plot actually hinges on is as much the adventurousness of things themselves as it is the deeds or misdeeds of human actors.

It is the more explicit recognition that agency is 'democratically' distributed rather than concentrated in particular levels or categories of existence that characterizes the approaches that gather around the engagement with 'relational materialities'. This work is less obviously intent on terminating the being and the concept of nature, preferring to posit and pursue new ways of traversing the human/ nonhuman interface. What links its otherwise disparate strands is a concern with the way that entities – of any conceivable genus – interact with other entities, and how these relationships both shape their participants and compose entire worlds. This entails a turn away from sharp distinctions between the self and its others, the living and the inert, the born and the made, the conscious and the programmed, in favour of a recognition that real-worldly objects move along, cut across, combine or recompose such classifications (see Frow, 2001: 285; Bennett, 2004; Thrift, 2008: Ch. 7). Within the social sciences especially, such acknowledgements contribute to a generalized reassessment of the '*constitutive force* of things in social and political life': a turn to 'materiality' and 'the object' that is in part a reaction against the perceived over-indulgence in cultural and linguistic themes in recent thought (Braun, 2008: 670; Pels et al., 2002). Whether we buy into it or not, the sense of a need to loosen the hold of representation, discourse and textuality has clearly helped elevate a new generation of relational–material ontologies to a commanding position in current critical thinking around nature.

The two tributaries I focus on converge from different directions: Bruno Latour and fellow actor-network theorists arriving by way of the social study of science, Gilles Deleuze and Felix Guattari coming from a branch of continental philosophy concerned with the 'immanent' transformative powers of this-worldly things. Latour proposes a 'principle of generalized symmetry': an axiom formulated in conversation with Michel Callon which seeks to attribute capacities for world-making even-handedly amongst every kind of entity (Latour, 1993: 103; Callon and Law, 1989: 76). Actors – whether human or nonhuman, animate or inanimate, real or imagined – are to be defined not by any a priori category to which they may be ascribed, but by the difference they make to other actors and to the wider world (Latour, 1999b: 122). It is this renunciation of hierarchies of being in favour of a flattened ontology that brings Latour into broad accord with Deleuze and Guattari's fealty to the notion of an unbounded field of immanence in which all entities co-exist: 'a single fixed plane ... peopled by anonymous matter, by infinite bits of impalpable matter entering into varying connections' (1987: 255).

Latour's actors take shape and gain strength by forging alliances with other actors. Such associations may settle into networks: provisional but more-or-less enduring arrangements which enable mixed groupings of entities to achieve things they could never do alone. Deleuze and Guattari use the notion of assemblage (or *agencement*) to make a case that the most novel structures or orderings come into existence not by way of stepwise development but through the coming together of previously unrelated objects or processes. In keeping with the syncretic spirit these theorists seem to share, researchers working the relational–materialist vein often fuse broadly 'Deleuzoguattarian' and Latourian concepts into generalized accounts of collaborative and emergent agency. In Jane Bennett's version, for example, 'a material body always resides within some assemblage or other, and its thing-power *is a function of that grouping*. A thing has power by virtue of its operating *in conjunction* with other things' (2004: 353–4, author's italics).

Claims about agency and identity being network-effects, it's fair to say, sit rather comfortably in the current anti-essentialist climate. In the corridors of critical thought, it is some time since anybody has publically championed things with pre-existing forms or stable identities. As Graham Harman reminds us, relational theories of reality have prevailed in philosophy throughout the last century (2002: 23–4). The real challenge lies in the imperative to include all the efficacious elements in any relational roll call and in the requirement to weight their respective contributions in unbiased ways. Here, the inclusive gesture of the new wave of relational ontologies – their willingness to account for direct action involving genuinely disparate entities – gives them a fresher air. It is an atmosphere which draws breath from the rich, permissive folds of *A Thousand Plateaus*, where Deleuze and Guattari depict the kind of events where 'a semiotic fragment rubs shoulders with a chemical interaction, an electron crashes into a language, a black hole captures a genetic message, a crystallization produces a passion ...' (1987: 69). One that takes more practical guidance from Latour's tracking of heterogeneous conjunctions, like the ozone hole in *We Have Never Been Modern* which 'links the most esoteric sciences and the most sordid politics, the most distant sky and some factory in the Lyon suburbs, dangers on a global scale and the impending local elections or the next board meeting' (1993: 1).

In their own way, what both projects insist on is the need to 'follow the things themselves'; to track the messy, variegated, and most often unpredictable entanglements that compose real-world situations, rather than resorting to pre-existent categories like 'nature' or 'society', 'subjectivity' or 'consciousness' to do the explanatory work. The problem with modern thought and practice, Latour argues, is that it has assumed the self-consistency of the natural, the social, the human and the nonhuman, and failed to register the inevitably miscegenous composition concealed by these crude divisions of being. Just as nature is always already permeated with human influences and transpositions, so too are societies or humans made up of a much greater mix of ingredients than most social scientists have hitherto assumed (Latour, 1993: 54). Hence Latour's question about what humans would be without plants, lions, plankton and so on (1998: 231). Whereas spokespeople for modernity have strenuously sought to purify nature of its social implications and society of its nonhuman infusions, the reality is that '(e)verything happens in the middle, everything passes between the two ...' (Latour, 2003: 37; see also 1993: 37). Or as fellow science studies scholar John Law puts it, '*Contra* appearances, nature is always entangled with culture and society. To negotiate the structure of one is to negotiate the structure of the others' (2004: 121).

For Deleuze and Guattari, the different kinds of matter which make up the universe tend to get captured by and locked into relatively homogenous aggregates which they term 'strata'. This generates an ontological schema with no obvious counterpart in Latour's thought. But Deleuze and Guattari also stipulate that there are movements which constantly cut across these belts, drawing elements from different layers into new encounters and assemblages (1987: 40). It is vital for Deleuze and Guattari that strata such as the physico-chemical, the biological and the socio-cultural do not simply follow each other in a one-way, developmental succession, but are mutually open and available for generative re-orderings. Thus 'very old strata can rise to the surface again' (1994: 58). Or newer strata can host constituents carried over from earlier formations, such as when 'cultural or technical phenomena provid(e) a fertile soil ... for the development of insects, bacteria, germs' (1987: 69). While it is important to note that Deleuze and Guattari posit relational structures that are both more stable and more volatile than Latourian networks, they too insist that the complex determinations and becomings that concern them are 'as much artificial as natural' (1987: 406; see also Deleuze, 1995: 155).

But what kind of 'worlds' are formed out of all this rampant interactivity? Both the more social scientific relational materialist approaches and the philosophical interventions of Deleuze and Guattari partake in the flattening of vertical hierarchies of being into an unlimited horizontal plane. Both trace the trajectories of disparate objects and explore the transversal mixings of different zones of reality. But do they do this in the same way, and with the same consequences? In the following sections, I attend more closely to the way that Latour and those influenced by his work propose that 'worlds' or 'realities' are formed – particularly at the global scale that prevails in so much contemporary social analysis. And I begin to draw out some of the more questionable implications of the leveled, all-inclusive and symmetrical ontologies purveyed by actor-network theories (see Lorimer, 2005: 88).

Ways to make a world I: Latour's guide to composing a cosmos

The key to Latour's way of thinking about worlds, globalities, cosmoses is his stipulation that we must set forth from concrete interactions and work up to more composite and encompassing entities. Actual relations are always 'localized', not in the manner of a crude spatial fixity, but in the sense that they consist of a unique, specific and situated connection between two or more actors. In this way, a generality like the 'global', or 'society' or 'nature' must not be taken as a point of origin or a pre-given context of subsequent action, but as an emergent property of particular relations.

The basic diagram for the constitution of a world is set out in *The Pasteurization of France* (1988). Here, Latour demonstrates how disease-inducing microbes came to have a presence which they formerly lacked, not only by virtue of being manipulated under experimental conditions, but as a result of Louis Pasteur's canny construction of a far-ranging and enduring set of networks. Through these channels, the initially 'local' existence of 'the bacillus' is progressively amplified in such a way that it comes to matter in social life. Effectively, microbes enter nineteenth-century French society. On these grounds, Latour makes his case that science does not so much represent an exterior reality as perform a worldly intervention – both by 'enacting' the objects it purports to describe (with the help of the microbes themselves), and by extending this enactment into an alteration of the very composition of the world.

Similarly, today's 'global' environmental controversies emerge from a concrete, situated conjunction of elements from which they must be progressively protracted into fully fledged globality. Like the ozone hole, with its disparate tributary factors, Latour has described the way global warming gets composed 'through the action of each of us, with all the oceans, high atmosphere and even the Gulf Stream – as some oceanographers argue – participating' (2003: 32). Bruce Braun teases out the logic behind this model: showing how discursive constructions of 'global nature' take shape in particular places and only come to be experienced as global as a result of successful mobilizations which reproduce localized achievements at many other sites:

> The 'global biological' is thus the *effect* of the extension of technoscientific networks, by which a 'local epistemology' becomes ubiquitous …
> To the extent that natures can be said to be global, then, it is only in and through these spaces of assemblage, which give them their specific biosocial and spatio-temporal dimensions. (2006: 650–2)

Latour himself is unequivocal: anyone who would make a claim for 'globality', for a 'cosmos', for 'nature' or any other expression of unified reality must be prepared to lay out the full quota of components from which it is to be assembled and all the procedures by which its unity has been brought about: 'To think in truly "global" fashion, they needed to begin by discovering, I want to say they need[ed] to begin by discovering the institutions thanks to which globalism is constructed one step at a time' (2004b: 3). He has no patience with those whose visions of the world fail to fulfil these criteria. Political ecologists, in particular, are admonished for fast-forwarding to a conception of all-embracing planetary oneness, like the 'worthless' and 'wretched' Gaia hypothesis, which presents global nature as a 'higher unity' to which human life is expected to acquiesce (1998: 227, 233). 'Where "global thinking" is concerned, they have come up with nothing better than a nature already composed, already totalized …', Latour concludes of the radical ecological project (2004b: 3).

In much the same way, the entire edifice of modern natural science comes under attack for its assumption that there is a single, unified nature upon which all scientific understanding must ultimately converge. Scientific naturalism, in this sense, is inevitably mononaturalism: the belief that *we all live under the same biological and physical laws and have the same fundamental biological, social, and psychological makeup*', which is coupled with the conviction that only science has the power to reveal these universal truths

(Latour, 2004a: 458, author's italics). The trouble with the scientific world view, like radical ecology's whole earth phantasm, is that it prohibits any understanding of the actual processes by which worldly coherence is necessarily achieved. Or as John Law puts it, in relation to the narrating of earth processes by the science of geology: 'what comes into view is a reality out-there that is independent, prior, single and determinate' (2004: 137).

But the disavowal of any prior or independent globality and the insistence on the identification of the institutional mediation of any postulation of global nature have some troubling ramifications, even according to ANT's own most cherished principles.

We need to recall that one of Latour's most celebrated pronouncements is his early claim that nonhuman things must be credited with an independent existence and interests of their own. '(T)hings-in-themselves', he proposes in the manifesto-styled *Irreductions*, 'get by very well without any help from us' (1988: 193). They do not need scientists or any other human interlocutors to stand in or mediate for them, but are quite capable of 'fomenting their own plots, forming their own groups, and serving other masters, wills, and functions' (1988: 197). And in so doing, other-than-human entities – alongside their human counterparts – are credited with the ability to make alliances, to forge and extend networks, to such an extent that it can be said that 'Every actant makes a whole world for itself' (1988: 192).

These are themes Latour has cheerfully revisited in recent years. 'So I have always been perfectly happy to speak, like Alphonse de Candolle, of "plant sociology" or, like Alfred North Whitehead, of "stellar societies"', he announces (2004a: 451): possibilities other theorists have embraced heartily. Graham Harman is so taken with the permitting of other-than-human actors to orchestrate their own relationships and build their own self-standing worlds that he proclaims it a breakthrough in metaphysical thinking: 'Latour gives us the first philosophy ever known in which the relations between objects are both a puzzling difficulty *and* are not monopolized by some tyrant entity, whether human or divine' (2009: 102). And Harman is far from alone in conceiving of this positing of the radical autonomy of the other-than-human as a profoundly promising and liberating move.

The limits of co-enactment

However, a number of otherwise sympathetic readers have noted that in practice it is difficult to find evidence of genuinely independent nonhuman activity in Latour's work or in related writings. Commenting on a recent work which draws on ANT to explore the human and other-than-human co-production of a specific geographical region, Doreen Massey (2005a) commends the author for the richly detailed way in which he weaves together a range of heterogeneous forces in the making of place. But she also finds cause to question 'the assumed balance of forces between human and nonhuman', and ponders the passing over of long-term earth processes like plate tectonics and other forms of place-making that have occurred and still occur beyond the scope of human involvement (2005a: 355–6). Analogously, Sarah Whatmore observes that nonhuman animals sit 'uneasily with the extended casting of social agency figured by ANT' (2002: 36). And even Harman concedes that despite the hypothetical embrace of other-than-human autarchies, 'only the most flickering hints of networks devoid of human involvement' can be found anywhere in the Latourian corpus (2009: 124).

This may be more than an accidental oversight. If it is not permitted for human interlocuters to speak of non-human worlds without documenting their own role in the description, translation and inevitable re-composition of these realities, then it is hard to imagine how a domain fully independent of the human can legitimately receive attention as anything more than an abstract possibility. To engage substantively with an inhuman region in and for-itself would by definition repudiate the entanglement that attends all such intervention, according to Latour's logic, thereby constituting an act of purification of the human presence. And yet, as I suggested in the introduction, if we pursue the injunction of actor-network theorists to follow the things themselves, it is inevitable that sooner or later we are going to be drawn into realms which precede, antecede or otherwise exceed human influence – as the current understanding of issues like global climate change makes all too apparent.

In practice, Latour circumvents such dilemmas by extrapolating from the unequivocably transformative milieu of the laboratory to the world-at-large so that 'the thick of things' inevitably appears as an interzone of human–nonhuman co-enactment. He does this in a dual sense, both by tracking the actual processes by which localized techno-scientific interventions are systematically networked into globally scaled propositions, as we saw above, and by arguing that the uncertainties accompanying world-altering events like climate change or ozone depletion effectively turn the entire planet into a vast experimental lab. By contrast, philosopher of science Isabelle Stengers, with whom Latour is in frequent conversation, is much more precise about the limits of human co-enactment with nonhuman forces. However, much lab science is credited with engineering its own objects of concern. Stengers argues that we must not lose sight of the independent 'force of things' which endures beyond the institutions that specialize in scientific experimentation. 'For everything changes when one leaves the laboratory', she insists (2000: 128).

The difference between Stengers and many of her fellow science studies scholars becomes even more pronounced when she turns to the question of climate change. Where others emphasize the human–nonhuman co-construction of climate, she drives home the point that issues of global ecological transformation compel scientists to look deeply into the past history of the earth. This much longer purview encourages us to conceive of the planet not just in terms of our own interchanges with it, *but in and for itself*: 'Of the Earth, the present subject of our scenarios, we can presuppose a single thing: it doesn't care about the questions we ask about it' (Stengers: 2000: 145). As Stengers argues, we must be careful to distinguish between those modes of producing knowledge which palpably have an influence on the phenomena they study – because these entities are present, have interests of their own, and are thus *not indifferent* to out interrogations – and those knowledge productions which deal with phenomena whose history or spatiality is not coextensive with the situation in which they are being researched – and which therefore 'have a stable identity in relation to the type of intervention that lets them be studied' (2000: 146). Out in the field, researchers do not encounter phenomena which they themselves have conscripted into bearing witness, but must contend with a terrain that stubbornly 'preexists the one who describes it' (2000: 144).

It should be stressed that, for Stengers, having 'a stable identity' in relation to scientific study does not imply stasis or stability per se. It merely means that whatever instabilities obtain do not issue from the concrete, spatio-temporally localized impacts of the research process. In crude terms, taking core samples from 200,000-year-old ice does not alter the composition or the dynamics of a Pleistocene glacial. Or to put it more generally, a contemporary anthropic intrusion cannot co-enact or co-constitute an event with which it is not co-incident. For Stengers, it might be said, geoscience is inclined to speak of a world which is 'prior' and 'independent' without implying that it is 'single' and 'determinate': it encounters an earth which is very much 'already composed' without it thereby being 'already totalized'.

In a recent and surprisingly receptive response to warnings about the current environmental predicament presented by Gaia theorist James Lovelock, Latour turns explicitly to thinking about the earth and what it means to be an 'earthling'. Picking up on the theme broached earlier by Serres, he makes a strong case for humanity's arrival as a geological force, comparing the dangers we now pose to the planet with 'the impact of a major meteorite' (2007: 2). Yet, in spite of the significance of decisively pre-human events and formations in his argument, Latour uses the opportunity to rehearse the inescapable entanglement of the human and the more-than-human and reassert the folly of any commitment to unravelling these forces. In this way, he returns us once more to the prevailing theme of science studies' version of relational materiality: 'the production of humans and nonhumans simultaneously' (Latour, 1993: 103).

Latour's reluctance to probe regions of existence outside of human–nonhuman co-constitution, I will be suggesting, may have more to do with political preferences than ontological ones. Or rather, it concerns his conceptualization of ontology *as politics*. There are important differences here with regard to Stengers, for whom the pre-existence of the terrain in which the earth sciences operate clearly implies that their endeavours to present phenomena and provide proof 'are no longer an affair of power, but an affair of a process that one must *follow*' (2000: 145, author's italics). Her sense of 'following' as a kind of responsiveness to the problems posed by a complexly folded and dynamic terrain draws explicitly on Deleuze and Guattari, just as it recalls her collaborative work with physicist Ilya Prigogine on the essential irreversibility of the material becomings of the earth and cosmos (2000: 155, Prigogine and Stengers, 1984).

In this way, Stengers' work encourages a rethinking of the earth in both its objective and grounding capacities in ways that are diminished by Latour's restriction of 'globality' to a manifestation of sociomaterial networking. And yet, we must not forget that it is Latour himself who has provided some of the most compelling reasons why our own species should never be granted a monopoly on worldbuilding or 'cosmogenic' activity. In the next section, I want to look at some social theoretical and philosophical work that converses with the earth and life sciences in order to explore the possibility of becoming *even more Latourian* in our pursuit of things themselves and our attribution of world-making capabilities. This means considering not only how nonhumans make worlds *of their own*, but how they provide worlds *for others* – a move which brings us back to the 'vital materialist' thinking of Deleuze and Guattari.

Ways to make a world II: building realities from 'below'

Where and what were microbes before Pasteur? In answer to his own question, Latour replies: 'After 1864 airborne germs were there all along' (1999b: 173). For all its counter-intuitive cunning, this stratagem only enables us to follow things so far. It permits us to track nonhuman entities back and forth through human-instigated networks, only to relinquish them at the moment their full autonomy might blossom.

What if we were to follow the prescription of classic actor-network theory and pursue microbes deep into the associations they forge with no help from us? Picking up where Latour leaves off, Myra Hird offers us a book-length 'sociology' of bacterial life. *The Origins of Sociable Life* (2009) draws on research in the laboratories of evolutionary biologist Lynn Margulis, though this is less a study of what scientists actually do than an account of the deeds of bacteria. Hird guides us through the rich world of microbial evolution and diversity, energy conversion and technics, sensing and communication, sexual behaviour and even politics. She reminds us that microbes reigned supreme as the earth's sole living inhabitants for nearly three billion years – during which time they invented all the major forms of metabolic processes that terrestrial life now depends upon (2009: 22).

Following Margulis's now widely accepted theory of symbiogenesis, Hird explains how all multi-cellular organisms are composed on a base of complex bacterial communities (2009: 62–5). By tracking the prolific and promiscuous lives that are the vital components of our own bodies and our bio-physical environments in this way, we are invited to relearn what it is to be human. More than this, we get a sense of an unthinkable multitude of microscopic lives whose daily existence will likely remain forever beyond our knowing or experience. Hird is unequivocal: 'the vast majority of microbial intra-actions have nothing to do with humans' (2009: 26). This is hardly surprising, once we hear that there are an estimated 5×10^{30} bacterial cells on earth. But the fact that most of life's *agencement* or relational becoming has barely anything to do with 'us', Hird argues, is all the more reason to 'take the biosphere seriously as entangled actant' – which is how she suggests her scientist collaborators actually conceive of the world (2009: 2). This resonates clearly with an earlier reflection of Andrew Pickering's that when we look directly at the kind of tangled, open-ended worlds which evolutionary biology reveal to us, what we encounter 'are precisely the kinds of assemblages of multiple and heterogeneous entities' that he and fellow science studies scholars have been talking about (2001: 9–10).

In keeping with a particular model of studying science championed by Latour, much of the relational materialities literature – including engagements with biohazards in a globalized world – puts the stress on the processes through which heterogeneous entities are recruited, and enrol themselves, into novel confederations. Because science as a worldly practice remains pivotal to most of this work, and by way of the central premise that scientific research invariably transforms whatever it encounters, I have been suggesting, this mode of inquiry is rarely disposed to dwell on what nonhuman entities get up to in the absence of human incitement or orchestration. Hird's 'microbial sociology', by contrast, channels a tradition of feminist engagement with science which permits itself to be more enthralled with the phenomena and events which intrigue scientists than with the antics of the white-coated ones themselves. Such an approach tends to make 'collateral use of the sciences', as Elizabeth Grosz puts it (2004: 157): it characteristically probes the enigmatic, unresolved and contrary findings of selected scientific investigations in order to provoke social or philosophical thought to view its own objects in alternative ways. In a formulation I would happily extend to the earth and astronomical sciences, Grosz avers: '(b)iological discourses are no more "dangerous," "ideological," "biased," or "misleading" than any other discourses or models; we ignore them only at the expense of our own disciplinary discourses and political models, only at the expense of our own growth and self transformation' (2005: 28).

In significant ways, much of this 'corporeal feminist' research inherits and extends the concern of the French philosophers of the 1960s with forms of iterability, communication and generativity that subtend the more specific field of human culture or language. Unlike so many intervening post-structuralist and anti-essentialist thinkers, recent feminist theorists of flesh and matter share with their continental precursors an insistence that the world is not simply a 'reality effect' of language or culture or science or any human endeavour but is the outcome of its own inherent capacity for assembling and articulating itself. It is, as Vicki Kirby echoes Derrida, 'the worlding of the world' that is of prime interest, and not simply its construction by more or less astute social agents (1997: 61). Biology (and matter more generally), in this way, is viewed as a kind of intertexture – a weave of differential forces – that is constantly generative of new forms (Kirby, 1997: 78; Grosz, 1998: 191–2). Beyond mere forcefulness, biological life does not go in need of any extraneous observer to grant it meaning or intelligibility. It not only performs or enacts itself but has its own versions of articulateness and communicability. Resonating with Latour's early musings, before he swerved from his own most intriguing insights, Kirby speaks of 'corporeal existence (as) generative and generous in its inclusiveness; an infinite portioning, *mediated from and within itself*' (Kirby, 1997: 146, my italics).

With an eye to the current concern with biological hazards, the implication of this take on embodied life is that the threatening unpredictability of certain living things is best seen as an ongoing manifestation of what life has always done: generate novel forms and behaviours, probe new pathways and spaces of possibility, proliferate itself. As Grosz argues, organismic life by definition contains potentials in excess of what can be realized in any existing context, evolution being the expression of this superabundance in acts of self-mobilization beyond a given situation (2005: 81). Those writing within a broadly relational materialist frame are certainly no strangers to these thematics. Where the overlap with recent feminist writings on embodiment and materiality often occurs – in the biosecuritization literature and beyond – is through the shared uptake of the Deleuzean notion of virtuality. The virtual is often marshalled as a way of expressing the essentially unforeseeable trajectories of life: its intrinsic capacity to enter into permutations which cannot be read off the present. As Paul Rabinow describes the contemporary predicament vis-a-vis infectious disease outbreak: 'Today we seem to be in (an) antechamber, awaiting the descent into catastrophe through the single episode whose virtualities were and are incalculable and which may or may not be part of a series or regular pattern' (2008: 282).

For those tutored in actor-network theory's punctilious pursuit of objects through close-knit nodes and strung-out reticulations, the concept of virtuality offers a warm blast of the boundless and the ineffable. While Latourian networks might be prone to periodic breakdown or break-out, Deleuze's resuscitation of the Bergsonian virtual proposes an immeasurable multiplicity which constantly infuses every extant thing or arrangement of things (Deleuze, 1990). Conceived as a limitless reservoir of promise of which any existing being is a localized incarnation, the virtual exerts a constant pressure on the actual to veer off-course into something other than it is. Most commentators agree that the notion of the virtual helps us get beyond any lingering assumption that matter or life needs an external source of motivation (a deity, or god-like powers appropriated by human subjects), and that it injects a sense of open-ended futurity which provides an alternative to the modernist fixation on the future as linear accomplishment of known possibilities. It is also widely accepted that Deleuze's attribution of a 'certain vitality' to matter encourages us to see continuities rather than sharp divides between the spheres of physico-chemical elementality, organic life and human existence.

Beyond these basic points, however, the question of how the realm of the virtual relates to actually existing strata or entities excites widely divergent interpretations. For some readers, Deleuze deftly catches an early wave of the scientific appreciation of the emergent and self-organizing properties of matter and life (see De Landa, 1992, 1997). For others, his investment in virtuality entails a less-than-desirable secreting of the true source of 'becoming' in a dominion far beyond the grit and slog of ordinary material existence, thus derogating the richness of the concrete (Harman, 2009: 30, 101; Brassier, 2007: Ch. 6). What is certainly pronounced in his work is the sense that the fate of actual embodied beings is very much subservient to the broader sweep of an inexhaustible creative evolution – or what Deleuze and Guattari refer to as the 'flux of invincible life' (1986: 41). Whatever we make of this affirmation of generalized creativity, it needs to be stressed just how incompatible it is with Latour's stipulation that what must be accounted for in the composition of reality is nothing but the assertions of specific, individualized actors. 'Since Latour is committed to a model of actants fully deployed in alliances with nothing held in reserve', Harman cogently reminds us, 'he cannot concede any slumbering potency lying in the things that is currently unexpressed' (2009: 28).

Deleuze and Latour's positions have different consequences, as we will see, for the way we conceive of human subjects, and what befalls them in an inconstant universe. They also have differing implications for how worlds get made. While virtuality's 'all-encompassing murmuring' may resound in every actualized object (see Badiou, 2000: 35), it is nonetheless crucial to Deleuze and Guattari's ontology that heterogeneous elements, at least provisionally, settle into relatively distinct strata. While it may be possible to move across and combine strata which are spatially and temporally co-incident, as I noted earlier, their attention to 'singular' events that irrevocably transform organized bodies points to a fundamental irreversibility in their dynamical cosmos.[1] Ensuing foldings of strata erase the initial conditions, so that there is no going back – even if a newly emergent ordering turns out to be unsustainable and crashes or falls apart (Protevi, 2001; see also Goodchild, 1996: 68–9; Olkowski, 2009: 149).

In this way, each strata serves as the reservoir or substructure for the creation of subsequent strata, though it is a ground that is forever capable of ungrounding – and thus undoing what it founds (Badiou, 2000: 63). This idea that a swirl of interacting elements beds down into a relatively enduring field or layer which then offers provisions for what comes later is at the crux of my argument in this chapter. For my purposes, what is most important about Hird's 'microbial sociology' is her account of the way microbes have not only assembled 'worlds for themselves', but transform the earth for all who follow (2009: Ch. 6). As the progenitors of all terrestrial life and the energetic prime-movers of every known food chain, microbes built the biosphere from the bottom up – and still deserve most of the credit for its maintenance. They are also responsible for transforming the earth's atmosphere to its current aerobic state, look to have contributed substantially to the current extent of the hydrosphere, and have been major agents in the laying down and cycling of the lithosphere.

Other feminist theorists of matter and embodiment make similar points, in an even more general context. Nature 'composed of biological and material, and inorganic systems that sustain life' is constantly supporting, regenerating, transforming itself, but it is also what enables and provokes human culture, according to Elizabeth Grosz (2005: 43). Grosz has no hesitation about speaking of nature as 'the ground', 'condition' or 'field' out of which all life, including our social or cultural life emerges (2005: 44). Vicki Kirby also makes it clear that it is time to reclaim nature as ground from those who continue to demonize all grounding operations as forms of determinism or who would reduce nature or the ground to some kind of cultural–linguistic effect. She explicitly takes issue with a common assumption in contemporary anti-essentialist critical thought: 'that if the ground isn't solid and fixed, then it isn't a ground – if it moves and changes, then it must be the mere representation of a ground' (1997: 61). In the work of Kirby, Grosz, Wilson (1998) and other corporeal feminist writers, for all that nature is construed as a shifting, bottomless, interplay of differential forces, for all its abyssal instability and mobility, it still operates as the ground for that which now exists and that which is to come. Or rather, it founds and foments subsequent ventures of matter and life (including human life) precisely because of its own innate lack of fixity, its own self-differentiation, its own excessiveness.

It is difficult to imagine Bruno Latour, or those in his orbit, speaking of nature as a ground. For all the many advantages of Latour's treatment of each encounter between actors, each new alliance, each networking or world-building event as nothing but what it is at the moment of its occurrence – this prescription comes at a cost. Fortuitously using the example of the transformation of the biosphere and atmosphere by bacteria, Levi Bryant points up the price to be paid by Latour's unswerving commitment to a flat ontology:

> What is missed is the emergence of self-sustaining negentropic networks in which the actors in the network become *dependent* on one another in the replication or reproduction of the network. Just as Latour would like, these networks are composed of *heterogeneous* and autonomous actors, but insofar as the relations they enter into are characterized by negentropy, the network comes to organize subsequent adventures of actors in the network. (2009: unpag., author's italics)

The concept of negentropy – order emerging against the flow of the dissipation of matter-energy – is important here for the way that it signals an emergent level of organization, and hence, irreversibility. But even more telling is the reference to *dependence*. Whereas Latour's nonhumans are (at least hypothetically) permitted to construct whole worlds *for themselves*, Bryant empowers them to make and bequeath worlds *for others*. As is the case in Hird's narrating of microbial accomplishments, Bryant's microscopic multitudes transform planetary conditions for each other and for every life form to come. This means that successive living creatures, our species included, are completely and utterly reliant on the networking activities of these other entities: on actors who are mostly absent, beings whose bodies and inter-corporealities are by now deeply interred amidst the earth's ongoing stratifications.

If we are to take Latour's insistence on explaining how the global is constructed out of localized interactions 'one step at a time', I would argue that this is where we might begin: with the complex, inter-linked, world-building activities of trillions of tiny life forms. And even before that, with the congealing of an astronomical body out of swirling chemical elements. But this means that our flat-tened ontology needs the supplement of some significant layerings. Dependence on worlds made by others is another way of saying grounding. And grounding suggests a formative and fundamental asymmetry. However turbulent the ground may be, it implies a form of relating in which some actors rely on the achievements of other actors in ways that exceed any measure of mutuality or co-dependence.

From reciprocal relations to radical asymmetry

Across the terrain of contemporary critical social thought, and with a particular frequency in relational materialist camps, those who wish to speak of physical force or nonhuman agency while upholding prohibitions on any recourse to 'pure' nature, can select from the many hybridized or hyphenated formulations now on offer (nature-cultures, techno-natures, social-natures, cyborgs, quasi-objects). The popularity of such compound terms testifies to the pervasiveness of the idea that two-way traffic is the way to go. This goes beyond the matter of accepting that the respective realms of nature and culture have lately become 'inextricably entangled'. It reflects a more widely held – though rarely articulated – assumption that what is meant by 'relationality' is two or more parties engaged in some kind of *mutual* interchange or *reciprocal* encounter.

Though largely supportive of his overall project, Graham Harman makes a convincing case that Latour's version of a levelled-out ontology precludes any serious consideration of asymmetrical relations: which is to say the sort of event where one thing impacts upon another in ways that are out of all proportion to any inverse impression (2009: 208–10). Indeed, Harman has gone on to make a more general claim that unilateral or unbalanced influence is the rule rather than the exception. '(T)he model of symmetrical causation is narrowly biased in favour of physical collision, one of the few cases in the universe where symmetry actually occurs', he argues. 'In most other instances, causation flows in only one direction, even in relations among equals' (2010: 108).

While the relational materiality literature still tends to wield the evidence of a constitutive shuttling back and forth between the human and its others as if it were an ontological breakthrough, Harman is not alone in his disaffection for the co-relative model that underpins this mode of critique and analysis. As exponents of ANT have acknowledged, an application of semiotic theory informs the idea that purportedly opposed terms like nature and culture need to be understood as relational effects or outcomes rather than as 'given' (Brown and Capdevila, 1999: 32; Law, 1999: 3–4). Again, this implies that the authentic relationship of the terms in question is one of co-constitution, and thus that any insinuation of an uncompromised or uncontaminated condition on either side of the dualism must by definition involve an act of denial or purification of an unacknowledged 'otherness'. But for Clive Barnett, such logics of exclusion and othering have long since settled into a kind of post-structural truism. One which, he argues, serves to occlude such alternative possibilities as relationships are characterized by the 'radical asymmetry' of self and other or similarly differentiated terms (2005: 6–9; see also 2004: 512).

Perhaps the most thorough excavation and overhaul of the privileging of reciprocal or co-constitutive relations is to be found in philosopher Quentin Meillassoux's *After Finitude* (2008) – a formative work in the emerging speculative realist genre. Here Meillassoux puts forward a compelling argument that our most engrained and stultifying modern inheritance is not the binary opposition between humans and everything else, as we are constantly told, but an inability to think one side of this divide without the other. Not rigid dualism, but what he terms 'correlationism' has been the dominant tendency in Western philosophy for at least the last two centuries. By 'correlation', Meillassoux explains, 'we mean the idea according to which we only ever have access to the correlation between thinking and being, and never to either term apart from the other' (2008: 5). Ever since Kant cemented the idea that nature in-itself is inaccessible to the human subject, Meillassoux claims, philosophy has restricted itself to exploring the conditions under which an outer reality manifests itself to thought. What has become all-important, then, is 'the constitutive power of the reciprocal relation' between being and thought, to such an extent that any serious engagement with what the world might be like in the absence of a subject is effectively ruled out.

Meillassoux is not taking issue with the idea that humans are necessary entangled with or immersed in an extra-human reality. Thought needs being, he insists. Or in a more social scientific register, humans need a more-than-human world and society depends upon nature. The problem, as Meillassoux sees it, is with the assumption that this dependency works the other way round: that being needs thought, or that the world needs us. It is the assumption of symmetry or mutual reciprocity, he insists, that needs to be interrogated. As I have been suggesting, by way of earth and life science and their reception in certain fields of social and philosophical inquiry, there is plentiful evidence to suggest that vital earth systems got by for a long time without any thinking beings to make sense of them. This is a point iterated by Meillassoux to argue that the bond between the thinking subject and nonhuman being is a contingent rather than a necessary one. In this light, instead of chastising the physical sciences for their naive or politically suspect attachment to a world 'purified' of its inevitable human interferences, he celebrates the willingness of the modern sciences, and, especially, mathematics to countenance 'a world where humanity is absent, a world crammed with things and events that are not the correlates of any manifestation; a world that is not the correlate of a relation to the world' (2008: 26).

To drive home his point about the contingent relation between thought and being, Meillassoux focuses on the 'arche-fossil': his term for evidential traces of an earth that existed before humans or before any creaturely life. Though strongly sympathetic to the gist of his argument, Ray Brassier contests Meillassoux's reliance on a strictly chronological absence of human beings, arguing that the claim for radical asymmetry is even more robust if we follow the natural sciences and acknowledge that fully mind-independent realities are found across multitudes of times, spaces, scales or fields of existence. Accordingly:

> we are surrounded by processes going on quite independently of any relationship we may happen to have with them: thus plate tectonics, thermonuclear fusion, and galactic expansion (not to mention undiscovered oil reserves or unknown insect species) are as much autonomous, human-independent realities as the accretion of the earth. (Brassier, 2007: 59–60)

Like Stengers, with whom they share the idea of an earth largely indifferent to human intervention, both Meillassoux and Brassier's positing of intrinsically extra-human realities poses serious challenges to Latour's charge that modern science is fundamentally flawed by its imperative to purge nature of an always-already present human imprint. Instead of treating regions of being with no discernible human presence as phantasmic outcomes of a modern will to purification, we are invited instead to see them simply as the vast tracts of existence that are untouched by the necessarily limited reach of our inscriptions. This is not to belittle the importance of human–nonhuman co-enactments or enfoldings in the current juncture of the earth's history. But it does suggest that, along with the conception of particular socio-material assemblages of nature emerging at specific locations, we might need to think of the entire zone of human–nonhuman interchange as itself nothing more than a concrete, localized and contingent region in the midst of an overwhelmingly inhuman expanse.

Neither is this to necessarily condemn the Latourian version of relational materiality to what we might imagine to be an overflowing correlationist refuse pile. Harman (2009) launches a spirited defence of Latour as a sometime correlationist who is nonetheless a pioneer of a distinctly non-correlational valorization of mind-independent things thrashing it out amongst themselves. It's a claim we need to take seriously, especially in the light of Meillassoux's assertion that correlationism is not simply a premise or disposition we can ditch at will, but a tradition which we must work in and through.

In this context, it is worth returning to Latour's own clarification about his crusade for ontological even-handedness. '(T)he principle of symmetry', he explains, 'aims not only at establishing equality – which is the only way to set the scale at zero – but at registering differences – that is, in the final analysis *asymmetries*' (1993: 107, my italics). Arriving in the midst of *We Have Never Been Modern*, his polemic on the necessity of thinking of the human and non-human as co-constitutive, it's a moment of immense promise. Though it is not an affinity Latour himself would choose, this point resonates closely with Derrida's demand that we must not simply erase Western thought's constitutive binaries into a smear of sameness, his urging that we must be attentive to 'that strategic dissymmetry that must ceaselessly counterbalance the neutralizing moments of any deconstruction'. And his added stipulation that '(t)his dissymmetry has to be minutely calculated, taking into account all the analyzable differences within the topography of the field' (1981: 207 footnote 27).

When Derrida returns in more detail to non-symmetrical relations in *Specters of Marx* (1994), it is to explore the issue of how we are to deal with *inheritance*: something which comes to us from a past that we cannot change, even as its arrival presents us with a problem, a challenge, a task. Were Latour to take the plunge into the asymmetry he readily hails, he too might be led into the thematizing of that which comes to us from an anteriority that is not ours to enact otherwise. But he pulls back from this possibility almost as soon as he has prised it open, leaving us wondering what would happen if the dial was truly tuned to intensities far beyond the bilateralism of human–nonhuman exchange.

The trouble is that once acknowledged, asymmetry calls for more than a minor recalibration. It summons something in excess of the concession, quick to the lips of most relational materialist thinkers, that humans are not the only or even the main actors in any given scenario. Asymmetry is nothing if not abyssal (see Derrida, 1995a: 28). It changes everything. Radical asymmetry, as Harman, Brassier, Bryant and other thinkers associated with speculative realism would have it, is the necessary concomitant of moving through correlationism into the full admission of the autonomy of extra-human objects and forces. If nonhuman entities or things come before us, if they construct worlds of their own, then their worlds are inevitably going to be worlds others inherit. In this way, their constructions, productions, enactments become a condition of later existence – they 'organize subsequent adventures' of beings to come, however contingent or provisional 'we' and other later arriving bodies might be.

This means that the command to *follow* the things themselves has more than one meaning, as Stengers recognizes. Without an earth and its envelope of life, without a galaxy, a solar system and the ceaseless energy of the sun, human existence would be nothing. Without our species, the earth would still pulse with life and the sun would pump out light and heat, heedless and unperturbed. This is the bottom line of human being: we are utterly dependent on an earth and a cosmos that is, to a large degree, indifferent to us.

Conclusion: living with asymmetry

Why is it important to insist on the radical asymmetry of the relationship between human existence and nature? We know that everything humans create or compose ultimately derives from nature (Lingis, 2000a: 175). By now we are well aware that human agency has become a major force in terrestrial nature and that our techno-cultures are currently channelling nature in new and complicated ways. So why, at this juncture, summon a nature that retains its autonomy, that is envisioned as greater, older, more generative, more complex than we are? Why not stick with those mutual entanglements whose composition and repercussions play such a significant role in the current ecological and technological predicament?

As I will be trying to show in the chapters to come, conceiving of nature as a ground, an origin, a support has implications for the way we understand human agency, for how we think about politics and about ethics. What is at stake here is the core premise of critical, radical or progressive social thought: the belief that the realities we inhabit can and should be changed. Emphasizing the extent to which nonhuman nature has become enmeshed with human social spheres, whether in end-of-nature theories or ANT and other relational materialist ontologies, has consequences for the range of phenomena and events over which human agents have at least potential jurisdiction. When Latour pronounces that 'the very extension of science, technologies, markets, etc. has become almost coextensive with material existence' (2008: 7), he is not merely bemoaning an anthropic advance, he is signalling that little or nothing should be construed as being beyond the reach of alternative or renegotiated arrangements. Even when the intention is to demonstrate the impossibility of mastery and the ubiquity of nonhuman resistance, there is a presupposition that the relationship between society and nature, humans and nonhumans *might be done differently*. A 'material existence' that is contiguous with socio-technical networking is one that is amenable to being worked together in other ways; a cosmos which is assembled step by step is a cosmos that can be re-assembled step by step.

Paradoxically, then, the outcome of affording more agency to nonhumans has been a massive expansion of the dominions of being upon which collective human agency imagines it has purchase. For all its metaphysical audacity, this reflects a very conventional critical aspiration to redirect de-politicizing pressures into a radical magnification of the scope of politics. This is perhaps most conspicuous in the fusion of ontology and politics which is proposed in much of the relational materiality literature: a compounding that appears to posit 'being' itself – in the guise of a cosmic ordering open to reordering – as accessible to collective deliberation. The issue here is not so much that the process of constructing an ontology has a normative or procedural aspect to it – which is critical common sense – but the implication that 'being' or 'reality' or the 'cosmos' is thereby renegotiable *without remainder*.

The idea that nature or an earth or a cosmos subtends human life interrupts and problematizes this critical colonization of the entirety of material existence. Whatever threat progressive thinkers might see in this (re)turn to the notion of a ground, it is clear that the new philosophical appreciation of a generative and inaugurating nature has little in common with earlier recourse to a gathering and stabilizing soil. Whether in its Deleuzoguattarian, its speculative realist, its corporeal feminist or other guises (which are far from mutually exclusive), the recent resurgence of thinking around autonomous natural capacities for world-building puts the stress on the lack of fixity of the ground, and the provocations and challenges that an 'ungrounding of the ground' presents to all the entities which depend upon it.

Conceived in this way, an originary nature is anything but a foreclosure on the demands of politics and ethics. As Christopher Johnson cites Derrida: whatever is inaugural is 'dangerous and anguishing' (1993: 169). The problems raised by the radically asymmetrical relationship between nature and culture include those associated with the 'regionalized' instances of mutual entanglement that relational materialist researchers foreground, but they also greatly exceed that category. What arrives by way of asymmetrical causation comes as a gift, or a bequeathal or an inheritance rather than an exchange, with all the perilous promise that attends those offerings whose origin and final destination are beyond our grasp (Derrida, 1992a; Grosz, 2005: 67–70; Harman, 2010). We cannot simply excavate, render transparent, or recompose the messy, unstable, even violent play of material forces out of which we ourselves have emerged. And this means that alongside our capacity for action, the very condition of our active orientations in the world is a kind of primordial passivity, a susceptibility in the face of all that is not ours to make or even know (Grosz, 2004: 150). Or as Pheng Cheah puts it: 'The stakes are ... a thinking of the dynamism of materiality as a process ... suspended between the active and the passive, a dynamism that obeys an inhuman temporality which is incalculable by human political reason because (it is its) condition of possibility ...' (1996: 128).

These conditions of possibility are physico-chemical, biological, geological, astronomical. 'As symbionts we are gifted into heterogeneous assemblages', writes Myra Hird (2009: 85), reminding us of our bacterial origins. As late-coming earthlings, it might be added, we are gifted into an atmosphere, a biosphere, a hydrosphere, a lithosphere – substrata on which we remain utterly and unilaterally dependent. These pre-existing organizations of the elements retain a capacity to withdraw the support and sustenance they provide. Or they can offer us too much. Their gifts, like the surges of microscopic life that threaten our 'biosecurity' may be untimely, inconveniently placed or just too damned extravagant. If these offerings can undermine or overwhelm us, so too can we receive them without due care or respect. We can squander our inheritance, fail to acknowledge our debts, forget the bodies and the materials that have made us what we are (see Grosz, 2004: 2). Our accomplishments too can act as substrata for other beings, as Deleuze and Guattari helpfully point out. But this is not the same thing as levelling asymmetry into mutuality or replacing the excessiveness of the gift with the accessibility of an exchange.

In the chapters to follow, I will be exploring some of the implications of depending upon conditions that can be taken away, sometimes without warning. Much of the most exciting philosophical and social thought of recent years has found hope and possibility in various permutations of 'becoming': in the idea that there we are immersed in and part of processes of transformation and open-ended change. But the jittery, turbulent and often brutal dynamics of the materialities which subtend creaturely life also mean that disaster looms large. There is a high body count in some of my chosen topics. There are terminations or dead ends. In this context, the precariousness that Latour attributes to his networks take us only so far. The risk of an unravelling or disassembling of the alliances in which we are invested points up certain omnipresent risks, but does not quite capture the full un-worlding blast of a withdrawn ground. Or as disaster studies scholar Kenneth Hewitt muses on the catastrophic nature of his field: 'That is how the tell-tale *un*-words seem so readily to define our concerns – the language of the *un*anticapted, or *un*scheduled events; *un*certainty ...' (1998: 89).

Deleuze and Guattari's assertion that processes of destratification or deterritorialization constantly threaten entities with violent, wrenching transformations – the idea that 'every dynamism (is) a catastrophe' – draws us further in the direction of an inherently disaster-prone universe (Deleuze, 1994: 219). But even then, Deleuze's claim that even fatal upheavals come with the positive charge of a return to the ceaseless stream of generative matter-energy – and thus promise a renewal of becoming – seems to soften the blow (see 1995: 143). If death, annihilation, or even extinction is no more than 'a local and temporary setback, which life will overcome', as Brassier aptly notes, then questions must be asked as to just how catastrophic these 'catastrophes' really are (2007: 228).

The retraction of support from a ground, a field, a cosmos, I argue in the following chapter, carves deep fissures in our experience of the phenomenal world. It opens cracks which divide one being from another in ways that any pancake-flat ontology or slickly continuous plane of immanence is going to struggle to contain. Our attempts to bridge these rifts, I suggest, bring into play another sense of profound non-symmetry (see Bauman, 1993: 48–50): the gesture of empathy and compassion that reaches out across the chasm gouged by the earth's upheaval. No less than the unbalancing of our relationship with nature, the offer of help – without expectation of return or recompense – to those who have been laid low by the ordinary chaos of terrestrial existence also upsets the assumption of co-constitutive relations – and draws us deeper into the issue of how to live as best we can in an inherently precarious physical reality.

Note

1 Although, as Deleuze and Guattari insist, this does not imply any developmental or teleological drive: there is no suggestion of 'any kind of ridiculous cosmic evolutionism' (1987: 49).

3

After the Tsunami:
Vulnerability on a Volatile Planet

Introduction: facing disaster

If we look at it from a long enough perspective, as Deleuze suggested, then all of the earth's geological features are in some kind of motion. But, equally, if we take a narrower scope, then earth processes display phases of relative stability – or, at least, predictable patterns and rhythms. Zoom in to the scale at which most of human life is lived and many of the more punctuated geomorphological events will escape daily observation or even collective memory. These are the often considerable stretches of time and space in which the earth offers its support and sustenance – the kind of grounding that Husserl talked about. Emmanuel Levinas, another theorist broadly within the phenomenological tradition, has also explored the experience of entrusting ourselves to the embrace of the earth, but has delved deeper than Husserl into the embodied aspects of this inhabitation.

For Levinas, even before we have made sense of the world, even before we have fashioned a 'world' as an object of our sensing, we have been nourished by its flows, cradled by its firmness, awakened by its radiance (1969: 114, 2001 [1978]: 30). Prior to any act of possession, prior to any disclosure or action on our part, he proposed, is the simple fact of the earth's 'there-ness' and our bodily reliance on its elemental offerings.

Though it is his supposed preference for piety and self-denial that has attracted more attention, there is a warm undercurrent of 'enjoyment' coursing through the *ouvre* of Levinas. Along with eating, sleeping and reading, as he would have it, 'warming oneself in the sun' is one of those small pleasures that make life dear to us, as is 'the blue of the sky above my head, the breath of the wind, the undulation of the sea, the sparkle of the light ...' (Levinas, 1969: 112, 141). To feel the heat of the sun or the lapping of waves is to soak up an enlivening energy. It is to renew our contact with the earthly and celestial nourishments that are the source of life. All of which offers clues as to why so many people – those blessed with resources and mobility – had gravitated to the shores of the Indian Ocean at the time of year when sunshine and clear sky in the northern latitudes was in short supply. 'Lovers were lying on the beaches, swimmers were splashing in the cobalt blue waters, divers were exploring the coral reefs and fishermen were repairing their nets', as accounts would have it (Woods, 2005: unpag.).

This is what people – some people – were doing on the morning of Boxing Day 2004 when the great waves generated by the Sumatra-Andaman earthquake thundered across the sea and onto the land. This is the ordinariness, the 'there-ness', that was torn apart when a section of the earth lurched from relative stasis to mobility.

The Tsunami was triggered by the same geological instability that had carved out coastlines and raised the island arcs beloved of the region's sun-seeking visitors. As we have seen, it is only over the last half century or so that earth scientists have reached a consensus about the basic processes that generate and renew the planet's relatively solid outer surface: a 'settlement' that renders earthquakes a normal and unavoidable aspect of physical world-building. Geoscientists now agree that it is the movement of the tectonic plates that make up the earth's crust that give rise to many of the major surface features of our planet. The continuous upwelling of magma and its hardening into new slabs of crust forces the existing plates sideways, causing them to crunch into other plates. These colliding rafts of rock may grind past each other, or be pushed upwards into ranges and peaks. But sooner or later, in order to balance out the creation of new crust at submarine spreading centres, one of the convergent plates is forced downwards – or 'subducted' – to rejoin the magma circulating deep beneath the earth's surface (Colling et al., 1997: 114–15).

The quake that triggered the Indian Ocean Tsunami occurred at a subduction zone off the west coast of Sumatra; a site where the India tectonic plate, pushing north at around 6 centimetres per year, meets and slips under the Burma plate. As is usually the case, the sinking crust is propelled downwards in a juddery, stop-start fashion. For some 200 years, the Burma plate had been gridlocked, the strain slowly mounting. In the early hours of 26 December, the pressure gave way and a 1,600-kilometre slab of seabed suddenly subsided. The resulting massive displacement of water sent shockwaves rocketing through the surrounding ocean (McKee, 2005).

Seismologists had warned that the fault line was dangerously loaded with pressure and ripe for major readjustment. So too, in a very different context and register, had Levinas cautioned about taking the world's material substructure for granted. For Levinas, alongside it's 'thereness', the earth has a dark and withdrawn side. 'Enjoyment', he intones, '… runs up against the very strangeness of the earth' (1969: 142). Before going on to alert us '… to the fact that the plenitude of its instant of enjoyment is not ensured against the unknown that lurks in the very element it enjoys' (1969: 144). Like Husserl, Levinas returns us to the earth as the field, the ground, the subtending of human existence. But unlike Husserl's 'original ark' which primarily offers stability, his is a shaky platform, a ground which can unground, a foundation capable of retracting without warning the support it has previously provided.

In the last chapter, I argued that radical asymmetries in the relationship of human beings to the earth and cosmos put limits on what is open to being re-enacted or done differently. Perhaps more than any of his contemporaries, Levinas comes closest to connecting up this asymmetrical relation between humans and their physical environment – with the similarly non-symmetrical relationship between self and other. He is best known for his explorations around the idea that the formative moment in the human experience of togetherness is not some kind of mutuality or exchange, but an 'event' of being touched or moved by the sheer presence of an other that precedes any expectation of a return. Whatever relationship may ensue, sociability takes its impetus from this moment of unilateral opening.

Levinas consistently sought to think through this liaison between selves and others in terms of its inherent embodiment: his stated ambition being '(t)o understand the body starting with its materiality' (1987 [1947]: 56). To this prescription, Levinas added the equally salient insistence that '(t)o posit oneself corporeally is to touch an earth' (1969: 128). Taking cues from Levinas's thinking through the body – not just as a locus of action but as a site of impingement of forces beyond its control – I suggest, might help us to come to terms with the human experiential dimension of physical forces far beyond our measure.

In the course of thinking about inhabiting a volatile planet, my ideas were tested, twisted and wrenched into new shapes and intensities by the Indian Ocean Tsunami. The event of the Tsunami was a provocation not just about the dynamics of the earth but about the way people can respond to the plight of others in desperate need. The expressions of compassion and outpourings of generosity in the aftermath of the Tsunami were a powerful reminder that there is a lot more to confronting our susceptibility to forces beyond our control than acquiescence or fatalism.

But I have to admit also to feelings of frustration: initially with what felt like the inadequacy of writing in the face of so much suffering, but very soon after, out of growing unease with the way that many of my fellow 'critical thinkers' were engaging with the catastrophe. What I found disturbing was the speed with which the disaster of 26 December appeared to get processed into a critical narrative: how it was incorporated into a familiar storyline, into an 'economy' of causes and effects that preceded the event itself. How sense seemed to be being made of the loss of sense too hurriedly, too surely.

To put it another way, what concerned me about a certain kind of critical response to the Tsunami was the way that it seemed to rush through the moment of an uncertain but heartfelt response – the asymmetry of an opening – in order to reaffirm the importance of fathomable, identifiable, calculable relations. This chapter, then, is about bodily exposure both to physical processes directly and to the predicament of those whose worlds have been 'un-worlded' by the ordinary extremity of the earth. But it is also about trying to stretch out this vulnerability in order to take in the practice of writing – or thought, or research, or critique – so that 'our' position as respondents to a crisis is not simply one of observing from a safe distance (which is, of course, a luxury many of us do enjoy), but of being caught up in the machinations of the event. In response to the question of what prompts thought, writing, the creation of new concepts, Rosalyn Diprose answers: 'Something gets under my skin, something disturbs me, something elates me, excites me, bothers me, surprises me. It is this experience that sets off a movement that extends my world beyond the intimate and the familiar' (2002: 132). And this something, as Levinas weighs in, is inevitably a calling of myself into question, it must always be a learning as much as a professing or pronouncing (1969: 171).

Offering solace

Some of the early reports and most of the video footage of the Indian Ocean Tsunami came to a watching world from those vacationing in the region. We soon learned however, that it was local people who had taken the brunt of the waves and that overseas visitors were a tiny minority of the Tsunami's monstrous toll. In the coming months, commentators would point, again and again, to the presence of tourists in the disaster zone as a major factor conditioning the international response to the event. It was an observation that seemed to reveal a real need to find an explanation for the outburst of generosity which took place, at the same time as it managed to convey more than a whiff of censure and disapproval.

For those of us who like to see ourselves as 'political' (including, increasingly, in the environmental sense), global tourism is at best a guilty pleasure. Those 'northerners' who had found their place in the sun during the 2004 Christmas break were, of course, reclining under someone else's sun. As Georges Bataille once observed, it is not only plentiful sunshine – 'the flux and the fleeting play of light' – which makes for a pleasant stay, it is also a warm welcome – 'the passage of warmth or light from one being to another' (1988 [1954]: 94). This warmth and light can be given and taken in many ways, not all of which we might wish to celebrate. The industry that organizes this movement of pleasure-seeking bodies around the planet and the care they receive along the way, according to some calculations, is now the most lucrative on the planet. Like other sectors of a globalized economy, international tourism is premised on a set of carefully modulated transactions – hard currency in exchange for soft treatment. It's an economy that operates, at least according to its own premises, in an orderly, symmetrical and mutually beneficial way – a conditioned and careful hospitality.

Those shaky video images narrated in quivering voices record the moment on the morning of 26 December when this economy imploded. With the visitation of such a sudden and total sense of 'estrangement' on so many people, it ceased to be clear who was at home and who was a stranger, who was host and who was guest. The fabric of shared assumptions about what could be offered and what could be requested, where and when it should be supplied, and what its value should be, unravelled abruptly.

And yet, in the immediate aftermath of the Tsunami, even in its midst, as one set of relationships disintegrated, there were glimpses of the emergence of another kind of being-with-others; a kind of 'throwntogetherness' amongst all the tearing apart (see Massey, 2005b: Ch. 13). Many tourists, if they were lucky enough to be unscathed, joined the emergency relief effort. Some volunteered at hospitals and in morgues, or handed over money, clothes and medicines at the hotels where they were staying (*The Hindu*, 2005).

Others took up collections on return home, like the British tourist in Sri Lanka, carried several miles inland by surging waters, who set about fundraising for the people of the village where he finally came to ground (*The Observer*, 2005).

At the same time, people in the affected regions reached out to each other, across many gradations of difference. Journalist Amit Varma, who travelled through the state of Tamil Nadu in the days and weeks following the Tsunami, posted this story on his weblog:

> December 26 could have been the happiest day of Rafiq's life if the Tsunami hadn't struck – he was supposed to get married on that day. His *nikah* was fixed for noon, but the waves came in while it was still morning, and the marriage was cancelled. Rafiq was in the village of Parangipettai, close to a number of affected villages. Instantly, all the men of the community mobilised themselves under the Jamaat, their local organisation, and swung into action.
>
> They took all the veg biryani that had been prepared for the wedding feast, and went and fed it to the affected people. From that day until the day we met them, a week after the Tsunami, they fed breakfast and lunch to the affected people, making either lemon rice or veg biryani. They mobilised their funds superbly, and were well networked through mobile phones. If any village ran short of food, one phone call was all it would take to bring a volunteer rushing over with more food.
>
> Interestingly, even after the government set up its own operation, a few days late, the local people still requested the Jamaat to keep feeding them, and the Jamaat agreed. A deep bond had been formed between the villagers, who were all Hindus, and these Muslim men who rushed to help their neighbours. (Varma, 2005: unpag.)

We should not overlook the hidden work of women in this story, as in so many other accounts of hospitality and care (see Diprose, 2002). But neither should we be too hasty to pass over what is hopeful here and in related stories. In Malaysia, Alice Nah and Tim Bunnell (2005) report, news of the devastation across the strait triggered a new rapport in the previously fraught relationship between Malaysian nationals and displaced people from Aceh province. Many Malaysians approached Acehnese refugees to offer consolation over the Tsunami, and to discuss their more general predicament, while local Islamic groups worked with refugee community leaders to organize disaster relief. More generally, evidence and anecdote suggest that throughout the afflicted region, before organized relief arrived and sometimes well after the official relief effort was underway, it was neighbours and untrained local volunteers who provided vital assistance. As an Indian respondent reported in a review of the effectiveness of aid directly after the Tsunami: 'All kinds of cooked food reached us and it was in excess' (cited in Thomas and Ramalingam, 2005: 46).

Then there were the donations from the rest of the world, which UN emergency coordinators confirm were unprecedented in scale. Enough money was pledged by members of the public and by governments to cover the relief effort. More than enough, in some cases. Without even launching an appeal, the medical aid organization *Médecins Sans Frontières* received so many financial donations in the days following the Tsunami that it had to call a halt. When donors were asked if their pledges could be diverted to other humanitarian crises, over 99 per cent agreed. From a total of around $110 million received, this enabled some $85 million to go to other sites of need, including Niger, Darfur and the Kashmir earthquake (Batha, 2005).

But perhaps the most remarkable stories are those of the hospitality extended by the people of the afflicted areas to their seasonal visitors. Returning travellers reported that amidst the collapse of the tourist infrastructure, they were well looked after, or were treated even better than paying guests (BBC News, 2005). Many had been driven great distances by local people, sometimes by total strangers, so they could reach airports to make their way home. And there were stories of locals who helped their visitors in the search to locate families and friends, even before they sought out their own loved ones. Warmth and light, we might say, no longer traded, but given freely between bodies.

Finding fault

This being supposedly 'an age grown cynical and hardened to catastrophe' (Wyschogrod, 1990: 257), many people, positioned in varying ways in relation to the disaster, found something heartening in the response to 26 December, as indeed they have to the more recent tragedy in Haiti. For a while, the Tsunami looked to be not only a great wave in the physical sense, but a kind of surge, a fast-spreading intensity of feeling that swept up distant others into relations of attentiveness, care and giving. A wave of affect, we might say, at once global and very local. Or is that too naive? Now that so many of the promising bonds and alliances forged in the immediate aftermath of the crisis have revealed their fragility, it is harder to hold on to that initial optimism. But some commentators did not wait for the flood of good intention to recede. They mobilized almost immediately to confront the whole scenario of concern and generosity.

As soon as the extent of public donation and state pledges became apparent, critical voices demanded to know why this event had attracted so much attention, where no-less deserving causes had been left wanting. 'I am bewildered by the world reaction to the tsunami tragedy', wrote Terry Jones in an article entitled 'A man-made tsunami' in the UK *Guardian* a fortnight after the tragedy: 'Nobody is making this sort of fuss about all the people killed in Iraq and yet it's a human catastrophe of comparable dimensions' (2005: unpag.). Veteran journalist John Pilger announced in the same week: 'The victims of a great natural disaster are worthy (though for how long is uncertain) while the victims of man-made imperial disasters are unworthy and very often unmentionable' (2005: unpag.). 'The other tsunami is worldwide', he continued, 'causing 24,000 deaths every day from poverty and debt and division'.

Later, as the relief and recovery effort was subjected to scrutiny, left-liberal criticism became more pointed. As Mari Marcel Thekaekara reported in the *New Internationalist*: 'The Tsunami tossed up unnecessary, conspicuous, vulgar spending' (2005: 21). Earlier accounts of abundant handouts of food, unrestrained monetary donations and superfluous distributions of inappropriate used clothing have since been appended by evidence of an oversupply of replacement fishing boats, of the doubling up of inoculations against infectious disease, and even of an overzealous gathering of information and testimonials from traumatized survivors (Tarrant, 2005; Batha, 2005; Waldman, 2005). International NGOs came under assault for their insensitivity to local traditions and political complexities, for their lack of accountability and consultation with local representatives, and for their self-promotional behaviour, while intervening state actors – both local and international – were charged with capitalizing on crisis conditions to pursue unjust political and socio-economic agendas or to extend military presence in the region (Jeganathan, 2006; Korf, 2005; Glassman, 2005; Nanthikesan, 2005). In a more general sense, many critics chose to stress how projects of relief and rebuilding served to reinforce existing structures of inequality and injustice, a response exemplified by radical geographer Neil Smith (2005: unpag.):

In communities surrounding the Indian Ocean, ravaged by the tsunami of December 2004, the class and ethnic fissures of the old societies are re-etched deeper and wider by the patterns of response and reconstruction. There, 'reconstruction' forcibly prevents local fishermen from re-establishing their livelihoods, planning instead to secure the ocean-front for wealthy tourists. Locals increasingly call the reconstruction effort the 'second tsunami'.

This type of reaction has important continuities with the way that critics mobilized to shut down any insinuation that the Tsunami itself was a 'natural' disaster. It's worth recalling that almost immediately after the media dispatches revealed the extent of the destruction, critical commentators – from both within and beyond the affected region – were moved to point out that the real causes of the catastrophe were 'structural, not accidental' (Philip and Zacharias, 2005: unpag.). Some spoke of the inequalities embedded in informational infrastructures that prevented warnings getting through (2005: unpag.), or indicted developed economies for the drain on local resources that arose out of officially sanctioned arms trading in the region (McLaughlin, 2005: 22). Others highlighted the harm done to natural environmental defence systems by irresponsible coastal developments, viewing the disaster as 'the outcome of an insane economic system … that believes in usurping environment, nature and human lives for the sake of unsustainable economic growth for a few' (Sharma, 2005: unpag.). But most critics simply pointed to socio-economic inequalities: the global disparities that the presence of privileged Western tourists in the disaster-zone only served to accentuate. Writing of the Tsunami's victims in the Indonesian province of Aceh, Jim Glassman pointed out (2005: 165–6):

> … many of the population have lived in conditions of poverty or near-poverty throughout the years of economic boom. Those who lived in small coastal fishing villageseeking out a living from the sea were among these, and their susceptibilities to an event like the tsunami are part and parcel of this poverty.[1]

Having observed the burden of suffering falling most heavily on 'the poorest fishing communities in the most ramshackle of seaside dwellings', Chris Philo (2005: 444) couched it more questioningly. 'Why', he asked, 'is it these people, the planet's most vulnerable due to lacking resources available to others, who are so often the ones 'in the way'?

Now, this is by no means a question I want to take issue with. That vulnerability is unevenly distributed, in the Indian Ocean Tsunami and too many other disasters – and that there are identifiable and ultimately changeable causes behind this inequity are allegations that call for rigorous and relentless attention. This is, after all, the lesson that disaster studies has been trying to teach us for a long time. And this goes no less for the critical assessments of patterns of donation and programmes of aid. It is unlikely that anyone who takes the 'event' of generosity to heart would wish to elevate any aspect of giving or caring to a position above criticism. Who, after all, would not wish to learn from this tragedy, so as to render all their efforts of assistance more just and more effective, now and in the face of disasters to come.

But at the same time, all this mobilization to contain the 'excessive' dimensions of the disaster, with regards to both the forces which triggered the destruction and the forces which responded to it, is far from free of repercussions of its own. What appears to bind the drive to disavow the 'natural' genesis of the disaster with the rush to censure the generosity it induced is an unwavering commitment to a narrative that describes and explains the broad sweep of global injustice. What is important, from my perspective, is that the structures of social injustice and inequality that are summoned to make sense of the disaster are presented as preceding its onset, persisting through its unfolding, and enduring in its aftermath. The performative effect of this critique is to convey the impression that the real disaster, the main event, is the divisive structuring of global social life, leaving the Tsunami as a derivative and superficial phenomenon, whose main function is to throw into the relief the more profound realities that underlie it.

I don't want to suggest that there is anything underhand going on here. This is simply an instance of what critical thought does, and often does very well. Something gets under the skin of social and political critics too, and stays there. Continually incensed by the unequal distribution of power and wealth in the world, they – we – strive to strip away all deceptions, distractions and denials in order to expose the inner workings of injustice – and in this way to render visible the too-often concealed chains of causality and culpability that link privilege to underprivilege. In relation to the Tsunami and other disasters, as Philo observes: 'the vulnerabilities endured by certain peoples and places are almost always *caused* in one way or another by the acts, malign or unthinking, of others in other sites' (2005: 450, author's italics). An event like the Indian Ocean Tsunami provides an opportunity to flesh out this vital observation: both because the extreme conditions can play a part in sweeping away the usual occlusions of structured inequality, and because crisis situations are wide open to intensified exploitation and appropriation (see Klein, 2008).

According to this world view, such is the pervasiveness of asymmetrically structured linkages and flows that it is not only the ruses of the most powerful and unscrupulous operators that need unmasking. As Clive Barnett and David Land (2007) observe, it is pretty much taken for granted amongst the intellectual left that ordinary people engaged in everyday activities are complicit with major power-holders in the propagation of unjust and inequitable conditions. Largely through ignorance, or failure to inquire into the arrangements that make 'our' relatively comfortable existence possible (Philo's 'unthinking'), we persist in patterns of behaviour that perpetuate inequalities – differentials which are increasingly manifest at a global scale. The inference is that 'we' who are 'here' habitually disregard the well-being of 'others' who are 'there'; with the result that commitment to caring drops away precipitously as it moves offshore or away from home (Barnett and Land, 2007). Only by having the extended consequences of their daily deeds revealed to them, it is assumed, is there a chance that people will begin to take responsibility for their actions, forge new relations of solidarity with others near and far, and set about ameliorative or transformative action.

These are familiar intentions to many of us, if not as widespread or effective as we might wish. But this narrative found itself on the defensive when generosity took on the guise of plenitude or excessiveness rather than insufficiency, when acts of concern reached out across continents and oceans in advance of any critical directives or admonitions. In order to sustain the storyline in the face of the response to the Tsunami, critics resorted to evaluating all responses to the crisis according to the model of a pre-existing nexus of unjust social and spatial interdependencies, in the light of which, unsurprisingly, relief efforts tended to be rated less than optimal.

The assumption behind this interrogation is that all potential donors and aid workers should have been better able to assess the situation and weigh it against commensurate demands. As indicated by reference to the 'other tsunami', disasters of 'comparable dimensions' and the constant quantification of competing crises, left-liberal intellectuals stress the need for a kind of moral accounting at every moment of the event in question. Stipulating the necessity of such an arithmetic infers that behind the horizon of catastrophe, there persists a system of known and shared values stable enough to provide a baseline against which heterogeneous instances of need and suffering can be weighed up. An entire hospitality industry and all its constitutive exchange values may have been swept away, but another 'economy' – visible, calculable and available to critical thinkers – lives on.

A very early response to the Tsunami by writer and activist Rebecca Solnit (2005a) rehearses much of this critical framing of the tragedy: pointing to the structural conditioning of loss and suffering, highlighting comparative expenditures and corresponding injustices. But Solnit quite suddenly stops, takes breath, and begins to question the appositeness of discourses of blame and accusation in a time of profound personal loss. She then starts to probe the limits of what usually passes for politically committed critique:

> The relief will be very political, in who gives how much and to whom it is given, but the event itself transcends politics, the realm of things we cause and can work to prevent. We cannot wish that human beings were not subject to the forces of nature, including the mortality that is so central a part of our own nature. We cannot wish that the seas dry up, that the waves grow still, that the tectonic plates cease to exist, that nature ceases to be beyond our abilities to predict and control. But the terms of that nature include such catastrophe and such suffering, which leaves us with sorrow not as problem to be solved but a fact. (2005a: unpag.)

In this way, Solnit turns our attention back to those aspects of human vulnerability which cannot simply be overcome, which are part of the condition of our embodied being on a dynamic planet. By acknowledging the existence of forces which cannot be subsumed into the predominating model of social critique and the moral economy it imagines, she opens up the possibility of a form of ethical relating which exceeds causal connections. To put it plainly, Solnit reminds us that we live in a world in which, from time to time, we will be called upon to respond to things for which we are not responsible. That does not mean that we are devoid of complicity in the conditioning of these events, but it does mean that there is remainder: a major component of the event in question that cannot and should not be squeezed into the category of socio-political causation; a component with its own irreducible dynamics, and its own demands.

Solnit's evocation of a suffering which cannot be wished away by political thought and action points the way not only to an ethics which is incited by events that are irreducible to a topology of existing social divisions, but also to a kind of receptiveness to the needs of others which does not await an accounting in order to go forth. If we can get over the critical reflex to position all implicated parties in a field of pre-existing causal chains, and to rank all potential beneficiaries of our attention, then a host of other possibilities arises. A time and a space is opened for the disaster to be an event of its own, to be something that is genuinely unforeseen, and which thereby defies containment by any system or 'economy' set in place prior to its emergence. There is an opening too for the encounter with those who have suffered disaster (however mediated this may be) to have its own eventfulness, to exceed whatever has gone before or conditioned this meeting. And this has repercussions not simply for the way we think *about* disasters or *about* vulnerability but for how and why we think and write at all.

Estrangement from the earth

As a physical force, the Sumatra–Andaman earthquake was literally ex-orbitant. It generated a shudder of such magnitude that it nudged the spin of the earth, sheering a thin sliver from the length of one terrestrial day. At the human scale, it was no less excessive, jolting hundreds of thousands of lives out of their familiar and intimate orbits. The exorbitance of suffering, the feeling of losing our sense of who we are, shows up in the way trauma is depicted as a kind of radical dislocation. As we say in everyday English, someone is 'beside themselves' with pain or grief; they are 'shattered', 'broken', 'gutted', 'torn apart'. This is not far from Levinas's phenomenological figuring of trauma as 'being torn up from oneself in the core of one's unity', of 'absolute noncoinciding' (1998a: 49). Sociologist Kai Erikson describes the plight of the victims of disaster with whom he has worked closely in terms that suggest the very bonds of their social and physical being have come unstuck: 'they were torn loose from their cultural moorings – alone, adrift, floating like particles in a dead electromagnetic field' (1994: 235).

As Erikson and other disaster scholars attest, the experience of catastrophe makes strangers of ordinary people. People feel strange not because they have left home and entered some foreign domain, but because they have been let down and abandoned by their own home, their own world. Those who endure disasters large or small tend to feel estranged from others who have not shared what they have been through. More than this, they feel estranged from their own selves, as they lose the familiar outline and continuity of their own lives (Dikeç et al., 2009). Or as one of Erikson's traumatized survivors put it: 'The black water came down the bottom we lived in. I couldn't stand any more. It was like something was wiped over me and made me different' (1994: 231).

What was until recently a relatively limited literature around the traumatic effects of natural disaster has been greatly extended by the massive undertaking of therapeutic work and associated research dealing with the impacts of the Indian Ocean Tsunami (Goenjian et al., 2000: 911). In parallel with the other mobilizations of support we have already encountered, many thousands of mental health professionals and volunteers – both from within the region and beyond – headed into the disaster zone. They came to help deal with the psychological problems arising from personal injury, loss of loved ones, homelessness and displacement, and loss of livelihood. But there was something else they had to address, for which psychiatrist Anula Nikapota's observations, for all their simplicity, offer a useful point of departure: 'The devastating nature of the tsunami related to the enormity of the disaster, the suddenness with which it occurred, *the entirely new experience of the sea rising and coming on to the land*' (2006: 275, my italics).

Research from a psycho-social perspective has looked into the consequences of the destruction of 'place' that tends to characterize a large-scale geo-physical catastrophe (without, of course, being restricted to this kind of disaster). As one review sums up: 'In uprooting over 1.2 million people from their homes, the tsunami created one of the most abrupt and widespread "loss of place" incidents ever recorded' (Carballo et al., 2006: 218). The idea of 'loss of place', as geographers and other social scientists would agree, captures much of the experience of the undoing of the material and symbolic relations that are constitutive of individual or communal life. Resonating with the 'relational materialist' approaches I addressed in the last chapter, an understanding of trauma in terms of the unravelling of the bonds, associations or entanglements through which actors are shaped and sustained – including those which bind humans and nonhumans together – reminds us of the precariousness of all assemblages or networked accomplishments. Like the shock that accompanies the emergence and proliferation of dangerous biological agents through the connective tissues of global life, a geophysical event like the Tsunami points up the frightening underside of being hard-wired into heterogeneous material networks.

But somehow, storying an upheaval of the earth as a perturbing network effect doesn't quite capture its full corporeal or psychic impact. The earth as a ground, a foundation, is more than just one set of relations amongst others, and the loss of that ground seems to do something more or other than undoing the specificity of bonds and connections that configure 'place' – however important this might be. Research on earthquake survivors – especially those who have lived through aftershocks or a series of seismic events – point to acute anxiety associated with a loss of trust in the firmness of the ground (see Goenjian et al., 2000). In the case of the Indian Ocean Tsunami, unsurprisingly, similar anxieties are focused on the sea and coast (Carballo et al., 2006: 219). As Nikapota explains, drawing evidence from Sri Lanka:

> One of the major losses felt by everyone was the loss of the sea. The character of the sea had changed. In many of the coastal areas children were no longer allowed or in any way encouraged to go to the sea and many children were insisting they were too frightened to do so. In this they were reflecting adult views. Many of the adults we worked with were saying they didn't feel like wanting the beach. One man said, 'I always went down to the beach whenever I wanted consolation. Now I have lost that too' ... The fear of the sea was not limited to those affected. Many children and adults in coastal areas, which were not affected, nevertheless found looking at the sea painful, and walking by the sea difficult. (2006: 279)

For many local people, feelings of unease and distress were complicated by the disruption of maritime livelihoods and exacerbated by rumours of a second tsunami (Ghodse and Galea, 2006). In the case of non-local people caught up in the event, the experience of a dramatic overturning of a familiar and trusted element is also prominent in accounts of post-disaster distress and anxiety. In their longitudinal study of Swedish tourists who survived the Tsunami, Råholm, Arman and Rehnsfeldt (2008) describe a common storyline which includes initial disbelief and bewilderment at the physical world's irruption into chaos. Tied up with themes of groundlessness, this later comes to be interpreted as 'experiencing the very core of existence', or 'experiencing the darkness of understanding life' (2008: 603). What also surfaces in these reports is a strong evocation of the support and sustenance provided by the physical environment prior to the event of its upheaval. As the researchers sum up: 'The external context nourished the sense of security and closeness' (2008: 600). Or in the words of one of their respondents: 'it was fantastically beautiful. You kind of felt really safe' (2008: 601).

If only in a sketchy and circumstantial way, this gathering of fragments gestures toward the thematic of terrestrial support – and the dark underside of its sudden withdrawal – that Levinas opened up in his early work. We can lose loved ones, we can lose homes and familiar structures, we can lose the whole tangle of objects and relations that make up place. But we can also lose something more basal or elemental. Alongside all the forms of damage and distress it shares with other extreme events, geophysical upheaval seems to undermine a basic faith in the givenness of the earth – or the sea or sky. We might call this trust 'grounding' or 'security', or in Levinas's idiosyncratic terminology 'enjoyment'. But however it is designated, the disappearance of the 'there-ness' of the elements is sorely felt. This is a stark reminder that human corporeality 'touches an earth' in deep, formative ways. And that we remain, through this enduring contact, not only somatically exposed to sudden movements and displacements, but psychically vulnerable to the anguish of a profound abandonment.

The excess of the other

While Levinas's speculations about the deep-seated rumbling of our earthly foundations have only rarely received sustained attention, his insights into the way that the plight of a fellow human being could reset the course of one's own life have been hugely influential in philosophy and social thought. Just as our embodied and sensuous condition condemns us to feeling pain of our own, he observed, so too are we exposed to the suffering that is expressed in the face, the eyes, the cry of an 'other' (1969: 206–97, 1987 [1947]: 68–71). To allow someone else's needs, someone else's trauma to make a real impression on us constitutes a 'risky uncovering of oneself' (1998a: 48).

And to even start to think this way poses a challenge to the idea of an autonomous, self-directed subject – thus opening the way to a notion of 'being as vulnerability'. Arguably, for Levinas this is as much a claim about the ontological condition of 'corporeal life' as it is a purely ethical imperative (1998a [1974]: 50; see also Harrison, 2008: 426), though this is not to imply that a particular mode of response is inevitable, or even that the one who is called upon will answer at all. What it does mean is that a summons from an other in distress tends to descend on us from beyond our usual sphere of operations, from outside our 'comfort zone'. 'It comes to me from elsewhere, unbidden, unexpected, and unplanned', as Judith Butler puts it. 'In fact it tends to ruin my plans ...' (2004: 130).

Something which unexpectedly messes with *my* plans, throws *me* off course, it can be argued, is not simply a response to a disaster. It is part of the disaster itself, part of its shock, its surprise, its forceful-ness. Though it may seem like a gross exaggeration to suggest that responding to those who have endured a traumatic event is anything like going through the event oneself, the point Levinas wants to make is that it is precisely our inability to truly share what others have been through that troubles us, haunts us, provokes us into our own transformation. As Levinas's close friend Maurice Blanchot puts it, a response to an other's predicament '... presupposes an overturn-ing such that it can only be marked by a change in the status of "me"' (1995 [1980]: 25).

This about-turn in agency may in fact be so commonplace that most of us take it for granted as we go about lives filled with give and take, helping and being helped, caring and being cared for. But the very notion that the 'weak' might transform the 'strong' – against the latter's best interests or intentions – has enormous consequences for critical thought and practice. John Caputo describes Levinas's core insight as 'a gripping tale, very moving and very powerful, a tremendous and salutary shock ... to contemporary philosophy' (1993: 79). Amongst other things, it offers a vital supplement to the idea that what social scientists and philosophers characteristically refer to as 'power' is always weighted in favour of the privileged, well-resourced, best-positioned. Without denying in any way the pervasiveness of inequality or the unjust exercise of political force, Levinas declares, with regard to the 'stranger', the one who is visibly dispossessed and distraught: 'Over him I have no *power*' (1969: 39, author's italics).

Although it may not stand up well in the social–structural or insti-tutional arenas in which power relations are usually analysed, the idea that those who are otherwise empowered and enabled may be 'held hostage' through their voluntary deferring to the needs of an other offers a markedly different point of departure for thinking about social forces and bonds. As Levinas would have it, it is not the wielding of force but its withholding – the putting aside of arms and lowering of defences – that is 'the condition for all solidarity' (1998a:

117; see also 1969: 198–9). What he is emphasizing here – the instant of receptiveness, the formative importance of a capacity to be moved, swayed, touched by others – would seem to be precisely what so many left-leaning commentators found so hard to affirm in the immediate aftermath of the Tsunami. It is what they struggled to defuse and recontain within a conventional critical modelling of differentials of power and wealth.

But what is both poignant, and troubling, about this discomfort with the exorbitance or asymmetry of generosity is that it is precisely this responsiveness to the suffering of others, as Levinas would have it, which is the deep and secret source of the will to justice – that same sense of justice to which radical or progressive thinkers are so solidly committed. To use what even he admits is a 'worn-out and ambiguous word', Levinas proclaims that 'Justice comes from love': its originary impulse is the singular desire to reach out across the rift gouged by inequality (1998b: 92; see also 31). This is perhaps the very incitement we might divine at the heart of the question of 'why it is these people, the planet's most vulnerable due to lacking resources available to others, who are so often the ones "in the way"'.

The broader point to be made here is that Levinas's conception of a radically constitutive vulnerability is not opposed to action, to deliberation or calculation. In one respect, his insistence that we are susceptible to the needs of the other in advance of being decisive and agential, like that of his thematizing of our dependence on the earth's offerings, is a counterweight to Western thought's fixation on active and intentional subjectivities. But for all that Levinas prioritizes the receptive moment in order to reclaim the passion and passivity of being-for-another from its previous obscurity, he is aware that the burden of judgement is ever present. Because there is always more than one other who may make demands on us, even if only one face appears before us, right from the outset we are compelled to make choices, to weigh up options, to consider outcomes (Levinas, 1998b: 9).

In this way, according to a logic later thinkers have filled out, the surrender to the demands of others is an incitement to purposive action, not its refusal. It is our *inability* to truly know and share the 'estrangement' of the other that spurs us to think and act. 'This incomprehensibility', as Derrida teases it out, '… is not the beginning of irrationalism but the wound or inspiration which opens speech and then makes possible every logos or every rationalism' (1978: 98). A catastrophe like the Tsunami drives home just how crucial this movement is between the loss of sense and the attempt to remake sense (Clark, 2005a). As Blanchot reminds us, the literal meaning of *dis-aster* is the loss of a star, the parting from one's guiding light (1995: 2). '(T)he disaster', he exclaims '... overflows every variety of thought' (1995: 5). The disaster is the event so severe that in its tearing away of the foundations, structures and relations that make the world legible, it also deprives those it afflicts of their capacity to absorb and process the event, to render it intelligible.

And the Tsunami was indeed an opening of speech, writing, presentation of every kind – from the 'superabundant photographs' to which Solnit refers (2005a, unpag.) to the prolific documentation that a Sri Lankan refugee speaks of. 'They have come and written and written and gone', the Tsunami survivor recounted to a reporter of the officials who had passed through her camp. 'Everybody's writing endlessly' (Nageshwari, cited in Waldman, 2005: 14). But this is in many ways understandable. If a response is to be effective, which is to say responsible, then it needs to be informed, as well-informed as can possibly be. As Derrida asserts, 'one can't make a responsible decision without science or conscience, without knowing what one is doing, for what reasons, in view of what and under what conditions' (1995a: 24). Or as Gayatri Spivak puts it: 'The call is a gift, but the response is, unavoidably, an exchange effect' (1994: 45).

We have Blanchot to thank for the idea that the disaster might be seen as a gift (1995: 49–50). By this, he means that the very destructiveness of the disaster, the loss of sense that ensues, is also, in a strange and paradoxical way, generative. It starts the world turning again. In conversation with Levinas's notion of 'being as vulnerability', Blanchot is pointing to the way that the disaster does not merely throw into relief or disarray previously existing structures and arrangements, but gives rise to the new. This is not the same thing as saying that there is only the fullness of production or generativity in the universe (see Wyschogrod, 1990: 210). But it is to say that the disaster demands change, precisely because of its profound rupture with the past, because of the impossibility of recasting it into positivity, of redeeming it, or even of making sense of it. There is no way to know that change will be for the better, just as there is no guarantee that the call will elicit a response, or that those who offer assistance will give enough, or that their gifts will be appropriate or welldirected. But if a response is a genuine opening, if what is given is a part of the one who gives, then it is also a contact, a kind of touching, an obligation. In whatever small and veiled way, it sets something in motion – without expecting that movement to involve any reply or reciprocation: it is an 'adventuring outside oneself … *(w)ithout hope of return'* (Derrida, 1978: 95).

Those who pass critical judgement on acts of generosity, then, are far from fully misguided. It is just that in their rush to restore sense, they tend to move too quickly through the obscure and enigmatic potency of the disaster. This is what Levinas is getting at when he suggests that '(c)larity is the disappearance of what could shock' (1969: 124). Arguably, any mode of truth-telling or sense-making that airlifts its axioms, concepts and laws into the disaster zone without allowing itself to feel some disorientation, has evaded the disaster's 'gift'. It has offered its guiding lights without having first ventured into what Spivak refers to as 'the risky night of non-knowledge' (1994: 25). And in this way, it denies its own core of vulnerability. Or, we might say, it imposes the symmetry of an economy of truth and understanding in place of the radical asymmetry of an opening into the unknown and unknowable.

The dark background of existence

The figuring of the disaster in terms of lost stars, un-worlded worlds, fissured grounds – even when it does not refer to *literal* cosmic upheavals – points to an abandonment deeper than the unravelling of connections or relations. As philosopher Slavoj Žižek writes: 'There is ethics – that is to say, an injunction which cannot be grounded in ontology – insofar as there is a crack in the ontological edifice of the universe: at its most elementary, ethics designates fidelity to this crack' (1997: 214). Ethics, Žižek is suggesting, must be true to this rupture; it must attend to a discontinuity that it knows to be too profound for any truth or technique or project to paper over. This too, though in a different context and register, is Levinas's lesson: that the ethical relationship is a working across differences that cannot ever be fully accommodated or processed into shared understanding or identification (1969: 194, 292). This is why Levinasian responsibility is *infinite*. And in this way we can see that the disaster demands of its respondents a negotiation of at least two starkly contrasting temporalities. There is the need to act immediately and decisively in the white heat of the event, and the endless patience required of bearing witness to and working towards a forever unattainable mending (see Barnett, 2005: 10–12).

But Levinas's insight that the other 'overflows absolutely every *idea* I can have of him' (1969: 87) has implications beyond the encounter of a self with another human being. If we return to his earliest work, where he introduces the idea of the earth as a ground or reservoir of support, we find an anticipation of this notion of a contact or even intimacy that retains a trace of insuperable distance at its core. When Levinas makes the point that 'knowing is a relationship with what above all remains exterior' in *Existence and Existents* (2001 [1978]: 87), he is speaking not only in the context of self-knowing and interpersonal relating, but also of a more elemental or substantial otherness. As Graham Harman points out, it is here, in these underrated early explorations, that Levinas sketches out the ways in which the sensuous elements we depend upon have a depth to them that constantly eludes our full awareness (2002: 235; see also Lingis, 2001: xx). Conversing in important ways with Heidegger's sense of the withdrawn presence of our worldly surroundings, Levinas directs our attention '… behind the form which light reveals into that materiality which … constitutes the dark background of existence' (2001: 54–5).

As we saw earlier, Levinas makes the case that the play of our relations with a sustaining world can also be interrupted. There are times, such as if we find ourselves stumbling through the darkness of night, when the vertigo of formlessness envelopes us, and we are bereft of the usual givenness of the ground – at least until the sun's rays again cast the world into clarity and substance (2001: 52). It is through this intimation of a world which can un-world itself that Levinas comes to a more general point. Just as there is something insurmountable and insatiable at the heart of even our closest friendships, so too in our relationships with objects is there a kind of separateness 'which can indeed be traversed, but remains a distance' (2001: 35, 39; see also Harrison, 2008: 436). Or, as he later develops this insight: 'What the side of the element that is turned toward me conceals is not a "something" susceptible of being revealed, but an ever new depth of absence, an existence with existent, the impersonal par excellence' (1969: 142). The risky night of non-knowledge, in other words, is always with us.

It is not all grim. In the play of lucidity and concealment that he sketches out, Levinas endorses the world's 'anonymous rustling' that slips in and out of the reach of our knowing (2001: 61). The other side of this to-ing and fro-ing of accessibility, as we saw in the opening passages to this chapter, is that he also attuned to the allures and enjoyments of earthly existence, happily affirming a 'joyous appetite for things which constitutes being in the world' (Levinas, 2001: 27). Alongside the foregrounding of a visceral responsiveness to the entreaties of the stranger, then, is Levinas's no less important thematizing of the 'sincerity' of human lives in their exposure to and immersion in the elemental (2001: 36). Or, as Harman inimitably sums up: 'Levinas brings us to a point where it is no longer a mark of urbane sophistication to take a smirking ironic distance from the most colourful details of the earth' (2002: 237).

There are vital points in Levinas's work when the theme of a nourishing elementality converges with his more acclaimed concern with an inter-human otherness. In a well-known passage in dialogue with Pascal, Levinas reflects on the deep-seated indebtedness we might feel for our enjoyment of a 'place in the sun'. It is one of his more apparently political offerings, for he immediately suggests that the ground we inhabit, the section of the earth that sustains us, may well have come at the cost of denying someone else the same comforts. Or indeed, that our very existence is premised on a whole series of seizures, displacements, or appropriations: 'My being-in-the-world or my "place in the sun", my being at home, have these not also been the usurpation of spaces belonging to the other man whom I have already oppressed or starved, or driven out into a third world …' (Levinas, 1989: 82).

While these words seem to speak directly to the circumstances through which Western tourists found themselves on the shores of the Indian Ocean, luxuriating under someone else's sun, there is more at stake here. Levinas is not only, or even primarily, talking about the kind of traceable and presentable causal connections between privilege and dispossession which polemical writers held up to scrutiny after the disaster. He is gesturing towards a deeper and more obscure entanglement, and the sense of responsibility that might flow from it.

The debt Levinas has in mind accompanies us from our very inception (1998a: 87). It is what we 'owe' others for the paths we follow, for the languages that speak through us, for the very flesh of our bodies. If these gifts – which give us a present and future – well up from the past, it is not simply from a past that can be made present, brought to light, or tallied into an account. It is an abyssal past, not a recuperable one. 'Men have been able to be thankful for the very fact of finding themselves able to thank; the present gratitude is grafted onto itself as onto an already antecedent gratitude', professes Levinas (1998a: 10). While we have no chance of fully comprehending or calculating the work, the care, the love that has bequeathed us our place on the earth, what is inescapable is our utter reliance on others who have come before us or who walk beside us. For it is they who enable my 'being at home', they who have imparted me with the 'well-trampled places' which provide my everyday support (see Levinas, 1969: 138). But remembering what Levinas has also said of the raw elementality that underpins our repose, of the fecundity and light that lends us our love of life, we have good reason to extend our 'already antecedent gratitude' still further: on beyond human others, beyond any living beings, on into the anonymous exteriority of the supporting earth, the gentle breeze, the rolling ocean, the sparkling light.

For all that Levinas conjures a sense of the subterranean murmuring of the elements, it would be an exaggeration to enrol him as a theorist of volatile earth processes. He is not, like the Immanuel Kant of the forthcoming chapter, an amateur seismologist with recurring anxieties about geological upheaval. Given his experiences in war-torn Europe, we would hardly expect geohazards to have been Levinas's priority. But there is something in those early musings on the encounter between the embodied human being and its terrestrial subtending that deserves reclaiming. This is especially so at present, in the light of a growing discontent in some circles of critical philosophical inquiry with the theme of 'otherness' in the Levinasian fold: an ever-more fashionable impatience with the absoluteness of his conception of alterity and its 'otherworldly' implications (see Badiou, 2001: 18–20; Hallward, 2003: 255–6; see also Clark, 2010b).

At a time when the instability of the earth is presenting itself to us in novel and alarming ways, and vast new sources of human (and more-than human) vulnerability appear on the horizon, we would do well to hang on to the decidedly this-worldly concern of Levinas with the elemental underpinning of our existence. While care must be taken not to simply map '(t)he adventure separation opens' (Levinas, 1969: 292) onto the repercussions of a physically rending planet, the singular crossing in his work of the thematic of the 'strangeness of the earth' with the sensuous, earthy enframing of 'the stranger' needs to be drawn out. As we will see in later chapters, it is a task that philosopher Alphonso Lingis has already taken on with immense verve.[2]

As Lingis (1994) would have it, when we encounter a stranger we cross paths also with the journeys they have taken, the elemental forces they have lived with, the extremes they have weathered. Extrapolating from Levinas's insight that the exposure and susceptibility of the embodied subject is originary rather than contingent or derivative, this serves as a timely reminder that we do not simply live in the path of future upheavals, but that we – all of us – are always already downstream of the disaster. Past catastrophes, that is, and all the meetings, openings, obligations and assemblages they incite, are part of who and what we are – just as the effects of the Tsunami will mark those who endured it and will be passed on to others in ways both visible and imperceptible.

In the following chapter, I dig deeper into the constitutive role of the natural disaster, and the traces it leaves on thoughtful but fragile bodies. With particular attention to one major event in early modern European and North Atlantic history, I suggest that the ordinary tumult of earth processes may have played a much bigger part in the formation of the modern subject than we are usually led to believe.

Afterward: expressing gratitude

A rapid assessment report on the Indian Ocean Tsunami jointly produced by the Sri Lankan Green Movement and a UK-based disaster and development research centre begins with the following words:

> The Disaster Management and Information Programme firmly understand that every one has drunk from other people's wells and has been nourished by other people's ideas, and therefore is happy to feed the hunger or satisfy the thirst of people they may or may not ever encounter. (Disaster Management and Information Programme, 2004: 3)

The report went on to announce that the information they were providing was free for anyone to reproduce, by any means, for whatever purpose they wished. Generosity, in whatever medium it appears, begins with a welcome. Such generosity feeds and nurtures itself on gratitude, sociologist Arthur Frank suggests (2004: 142). And that gratefulness may be boundless. Beneath the flow of words and the circulation of ideas is the tapping of water from another's well, the well which is topped up by countless drops of rain percolating through the pores of the soil and the silent ebb of subterranean streams.

Gratitude is an outpouring of enjoyment in existence, a flow we cannot consciously turn on or off, any more than we can decide not to feel the pain that seeps through the receptors and pathways of our nervous system. Feelings of gratefulness just happen, though all the effort that has been devoted to theorizing a non-indifference to the pleasure and pain of others suggests a quiet hope that its passage might be smoothed. Perhaps, in a more or less diffuse way, visitors to the Indian Ocean felt a certain gratitude for the place in the sun that they had found – before the shock waves surged across the beaches and through the hotel gardens and foyers. What floats gently beneath the surface of accounts of the tragedy by tourists is an appreciation for the hospitality they received – before, as well as after, the Tsunami. It is a warmth of feeling that seems superfluous to the contractual obligations that, as any clearheaded analysis would tell us, structure the tourist economy – as if these guests simply felt gratitude for having shared someone else's sun, and thankful for the support and sustenance that made this possible. As well as just being grateful to be alive.

To take into account the unaccountability of generosity and gratitude is not to ignore those aspects of our relatedness to others that we can measure up and find wanting. How some of us came to be reclining on distant beaches, or had money and wardrobes of clothes to give, can be explained in terms of global economies whose inequitable flows can be identified and even computed. That all the earth's surface now presents itself as potential places in the sun, for a few of us at least, is something for which we could feel a vast and immeasurable gratitude. It is a gratitude expressed as generosity in the face of disasters both chronic and sudden. And this generosity, we need to acknowledge, will fall short, overshoot or stray from its target, this being the inevitable fate of the gift in all its guises (Frank, 2004: 2). To confront the inherent insufficiency of giving is also to invite a response from those who are on the receiving end, such as we have heard from individuals and communities afflicted by the Tsunami. For if generosity is truly an opening of oneself, then it also makes the one who gives vulnerable. The donor too must be prepared to feel hurt, to be chastened, criticized, even rejected. Only in this way might they – we – learn to give responsibly, as well as responsively.

Such lessons, painful and searching, are the gift of the disaster – the event which ends the world and starts it turning anew. 'The disaster', which, in the words of Blanchot (1995: 1), 'ruins everything, all the while leaving everything intact'.

It was such a strange day. The sun was shining and it was warm. Then the tsunami came and destroyed everything. Afterwards when I looked out across the wasteland, I couldn't help thinking that it was strange that the sun was still shining. (Mezubar, Tsunami survivor and volunteer worker, Banda Aceh cited in British Red Cross (2005: 6))

Notes

1   There seems to have been resistance from local people themselves to the constant reference to their poverty, as reported in a post on *The South-East Asia Earthquake and Tsunami Blog* a week after the disaster:

> Most of the people affected are fisher people – they are not 'poor' in the sense of the word. One woman said 'We may live in huts – but you should have seen the inside – it was full of stuff – we had men working in Dubai and we had motor boats, TV, VCRs, jewellery and pattu podavais. All that is now gone'. (posted by Kartik, 01/01/2005)

2   For a provocative extension of Levinas's engagement with loss and trauma far beyond the domain of the human, see Brassier (2007: Ch. 7).

4

Quaking:
The 1755 Lisbon Disaster and the Modern Subject

Introduction: chasms and crevices

Starting as a hairline crack, the jagged cleft forked its way to the far end of the gallery, deepening as it went. Artist Doris Salcedo's installation *Shibboleth* cut through the concrete floor of the cavernous Turbine Hall of London's Tate Gallery, severing reinforcing rods and everything else in its path. Confronting what looked disturbingly like real, seismically inflicted structural damage, reviewers seemed relieved to point out that at its deepest it went down no more than a few feet. While it may have been the case that throughout its 167-meter length the fracture remained narrow enough to hop over with ease, you could cross it as often as you liked, but a sense of the ground opening abyssally beneath your feet never quite went away. Even now that the exhibition is over and new work has taken its place, that re-concreted rift is still visible from the viewing platforms above: a ghostly trace likely to be there for the duration of the building.

Reminiscent of the void that dissects Daniel Libeskind's Jewish Museum, Salcedo's fissured foundations speak of a gap that can never be fully bridged, a missing presence that cannot be filled and made whole. Like Libeskind's architectonic rift which figures for the wartime destruction of the Jewish community of Berlin, Salcedo is gesturing toward social divisions: schisms cruel, deep and enduring. Both works grapple with the impossibility of representing that which cannot simply be made present again – the chasm in built space doubling for communal trauma, bodily laceration that will not heal, an eternally open wound.

In the last chapter, we looked at events so shocking that they threaten to undermine the very concepts or categories we rely upon to understand the world. As Jean-François Lyotard poses it: 'Suppose an earthquake destroys not only lives, but the instruments used to measure earthquakes directly and indirectly' (1988: 56). Lyotard is using the idea of seismicity figuratively here, to give an impression of something happening that rocks the very foundations on which thought and practice base themselves yet at the same time demands a response, compels us to think and act anew. In fact, most of the theorists I drew on to help make sense of the loss of sense that was the Tsunami made their original interventions not in response to any disturbance in the natural world but in reply to horrifying acts perpetrated on human beings by their fellow humans (but see Turner, 2006: 26).

Living through or after what Levinas referred to as a 'century of unutterable suffering' (1998b: 80), artists, writers and theorists have sought to develop ways of presenting the unpresentable, of depicting atrocity and its grievous impacts in ways that neither convert it into a spectacle nor reduce it to the familiar and assimilable. They have tried to hold open that which is unresolvable, unthinkable, unfathomable, so that we remain in close proximity to distances that cannot and should not be closed.

For all that it is horrors of our own making that have come to weigh so heavily on the moral and political conscience, figurations of societal crisis and inter-human violence return frequently to the topos of natural disaster. To capture the sublimity of human suffering, the profundity of social divisions and communal losses, commentators and practioners still turn to the tropes of geological dynamism, dipping into a lexicon of seismic shifts, fault lines, eruptions, upheavals, fractures, fissures, abysses, chasms and rifts in order to conjure the most deadly threats to the vitality of human life (see Clark, 2007b: 1134) .

But then there is Alberto Burri's *Cretto*. *Il Cretto* (*Crevice*) is a controversial work of land art, 40 hectares plus of glaring white, hard-edged, concrete slabs, divided by pathways equally devoid of traces of life or embellishment. With its grid-like structure and near-inhuman minimalism, this would appear to be a paradigm of modernist austerity. Yet Burri is an artist whose reputation was built on a conscious deferral of the primary gesture in the creative process to the forces of nature. His more intimate works, paintings also known as *Cretti*, involved the covering of the picture plane with a paste of materials that cracked and crazed as they dried, leaving the final patterning of the pictorial surface beyond the artist's control (Rozner, 2009: unpag.). And that play of responses between human and nonhuman elements is just as much the defining character of the outdoor *Cretto*.

The great *Cretto* is a monument to the hill-side town of Gibbellina in western Sicily which was totally destroyed with considerable loss of life by the devastating earthquake of 1968. A second Gibbellina was built from scratch 18 kilometers away, closer to rail links and *autostrada*. Burri, invited to contribute a public artwork to the new town, came up with a more grandiose proposal: the entombment of all the rubble and ruins of the abandoned town in a massive, impervious structure that mapped onto its ground plan (Ingersoll, 2004). In many ways, the *Cretto* resonates with other cultural or artistic figurings of cataclysm – with its refusal to let a harrowing loss dissipate into obscurity, its insistence on confronting us with the stark absence of life where once there was vitality, its cavernous wounds which will not ever close. But in other ways, the artwork is a strange inversion of the use of the fissure, the chasm, the upheaval in so much late- or post-modern thought and practice to figure for that which is most decidedly non-natural.

Amongst other readings, *Il Cretto* might be taken as an assertion that the forces of the earth have not been eclipsed by other forms of endangerment; a reminder that they too deserve a response – a reply that neither lays disaster to rest in a safely distant past nor encourages the suffering of others to be consumed as an arousing but ephemeral spectacle. With its brutal mineralization of the landscape, the monument refuses the consolations of revitalization, even as its lifeless avenues constantly reconnect the gaze to the verdant countryside beyond (see Rozner, 2009: unpag.). If it stands as an acknowledgement of the frightening forcefulness of the earth itself, so too does the *Cretto* seem to answer back with a boldness that confronts earth processes on their own terrain and scale. In Burri's own words; 'strength like history had to emerge from the comparison of the great civilizations of Segesta, Selinunte, Motia and the ruined world of the poor and the dead' (cited in Rozner, 2009: unpag.), suggesting an intention to distil something enduring and potent from the detritus of one small, fragile village.

Recalling Serres' evocation of civilization as 'colossal banks of humanity', or the geologist Antonio Stoppani's earlier depiction of humankind as a 'new telluric force' (cited in Crutzen, 2002: 23), *Il Cretto* seems to find something in ordinary human achievement that itself has the intractable presence of a tectonic plate. This makes it less a reconciliation with nature than a gesture of defiance, a response to the catastrophe that both recognizes and rages against the precariousness of human settlement – or of human life more generally. As Alphonso Lingis observes, in an unrelated but resonant context:

We stand on top of the mountain and it does not seem to us that simply there are so many lines extending across the field of our vision, as when we stand in front of a map or a painting, it is because we feel the distance, the vastness of the space. In the movement of the wind in the fields below and in the clouds above, we feel the force of geological and cosmic time. (1998b: 120)

It is precisely the might of the geological or the cosmic that the *Cretto* encapsulates in a literal way that is – like Lingis's own philosophical engagements with an elemental forcefulness – all too rare in an era still in thrall with the ambivalent capacities of the anthropic. As the tone of commentaries on the Indian Ocean Tsunami suggested, we live in a time when critical intervention is marked by a reluctance to allow the physical dynamics of our planet, or even the plight of those caught up in these changes, to speak to us in direct ways. An unwillingness that is, to permit natural elements or entities, in and of themselves, to disturb or challenge or incite us. 'For contemporary observers, earthquakes are only a matter of plate tectonics', as philosopher Susan Neiman sums up: 'They threaten, at most, your faith in government building codes or geologists' predictions. They may invoke anger at lazy inspectors, or pity for those stuck in the wrong place at the wrong time. But these are ordinary emotions' (2002: 246).

Whatever progressive intellectuals might say to the contrary, the Tsunami, I argued, threw up a wealth of evidence of ordinary people in many different places being thrown off course by a geological event – often as a result of their encounters with others who had suffered in ways they had been spared. In this chapter, I want to dig deeper into the issue of why it is that modern Western philosophical and social thought is resistant to the attribution of generative or originary significance to natural processes. Why it is that we are so much more likely to read, for example, that 'September 11 has ruptured irrevocably the context in which we as intellectuals speak' (Buck-Morss, 2002: 2), than we are to hear that the subsidence of a piece of the earth bigger than half the world's nation-states that took a third of a million lives might have revised the way we think about our planet and its inhabitation.

Neiman's prognosis of the impact of seismic events that I cited above is in fact more nuanced than it first appears. Far from simply disavowing the ontological impact of volatile earth processes, she identifies a paradox at the core of the modern idea of the subject. It is the destruction of the city of Lisbon by earthquake, tsunami and fire in 1755, Neiman suggests, that is pivotal to the emergence of a subject desperate to believe in its own self-determining qualities. Thus, it is less the capacity to dominate outer nature or inner nature so much as a sense of the vulnerability of the thinking being that drives the quest for a subjecthood capable of rising above the threatening forces of the earth and cosmos. Taking Immanuel Kant as the exemplar of this turn, I want to build on Neiman's case that the definitive auto-affective characteristics of the modern subject conceal a very real sense of human frailty in the face of a nature that showed itself to be terrifyingly violent just at the moment when its victims and its audience were at their most exposed.

Kant's settlement, as we will see, involved putting up a barrier between a sphere of nature that is left to its own necessities and a realm of human existence where we are free to compose our own principles. It is he, then, who gets the credit or the blame for firmly establishing the idea that freedom *is* where nature *is not*. Henceforth, we do not take our directives, our moral imperatives, from outer nature, but only from the inner logic of categories we have decided for ourselves. One of the major repercussions of this turn is that any kind of encounter between objects or elements in which no humans are present ceases to be of interest to critical observers. As Graham Harman explains:

> any sort of communication between substances that does not involve human beings is banished to an unknowable, barely mentionable place. Kant simply has far less to say about the collision of rocks than Bruno, Descartes, or Leibniz. The single remaining gap between human and world banishes any more general treatment of causation, which is now left entirely to the physicists. (2005: 92)

This is the 'settlement' that gives rise to the idea that thinking beings are restricted to accessing only the correlation between their thought and the outside world, and not what things get up to 'in themselves', and to its practical concomitant – that nonhuman nature should have no direct bearing on the ethical, political or cultural strivings of human agents.

It is the cataclysmic events of the mid-twentieth century that go by the proper name of Auschwitz or the Holocaust, Neiman contends, which proved the final blow for the hopes and ambitions that attended the modern self-willing subject. But at the same time, as we will see, the shift in emphasis to the deadly repercussions of this constitution of subjectivity has served to further obscure the role of independent natural forces in its formative moments. One of the implications of this occlusion has been that, amongst all the momentous questions provoked by human-induced catastrophe, the self-defensive separation of the 'is' and the 'ought' has tended to go untroubled. Even when the worst pathologies of modern individual or collective subjectivity are being laid open to scrutiny, the assumption persists that allowing nature to have any direct impact on humankind can only mean a nostalgic and anti-progressive recourse to the determinations of the natural referent.

But this is not the only option. Picking up on what I have already said about the radical asymmetry of the human and the natural, and what we have learnt from Levinas about the obligation of self to an other, I want to make a case for acknowledging the imperatives that come to us directly from the 'otherness' of nature. Following the leads of Alphonso Lingis, as well as those of the speculative realist philosophers, I argue that it is possible to sift through the Kantian inheritance in ways which once more open up the possibility of generative encounters with natural forces and processes, and in this way unsettle the divide between 'is' and 'ought'. Nestling within Kant's formidable subject, as Lingis has suggested, is another, more pervious being, responsive to imperatives that come to it from far beyond its own inner domain.

To go beyond Kant's subject, then, we may first need to get in closer – a move anticipated by Deleuze and Guattari's intriguing suggestion that Kant is an inspiration for their own 'geophilosophy': their attempt to productively bridge the divide between the human subject and a forceful earth and cosmos. 'Kant is less a prisoner of the categories of subject and object than he is believed to be', they suggest, 'since his idea of a Copernican revolution puts thought into a direct relationship with the earth' (1994: 85). In other ways, I argue, Kant's own thought was in a 'direct relationship' with a dynamic earth long before the critical turn that established him as a philosophical force.

Lisbon, 1755

Michel Serres may have written eloquently about his personal experience of an earthquake, but he is not the first philosopher to feel the shock waves of a seismic event. Harman's claim that Kant has little to say about the collision of rocks has a ring of truth with regard to the philosopher's mature or 'critical' writings, but even there, his relative silence about lithic instability may be more a repression than a categorical omission. Or to put it another way, Kant actually knew a great deal about the threat of cracking ground and colliding rock, so much so that one of the aims of his major works may have been to elevate the human subject to a position where it is safe from being crushed and buried by the earth's upheavals.

As Walter Benjamin pointed out in a 1931 radio programme, Kant helped invent the science of seismology, as evidenced by a slim volume written in 1756 by the then little-known scholar bearing the earnest title *History and Physiography of the Most Remarkable Cases of the Earthquake which Towards the End of the Year 1755 Shook a Great Part of the Earth* (Kant, 1994 [1756]; Ray, 2004: 8). The seismic event Kant writes about is best remembered in the West for the destruction it wrought on the Portuguese capital. On the morning of 1 November 1755, Lisbon was rocked by three huge tremors that opened giant fissures in the town centre and brought down many buildings. The enormous loss of life that ensued was made worse by the fact that it was All Saints day, and the quake caught a large proportion of the populace crowded into the big, brittle structures that were their places of worship.

The death toll escalated as fires erupted, ignited, as some accounts would have it, by toppling altar candles. Many of the survivors stumbled down to the open spaces of the waterfront. Here, like the baffled onlookers around the Indian Ocean shoreline 250 years later, they caught a glimpse of a hidden world suddenly exposed by the withdrawal of the sea: the portside seabed littered not only with floundering marine life but with the ghostly hulks of shipwrecks and lost cargo. Shortly afterwards, several massive tsunamis engulfed the downtown area, and surged up the River Targus, overflowing its banks into the stricken city. In those areas spared by the waves, the fires continued to rage for another five days (Neiman, 2002: 241–2; Ray, 2004: 7).

The tsunamis caused devastation and extensive loss of life along the coasts of the Iberian Peninsula, western Morocco, the Madeira and Azores Islands. Shaking from the quake was felt in France, Switzerland and northern Italy, the waves reaching Belgium and Holland, and crossing the Atlantic to strike Antigua, Martinique and Barbados (Kozak and James, 1998; Chester, 2001). As Voltaire (1756) put it in a poetic response to the event:

'Subterranean lightening swallows Lisbon

And scatters the debris of thirty cities

From the bloody shores of the Tagus to the sea of Cadiz'

(2009 [1756]: unpag.).

The destruction may have been geographically dispersed, but it was the fatal fusion of fire, water and shaking earth visited upon Lisbon that sent shudders of horror across Europe. With its strategic importance for the world's seaways, its wealth and cultural riches, its large and cosmopolitan population, the Portuguese capital was a European 'headland' in every sense. Popular reportage and intellectual reflection alike was swift and voluminous: 'All over Europe, the presses rushed into print countless eyewitness accounts; these pamphlets were hungrily consumed by people who had felt, albeit from a distance, the power of this disaster in the senses and the sympathies of their own bodies' (Ray, 2004: 8).

In the latter eighteenth century, Lisbon's destruction came to be considered by informed observers as the most momentous event to have occurred in Europe since the fall of the Roman Empire (Neiman, 2002: 240). In Theodor Adorno's words: 'The earthquake of Lisbon sufficed to cure Voltaire of the theodicy of Leibniz' (1973: 361). By theodicy, Adorno refers to a vision of the world as the product of a celestial architect, a view summed up in Leibniz's formulation that we lived in 'the best of all possible worlds'. Voltaire's poem expresses his emphatic disillusionment with the idea that the suffering experienced by the people of Lisbon could possibly be commensurate with God's greater purpose:

"All is well, you say, and all is necessary".

What! The whole universe, without this hellish gulf,

Without a Lisbon swallowed up, would have been even worse?

(2009 [1756]: unpag.).

Along with the swipe at Voltaire, what Adorno was getting at was a much more general turn away from a theistic moral and natural universe, in which 'Lisbon' has come to be seen as the tipping point. There is ample evidence to indicate that the intellectual foundations of the mid-eighteenth century were already in a precarious state (Neiman, 2002: 239). The challenge for exponents of theodicy was that every event of any consequence had to be slotted into a divine master plan, which in its blunter manifestations was taken to mean that those struck by misfortune must have attracted the attention of a vengeful deity. But on the face of it, the Portuguese capital seemed no more deserving of God's wrath than any number of kindred cities. To many pensive onlookers, the magnitude of death and destruction suffered by Lisbon appeared too extreme to have been divinely ordained, especially by a creator who had lately come to be seen as presiding over a harmonious and well-calculated universe (see Hamacher, 1999: 279–81).

And then there was the response to the crisis by those Lisbon authorities who stood firm on the divine plan. In the interests of a speedy appeasement, surviving local 'heretics' and other paragons of sinfulness were rounded up and conducted to what remained of the town squares. Voltaire, reputedly, was as horrified at the auto-da-fé that followed as he was by the fiery course of the quake itself (Neiman, 2002: 324).

The alternative to the various theodicies on offer was the acknowledgement that the disaster, for all its capacity to test the will and tear at the emotions, was a work of nature, an event of purely earthbound causality (Neiman, 2002: 60). This is where the youthful Kant staked his allegiance. His *History and Physiography* of the 1755 catastrophe opens tentatively by paying its dues to the creator who set up the laws of nature. But the Königsberg philosopher-scientist concludes his piece by underscoring the folly of believing that whatever follows from these laws is the work of a divinity who bothers to meddle in the daily concerns of humanity (1994 [1756]: 29–30). God, Kant seems to be saying, has better things to do. Effectively, we are on our own amidst the best and worst that nature has to offer, and it is up to us to try and comprehend these variable forces, to accommodate ourselves to them, and to show consideration when they lay others low (Kant, 1994 [1756]: 25–6, 29).

If we accept that there is no ulterior motive behind the earthquake, if it has no meaning other than what we make of it, then what has taken place is a severing of the domain of morality from the realm of nature. As Neiman explains:

After Lisbon, the scope of moral categories contracted. Before Lisbon, they could be applied to the world as a whole; it made sense to call earthquakes evils. Afterward moral categories were confined to one small piece of the world, those human beings who may be able to realize them. (2002: 240)

This disinvestment of moral meaning from nature cements the definitively modern distinction between the 'is': the realm of nature or the cosmos, and the 'ought': the sphere in which human life conducts itself – a move initially taken up with more commitment by Rousseau than the 'pre-critical' Kant. Henceforth, humankind is obliged to take responsibility for its own affairs, bereft of guiding principles or helping hands from on high. And it is this transition that might be seen as the wider 'dis-aster' of Lisbon: not only the falling away of firm ground under foot, but the loss of a divine guiding star. Like Lyotard's earthquake, Lisbon's concatenation of horrors signalled not only physical and corporeal annihilation but the collapse of a way of making sense of the event itself.

All of which left the rather substantial problem of how to live on once God had been evacuated from ground zero. The issue was not only how to inhabit a moral universe that was free-floating. It was how to endure an existence that was at once unmoored and prone to being blown all over the place by vast, brutal and untameable forces.

Kant's shaky settlement

It is the work of the 'mature' Kant that is generally viewed as providing the first in-depth exploration of the opening rupture between nature and morality, as well as being credited with offering the best available guidelines for recuperating hope and self-respect from humankind's new-found isolation. In the Lisbon earthquake booklet, Kant had speculated that contemplation of the very horrors of the disaster might turn out to be a stimulus for 'self-improvement', a possibility he quickly consigned to 'more able hands' (1994: 5). Hands which turned out, later in life, to be his own.

In the trilogy of critical works, Kant advances the distinction between the realm of nature – in which invariant or mechanistic laws hold sway, and the domain of the human – where, at least potentially, 'moral' agents are free to formulate and pursue laws of their own making. Having earlier noted in the 'pre-critical' *Universal Natural History* that 'Matter has no freedom to deviate from the plan of perfection' (1981 [1755]: 86), Kant proceeds to demonstrate in the *Critique of Practical Reason* that 'the mechanism of nature (is) the direct opposite of freedom' (1967 [1788]: 117).

But how rational human subjects come to be in a position to choose their own course of action, how they attain and exercise their vaunted 'freedom', is a tricky question. Kant sets out a complex causal chain in which the faculty of thought commands itself to think, commands that we make sense of the external world and commands that we impose order on this world (Lingis, 1998b: 179–81). Our quest to establish our own laws follows an imperative – 'a command that the I arise and be in command', as Lingis sums it up (1998b: 183; see also Kant: 1967 [1788]: 106–7).

Kant is at pains to prove that thought takes its directive from within and not from any prompting by the external world. Nature must comply with our capacity to recognize regularity and order, and not the other way round: only because we are able to make sense of the empirical world can we infer nature is law-like and systematic, a proper cosmos rather than a swirl of chaos (Lingis, 1998b: 197; Guyer, 2005: 62). It is this sense of a necessary correspondence between our cognitive capacities and that side of the natural world that is accessible to us, cemented by Kant in the *Critiques*, that Meillassoux identifies as the pivotal moment in the establishment of the correlationist stance. Henceforth, 'instead of knowledge conforming to the object, the Critical revolution makes the object conform to our knowledge' (Meillassoux, 2008: 117–18).

This correlation is not just a matter for thought, but also a matter of practical action in the world. If the worldly actions we conceive of, following our own imperatives, are to have the outcomes we anticipate, then it is necessary that the material world we are acting upon complies with our instrumental intent as well as our knowledge of it. In order for us to assert ourselves, confidently and effectively, we have to believe that nature is pre-disposed to our plans: that '*(t)he world was made for our purposes, and we for the worlds*' (Neiman, 2002: 84, author's italics).

Again, this is not as simple as it may appear, for Kant both insists that it is not possible to ascertain whether the world has been constructed with our ends in mind and goes to great lengths to show that it is (Neiman, 2002: 83). Nowhere is this struggle to render nature conducive to human interests more intense than when he deals with events of extreme physical force. It is late in the *Critique of Judgement* (2005 [1790]), under the heading 'The Analytic of the Sublime', that Kant famously revisits the encounter with an awesome and threatening natural world. This time around, empirical detail is sidelined in favour of rational inquiry into the relationship between the humbling experience of excessive energies of nature and the cultivation of moral will. At the sensory level, Kant argues, the unruly might of the natural world impresses upon us an awareness of our own limitation and inadequacy, not to mention physical vulnerability. But he goes on to suggest that out of this negative experience comes something positive and ennobling. We are driven to step back and gather that force which is ours alone: the faculty for supersensible reasoning. In the words of Werner Hamacher:

> Only when the power of nature humiliates the capacities of human
> subjectivity does the one power of human beings 'that does not belong
> to nature' arise – a power that, for this very reason, no longer stands

under its laws. Only when human beings, as physical entities, are subjected to the violence of nature do they rise up as moral beings and transcend the forces that could destroy their physical existence. (1999: 274)

In this way, we apprehend our superiority over nature, experiencing our own will as itself even more immense, more limitless, more potent than those natural phenomena that previously belittled and bewildered us (Ray, 2004: 9; Kant, 2005 [1790]: 74–7). Given his insistence that the freedom of the human will is unobligated to the domain of nature, it is important for Kant to stress that the sublimity which prompts the mind's higher flight is not so much a quality of external nature itself, as it is a human sensibility: an inbuilt propensity for awe and wonder that is prompted but not determined by the phenomena it alights on. As he concludes: 'nature is here called sublime merely because it elevates the Imagination to a presentation of those cases in which the mind can make felt the proper sublimity of its destination, in comparison with nature itself' (2005 [1790]: 75).

It is at this point that commentators have discerned a hint of desperation in the canny attempt to redeem dignity from disaster. For it is in his discussion of the dynamical sublime that probing readers scent the return of Kant's repressed: the trace of the natural catastrophe that so perturbed the young savant 30 years earlier. Though the proper name of Lisbon is absent and seismicity is explicitly mentioned in the discussion of the natural sublime only in passing – 'the tempest, the storm, the earthquake, etc.' (2005 [1790]: 76) – Gene Ray detects its resonances in a stream of references to tremors, repulsions, agitations, abysses (2004: 9–10). The memory of the suffering and destruction wrought by Lisbon, Ray suggests, expresses itself in Kant's awareness of the dangers posed by physical annihilation for the whole project of human autonomy and self-responsibility, and in all the subsequent efforts he makes to recuperate the encounter with a volatile nature into something positive for human moral development: 'He needed to domesticate those eruptions of sublime nature, of which the Lisbon earthquake was exemplary in his own century, in order to neutralize the threat they posed to a myth of progress grounded in natural law and a purported human nature' (2004: 11).

Lisbon in all its singularity may have had a profound impact on Kant, but there is a broader context in which to view his reception of this event. Though they may have been overshadowed by his later priorities, Kant's more empirical natural scientific leanings never entirely receded. One of his ongoing concerns was with the question of how inanimate matter broke from the bounds of law-like regularity in order to give rise to living organisms, and eventually, to a being capable of thought (Kant, 1993 [1938]: 6; Grant, 2000: 42–3). At a very different scale, his explorations around the natural sublime remained tied to an interest in the cosmological and geological processes that had formed the universe in its totality, and that ultimately provided the substrate for all life on earth. He was in good company. The eighteenth century saw growing acceptance that the duration of the earth and the solar system greatly exceeded the three-or four-figure timescales that scholars had formerly adduced from biblical references (Rudwick, 2005: 125). An enthusiastic convert to the concept of deep time, Kant mused in the *Universal Natural History* that 'millions of centuries will flow by, within which always new worlds and world-orders form themselves one after another' (1981 [1755]: 154).

But the trouble with the newly unfurling temporal spans, along with the previously established immensity of cosmic space, was that it implied whole domains of existence in which no humans were present, vast stretches in which other-than-human objects were left to their own devices. In its decisive advance beyond any conceivable reach of the human, cosmological and geological nature flaunted its indifference to our purposes and our sensibilities (Kant, 1967 [1788]: 260; Meillassoux, 2008: 116–18). As Diane Morgan puts it:

> This confrontation with the dynamic world of magnitudes … wrenches us out of the world of anthropomorphised nature. No longer is the natural world conceived of as just serving purposes … no longer is it press-ganged into servitude to human concerns and needs … (2007: 40)

More than just a matter of scale, it was the dynamism that revealed itself in the expanded spatio-temporal frame that posed the greatest threat to the belief that nature was cut to human measure. Following the catastrophist turn in geology, Kant accepted the evidence that the earth had passed through major episodes of unrest: 'revolutions of nature', as he put it (1993 [1938]: 57). Over the course of the eighteenth century, the idea that the earth had a discontinuous genesis was lent weight by the collation of fossilized remains of extinct organisms, an archive whose cognitive and affective impact was enhanced by the absence of human traces amidst the apparently older strata. Not only had our planet been through such upheavals that whole categories of living things had been annihilated, but there had once been times without us – epochs thus bereft of a thinking being (Grant, 2000: 48). As Kant read them, these signs augured that our own future was far from assured:

> if our globe (having once been dissolved into chaos, but now being organized and regenerating) were to bring forth, by revolutions of the earth, differently organized creatures, which, in turn, gave place to others after their destruction, organic nature could be conceived in terms of a sequence of different world epochs ... How many such revolutions (including, certainly, many ancient organic beings no longer alive on the surface of the earth) preceded the existence of man, and how many ... are still in prospect, is hidden from our inquiring gaze. (1993 [1938]: 66–7)

No matter how determinedly he worked to conjure up a subject headstrong enough to rise above the convulsions of the earth and cosmos, the possibility not only of our supersession by new forms of life, but of our ultimate return to the very inanimate matter from which we had once sprung, continued to haunt Kant. As he pondered the cosmological sublime towards the end of the *Critique of Practical Reason*:

> The ... view of a countless multitude of worlds annihilates, as it were, my importance as an animal creature, which after it has been for a short time provided with vital power, one knows not how, must again give back the matter of which it was formed to the planet it inhabits (a mere speck in the universe). (1967 [1788]: 260)

Pushing further than most Kantian commentary, Iain Hamilton Grant draws out the full import of a cosmos that keeps breaking the bounds of what could reasonably be considered 'for us' – stressing just how much the resultant precariousness of humankind rattled Kant. If the universe derives its significance solely from the presence of 'moral subject', then the endangerment of this fragile being threatens the end of all freedom, all sense, all meaning – for all time. In the absence of humanity, as Kant himself exclaims, 'all of creation would be a mere wasteland, gratuitous and without final purpose' (cited in Grant, 2000: 50). If we think back to the cataclysmic destruction of Lisbon, and its indelible impression on the young Königsburg scholar, then it is all the more apparent that the prospect of the extinguishing of the human subject is far more than hypothetical: it is a possibility that has been rehearsed in full nihilating horror in his own lifetime.

It was this threat of thought's physical extinction that ensured no mere contemplation of nature's sublimity would suffice. For Kant, what was needed was not only a new kind of subject, capable of taking charge of its own inclinations, but also a very different earth: a natural order made over so thoroughly by the collectivity of self-willed agents that it would cease to pose a palpable threat to human existence. In Grant's words: 'the sublime necessitates that to survive the natural revolutions rumbling in the deep abysses of time, all of nature must be remade' (2000: 53). This is why Deleuze and Guattari would have recognized in Kant's programme a precursor of their own project of bringing forth 'a new people and a new earth' (Grant, 2000: 37–8). And it is for this reason that Kant was constantly drawn back to the need for a metaphysics of nature: his 'critique' preparing the way for an anticipated, but never fully realized programme of bringing philosophy to bear – in a practical, material way – on nature. This task was to involve not simply describing the physical workings of the natural world, but also laying out how the future transformations of this nature were to be brought into line with the further adventures of the self-legislating subject. From Kant's earliest to his last works, Grant insists:

> the metaphysics of nature, comprising mechanism, dynamics, geology, biology and physiology, remains a component of, rather than an obstacle to, the metaphysics of freedom. If therefore, metaphysics and physics are separated by a 'great gulf' such as divides nature and freedom, the faces of this sundered rock meet deep in the earth, and are not merely joined by the technological fix of analogical bridges. (2000: 38)

The disaster after Auschwitz

Along with its intellectual audacity, there is something rather courageous about Kant's attempt to conjure metaphysical optimism out of geophysical cataclysm. Beneath the exaggerated claims of autonomy, the often-repressed sensuous and somatic aspects of selfhood, the desire to lord it over nature, lies Kant's intuition of bodily vulnerability, an awareness that humankind is both individually and collectively bared to the elements. At a historical juncture when the sacred canopy was being rapidly rolled back, this exposure was experienced with an unprecedented intensity. In response, Kant sketched out a subject who could work on its own moral and practical advancement from behind a firewall offering protection from nature's full fury.

But deep down he seems to have figured that the ongoing upheavals of the earth would get to us in the end. And this meant that the stakes were extremely high. If the attributes and achievements we are rightly proud of – the capacities that are uniquely ours – could vanish traceless in the long-term temporizing of geological change, then the only option is to remake the world from the ground up. And no quaking, downtrodden being intimidated by stormy seas or shuddering earth was ever going to pull this one off.

These days, of course, it is much more fashionable to point out the strife that this sort of subjectivity has got us into than it is to dwell on the fix it was supposed to get us out of. From the other end of 'enlightened' modernity, looking back over the assorted ruins of our *grands projets*, Kant's faith in the faculty of reason has taken a battering. Worse still, it has been implicated in the run of catastrophes we have manufactured for ourselves over the intervening centuries. Theodor Adorno saw the self-mastery demanded by Kant's elevation of the rational mind as a denial of the frailties of the flesh: a violence perpetrated on one's self that too easily spilled over into violation of others (Cornell, 1992: 179). Just which atrocities he has in mind as the referent for this charge is spelled out when the Frankfurt theorist asserts that the horrors of Auschwitz make a mockery of the Kantian strategy of converting shock into an affirmation of the power of moral will (Adorno, 1973: 361; Ray, 2004: 11). Auschwitz, for Adorno, drives home the point that there are losses which are irrecuperable, suffering which should not under any circumstances or by any stretch of the imagination be set to the task of bolstering human dignity.

Adorno himself draws out the connection with Lisbon under the heading 'After Auschwitz'. To complete the passage I cited earlier: 'The earthquake of Lisbon sufficed to cure Voltaire of the theodicy of Leibniz, and the visible disaster of the first nature was insignificant in comparison with the second, social one, which defies human imagination as it distils a real hell from human evil' (1973: 361). In other words, the abomination of the death camps radically eclipses the catastrophe of Lisbon, because it is a disaster of our own making. If we lost faith in a divine plan and the harmony of the cosmos at Lisbon, after Auschwitz what remained of the faith humankind had in itself was irreparably shattered (Neiman, 2002: 250).

As a number of critical commentators have proposed, picking up the thread of Adorno's argument, this means that the epicentre of sublimity has forever shifted. What now stands for the formless, the unthinkable, the unfathomable – that which makes presentation itself quake and falter – is no longer nature's most violent displays, but the brutality we visit upon ourselves. Gene Ray puts it plainly:

> Once upon a time, encounters with the power or size of nature defeated the imagination and moved us to terror and awe. After Auschwitz, however, we have had to recognize such sublime effects among our own responses to this demonstrated human potential for systematic and unbounded violence. After this history, human-inflicted disaster will remain more threatening, more sublime, than any natural disaster. (2004: 1)

It is this conceptual distance between Lisbon and the Holocaust that Neiman is referring to when she suggests that 'earthquakes are only a matter of plate tectonics' inciting merely 'ordinary emotions'. From Auschwitz and Hiroshima, through the threat of cold war nuclear annihilation and the accident at Chernobyl, onto AIDS, international terrorism and global climate change, the figure of the unpresentable has continued to shift – but it has rarely wavered far from the thematic of *human-induced* disaster. Anthony Giddens' trope of a 'runaway world' and his observation that we have recently begun to worry more about what we can do to nature than what nature can do to us works this terrain (1999: 26). So too does Ulrich Beck's imagery of 'living on the volcano of civilization' (1992: 17).

Beck's claim that it is the very attempt to illuminate and secure the conditions of existence in the modern world that foments new kinds of chaos brings us back to the indictment of Kant's self-fortifying subject. Indeed, the charge made by Adorno that Kant's splitting away of reason from nature in order to shore up the modern subject resulted in 'self-preservation running wild' (1973: 289) offers an ideal epigram for the risk society storyline. For environmental theorists, taking a line of attack anticipated by Heidegger, Kant's insistence that only the presence of a self-conscious being gave purpose and meaning to the world serves to legitimate the reduction of the earth and its creatures to a means to human ends, with all the ravages that implies (Zimmerman, 1994: 44). Latour, too, censures Kant for failing to extend the imperative not to treat other thinking beings as mere means beyond our fellow humans into the realm of the other-than-human. This deliberate oversight, he argues, has discouraged any appreciation of the part played by nonhumans in the composition of our own collectivities. More than this, Latour contends, the strictures it imposed eventually precipitated '*generalized revolts of the means*', as disenfranchised nonhumans reasserted their own forcefulness and self-interest: this being the source of what we experience as ecological crises (2004b: 155–6, author's italics).

But as the age of ecological anxiety takes on the mantle of catastrophism, the whole trajectory of the displacement of natural sublimity by its human–induced counterpart ceases to look quite so clear-cut. For if indeed it is the *revolt of the nonhuman* that administers the final blow to the Kantian constitution of the subject, as Latour is suggesting, then the course of our modernity would seem to have followed a strangely circular destiny. If Kant's most pressing imperative was to find a way for human agents to successfully navigate the *'revolutions of nature'*, then effectively what Latour's framing of ecological crises does is to deliver us back into the very dilemma that first prompted his Enlightenment predecessor to renegotiate the nature–human juncture. For just as Latour likes to remind us that 'No one knows what an environment can do' (2004b: 156), so too, as we have seen, was Kant equally upfront that the number of 'revolutions of the earth' that had 'preceded the existence of man' would remain beyond our grasp, just as he willingly conceded that 'how many … are still in prospect, is hidden from our enquiring gaze'.

In other words, concern over the potential 'revolt of the nonhuman' has been one of Kant's imperatives, right from the beginning. As I have been arguing from the outset of this book, the message that is coming to us from the current environmental predicament – an insight we should have absorbed long ago from the earth sciences – is that dramatic changes of state are part of the normal dynamics of our planet. New knowledge about rhythms and patterns in physical systems, together with the growing sense of the inherent unpredictability of many such changes, is indicative that the question of 'what an environment can do' is becoming *more* rather than *less* problematic over time. In short, Kant's fear of 'natural revolutions' annihilating our species' achievements is not only empirically credible, but is most emphatically back on the scientific and popular agenda.

Though it is undoubtedly the case that a 'century of unutterable suffering' (which is by no means over) has transformed the horizon of the disaster, and that the prominence of extreme social pathology has had a corrosive effect on the self-conception of Western thought, what this *ought* to mean for our ontological and ethical receptivity to natural upheaval is by no means resolved. As disaster studies scholars remind us, all the evidence shows that human vulnerability to volatile earth processes has been rising sharply over recent decades, while at the same time, research in the field of psychosocial impact of extreme events has suggested that the effect of a natural disaster on its survivors is intrinsically no less traumatizing or easier to recover from than that of human–inflicted violation. Without wishing to enter into the realms of comparative evaluation of disaster categories – a strategy which would run counter to the thematic of incommensurability that animates philosophical and literary engagements with the 'cataclysm' – there are questions that need to be asked about the fate of the geophysical sublime over the last two centuries.

The point I want to make here is a relatively simple one. In repudiating Kant's *solution* to the potentially nihilating effects of terrestrial or cosmological change, we have also tended to bypass the *problem* that incited his project. But the problem itself has if anything advanced rather than receded. The idea that an elevation of concern with mass socio-political violence should effect a corresponding devalorizing of other-than-human catastrophics assumes a causal linkage that would seem to be in need of interrogation rather than acceptance and advocacy (which is not to question the connections established between social injustice human vulnerability to environmental variability). One of the questions we need to ask is whether the range of skills and interests of those intellectuals who currently engage with the ontological dimensions of disaster has implications for their own – explicit or implicit – prioritization of different types of extreme event.

However we rate Kant's 'armchair' scientific interventions, it is clear that he had a very high degree of literacy in the physical sciences of his time – reflecting an Enlightenment style of wide-ranging scholasticism that has largely succumbed to disciplinary specialization. There may be reasons, then, why contemporary social scientists and humanities scholars feel more open to events whose genesis and unfolding, for all the shock they induce, lies within a domain that is intellectually familiar. To put it another way, these days many more of us are fluent in the metaphorics of fracture and chasm than we are in the mechanics of actual seismicity.

It is important to recall that the Kantian settlement concerning the problem of human vulnerability in the face of momentous geophysical instability left its own architect deeply uncomfortable and in search of a more practically and logically satisfactory resolution. As Neiman observes, more generally:

None of the questions that tormented Europeans reflecting on Lisbon was ever directly answered or even directly rejected ... in proceeding as if questions were settled that were simply left hanging, theory left residues that cloud our attempts to eradicate evils today. (2002: 250)

While the pathological tendencies of self-directing and world-mastering subjectivity have been well raked over, Kant's scission of 'is' and 'ought' has remained largely beyond dispute – at least until recently. There may be a strong contingent in favour of ascribing intrinsic value to other-than-human entities, but few today show much enthusiasm for re-instating nature as a moral agent, a force for good or evil. But these are not the only options. The idea of a self that is primordially receptive to others, such that Levinas proposes, already 'fissures' the self-legislating subject with moral obligations that issue from a radical exteriority. Increasingly, the question is being asked as to why the emitting source of appeals or incitements needs to be a *human* other. Or indeed, why we should assume the *recipient* is one of us? In this regard, some of the latest revisiting of the 'is–ought' rift does not set out from the ruins of the Kantian categories, but instead takes Kant's notion of a self that responds to imperatives as a point of departure: as a constitution which might be deepened and extended rather than simply abandoned.

Earthly imperatives revisited

Deleuze and Guattari are not the only ones to have seen past Kant's auto-affective 'categorical' imperatives and recognized that his attempts to negotiate between geophysics and metaphysics literally prise open *'the problem of the relation of thought to the earth'* (Grant, 2000: 38, author's italics). With less of the grand ambition of bringing forth new peoples and planets, Alphonso Lingis has also returned to Kant and the fraught issue of a direct encounter between the earth and its inhabitants. What Lingis probes in Kant's thought are the issues hinging on what I have been referring to as 'radical asymmetry': the idea that the extent to which humans (and many other entities besides) are the products of cosmological or geophysical forces far outbalances any sense in which these processes can be considered products of our achievements.

Kant, as we have seen, sought to adequate the regularities and potentialities of the universe with those powers that defined our own species being, only to find, again and again, that the magnitudes of the geo-cosmic side of the equation defied containment in the categories provided by the self-willing subject. In Lingis's words: 'To act in the suffering one knows from the harsh edges of hard reality is to recognize that while one is the author of the formulation of their universal and necessary order, one is not the cause of the layout in which real things are found' (1998b: 203). Or as Neiman puts it, in relation to the same problem that tormented Kant: 'what affects us is not created by us' (2002: 80).

For Lingis, the fact that our sensible, fleshy bodies are open enough to the forces of nature to be at risk suggests that we must also be susceptible to the elements in other ways. It is not just Kant's unresolved wrestling with the crisis of a potentially thought-erasing cosmos that interests Lingis, then, but the very event of responsiveness: a theme he develops by way of a deep familiarity with Levinas's insights on an other-directed self and on the sensual experience of the elements. 'It is true that self-determination means being subject only to laws oneself formulates, he observes, 'but this subjection is itself commanded' (1998b: 200). And in this way, Lingis pushes on through the 'inner determining ground', to the ground beyond, the earthly imperatives that nudge, threaten and lure Kant's subject towards the task of setting its own directions: 'Then is not nature, which for Kant is an illustration of the force of the imperative known originally within in the sentiment of respect, indeed *the original locus of the form that is imperative?*', he asks (1998b: 208, my italics).

It is one such directive arising out of nature – the traumatic summons of Lisbon and its impression on the still soft and pliant form of the early modern self – which has been my guiding thread in this chapter. Our corporeal and psychic susceptibility to the dynamism of outer nature, and the problems it raises, I have been arguing, is not a recent supplement to the modern subject. It is as originary as any other formative force or element. In its literal fissuring of mid-eighteenth-century European life, a seismic 'readjustment' played a constitutive role in the emergence of the subjecthood bequeathed to us by the Enlightenment. And it has stayed with us, under our skin as it was under Kant's skin, disturbing us, inciting us, bothering us.

But Lingis wants to make something of our bodily and sensuous openness that extends far beyond the reach of a single event, however momentous that event may have been. Crossing the secret permeability of Kant's self-legislating imperatives with Levinas's primordial pregnability to a radical otherness, he blasts open the category of potential directives to admit the entirety of nature, any human and inhuman entities, all objects – fabricated and given.

Lingis would have all the surfaces of the sensible world sending out imperatives: the whole 'pageantry of things' variously cajoling, menacing, pressuring, enticing and exciting us in ways that prompt us not only to think, but to recalibrate our bodies, adjust our senses, alter our habits and rhythms, reroute our pathways (1998b: 100, 38, see also Harman, 2005: Ch. 5). His is a world, like that which haunted Kant, of vast and intractable forces which mock human pretensions of control, a macrocosmos composed of violent storms, meteor impacts and colliding tectonic plates. But it is also a universe replete with delights, diversions and inspirations: one which is as likely to lead us quivering with fascination as it is to leave us quaking with fear. In Lingis's own words:

> Sensuality is vulnerable and mortal from the start. But this suscepti-bility is not the vertiginous sense of the contingency of all being, an intuition into the nothingness in which all being would be perilously adrift, and which could be seen as a real possibility just beyond the thin screen of the actual being. The contingency of the sensuous ele-ment is in the very fullness and abundance of the present, which plugs up the horizons, the future. Coming from nowhere, going nowhere, it is here in incessant oncoming. It is not here as though grudgingly parcelled out by the malevolence of nothingness, but as gratuity and grace. Fortuity and goodness of the light, the play of iri-descent color, the resplendence of tones, the liquidity of the swelling forces! (1998b: 19)

For sure, things-in-themselves withdraw from us, as Kant recog-nized. But in Lingis's world, the faces these things present to us, the surfaces they flaunt, the myriad qualities they reveal, are just as real and just as important as whatever it is they conceal (1998b: 100). 'Each thing', he notes, 'has its own resonance' (1998b: 52). These resonances are not a consolation prize for an unrequited desire for essence, nor are they distractions from the main event that must be resisted. They are our point of contact, our opening to the cosmos, our invitation into worldly existence. And in this way, rather than joining the chorus of critical excoriation of the freedoms that the modern self-willing subject has claimed for itself, Lingis makes his own rather unique stand on the assertion that freedom lies in acknowledging our receptivity to a universe of colourful directives that come from without (Harman, 2005: 62).

Things witnessing each other

In many respects, the 'crusty' Kant, bunkered down for life in Königsburg, and the adventurous Lingis, flitting from one exotic location to another, are worlds apart (see Morgan, 2007: 36; Harman, 2005: Ch. 5). But their respective works hinge on a vital shared concern – the depth of our organismic vulnerability to the eventfulness of the world around us. It is this departure point that unites them even as they diverge: Kant conceiving of finitude, exposure and perviousness as fallibilities to be overcome, Lingis seeing these same characteristics as opportunities, the modalities through which we are moved by the richness and exorbitance of our surrounds. Kant struggles to patch together a subject who would not be swayed by the terrors or the temptations of a capricious cosmos, while Lingis has no hesitation about affirming our creaturely propensity 'to be moved by outside lures and threats' (1998b: 201).

But if we choose to make this move with Lingis, or with the early Latour, or with Harman and fellow speculative realists, there are serious consequences. Possibilities open up which Kant's 'critical' settlement nailed shut for several centuries. Possibilities, or rather provocations, which come up against assumptions upon which the 'progressive' thought of our own era still depends. One of the basic assumptions cherished by critical thinkers of many persuasions is the idea that reality is made rather than given. This belief, as I have been suggesting in previous chapters, is widely considered fundamental to and inseparable from the ideal that reality can and should be changed by collective human action. Lingis, however, happily concedes that much of the world is indeed *given* to us (without being intended for us). It is no disgrace, as he would have it, to experience reality as a density and obduracy beyond our measure, no shame to feel captivated and compelled by outside forces: 'What is given crowds in on us, imposes itself on us, weighs on us', he insists. 'For us to find ourselves is to find ourselves as subjects – not as spontaneous or creative source-points, but as loci of subjection. It is to find ourselves implanted in what has come to pass' (1998b: 120).

Does such obedience to outside stimuli undermine all that critical thought knows and loves about the human subject? Many contemporary thinkers vouch for the pivotal importance of incitements that arrive from an 'outside': from Giles Deleuze's 'fiery imperatives' (1994 [1962]: 200) or the '*external* provocation' that Jacques Derrida speaks of (1995b: 352, author's italics; see also Clark, 2003b). As it is with Lingis, such worldly demands are presented as stimuli to imagination, reason and ethico–political engagement, rather than as repudiations of the power of human thought and action. They are what turn us on, fire us up, set us loose. And in so doing, they are ultimately what urge us to construct imperatives of our own and what push us off in the direction of that which we come to experience as our own autonomy and self-determination. But where this does get tricky, where it really starts to grate against conventional critical thinking, is in the suggestion that inhuman things, physical things, natural things – and not merely human beings or social causes – might come to provoke and command us. This, for many liberal or radical thinkers, remains a step too far.

Just why this is suspect terrain takes us back to Kant's legacy. To argue for an extension of the sources of excitation of human conduct beyond the spheres of sociable life into extra-human realms is to come up against the steely barrier that has kept natural necessity apart from moral–political negotiability for more than two centuries. To speak of heterogeneous things that exude imperatives – and human beings that are receptive to these summons – is to conjure a world in which traffic flows from the dominion of the 'is' to the 'ought'. It is to conceive of a reality in which nature is not only a scene of moral action, but is also a source. It is not just to say that nonhuman things help compose our social worlds – which is no longer a problematic assertion in most quarters. Nor is it simply to argue that we must take consideration of these other-than-human things in our moral or political considerations, which again, is no longer especially controversial. Both of these options suggest an opening out, a deliberate and deliberative expansion of the sphere of intra-social operations to encompass other things. They expand the 'ought' to absorb ever more of the 'is', by way of extending the realm of the political–ethical or the normative to absorb ever more of the domain that used to be relegated to natural necessity.

What is more challenging, more threatening, is to speculate that there is a whole raft of characteristics and capacities that we once deployed to define our own uniqueness – such as commanding, attracting, resisting, negotiating – over which we have no monopoly; to suppose that such 'facilities' belong in the world as much as in our own being. And this really does have some important repercussions. Once we affirm the independent existence of things, and their raw, intractable ability to impact upon us, then we are also faced with the issue of how they impact upon each other (see Harman, 2002, 2005). Our inquiry overflows the issue of how we encounter the world, and spills into the question of what constellations or networks of things get up to amongst themselves. What then of the directives, the threats, the allures that nonhuman things present to each other? What of the 'fiery imperatives', the 'external provocations' that draw other kinds of responsive bodies into each other's orbit?

Here too, Lingis presses on, not content with commands that simply bind human subjects to a beseeching cosmos. For him, the orders, the allures, the 'oughts' that entice us into commerce with our sensuous environs are only a subset of a much greater consortium of things: an encompassing field in which '(t)hings witness one another', 'everything parts, everything greets every other thing again' (1998b: 100, 64, 86). So it is not just a matter of elements and entities which exhibit themselves to us, even as they harbour their own inner secrets, it is also a matter of things flickering between attraction and repulsion, disclosure and withdrawal, amongst each other – with or without our permission or our participation (see Harman, 2005: Ch. 5).

Exactly how other-than-human things encounter one another, how much of this process is accessible to human agents and what we can intuit or speculate goes on when no human agents are present, are questions that have largely been banished from Western philosophical agendas since the 'critical' Kant left his momentous impression on European thought. Today these issues are back, most explicitly in the work of those associated with the speculative realist 'moment' notably Meillassoux, Harman, Brassier and Grant – as well as in more suggestive ways in other contemporary interventions. Thrilling though it is to witness the resurgence of these maligned themes and categories, my intention here is not to advance the exploration of things-in-themselves. As I suggested at the outset, I'm happy to leave this to others.

But in many ways, my argument is dependent on these moves. While my concern is with the way embodied and collective human actors engage with 'volatile' terrestrial and cosmological processes, it is vital to this story that my human protagonists are caught up in a drama that is in the most part not of their making. We are, I have been arguing, intrinsically, inescapably, ensnarled in a mass of forces and objects that greatly pre-exist our emergence and have no need of our continued existence. If we are to come to terms with the radical asymmetries of our residence on 'a specific planet', in 'a specific universe', then the autonomy of the forces that shaped and continue to shape us needs to be at the core of our thought – and not simply hinted at in occasional concessionary flourishes. And this means that thinking through the independent existence of more-than-human constellations is not just a matter of philosophical curiosity, however important this is – it is also a matter of pressing practical concern.

'If global warming _isn't_ caused by man, doesn't that mean we're even more fucked?' – to return to Ivan's question. This is, essentially, Kant's question too – the theoretical and practical problem posed by 'the revolutions of the earth', returning in an era that is beginning to tremble with new insights about the inherent instability of our planet's climate. This is our Lisbon. Or perhaps it is the old Lisbon, unresolved, under our skin, resurfacing to urge and command us. *"The world is my world, and then of course it isn't"* ... ponders Susan Neiman. 'Is Kant's hesitation merely the result of theoretical worries?'(2002: 84) Of course, it wasn't then and it isn't now.

In the next chapter, I return to the issue of climate change and some of the political and ethical imperatives arising out of it. While the evidence of anthropogenic global heating might suggest that earth processes which we once believed to be autonomous of human agency are in fact 'co-enacted by us', I want to caution against any general recentring of global dynamics on an anthropic axis. Instead, I propose, we need to follow Kant and Ivan in the boldness of their focus on the bigger picture, the horizon that stretches far beyond the narrow district where humans are able to make their mark on reality. We need to ask, among other things, what might happen to our desire to even the scores, to make life just and equitable, on a planet that refuses to act as a level playing field. And this means looking once more at the crevices and chasms that the world itself opens up, and the way they fissure even the imperatives we like to believe are definitively ours.

5

Justice and Abrupt Climate Change

Introduction: justice beyond Copenhagen

In the last few chapters, the emphasis has been on physical processes with the potential to overwhelm human efforts and achievements. My intention in facing up to forces that exceed our measure or reach is not to disavow social agency, but to get it into perspective – with an ultimate aim of helping to understand when and where strategic human interventions are most effective. At the Copenhagen summit, we have just seen that relatively 'minor' or 'peripheral' actors *can* make a difference – or at least that they can insist on raising issues that will make a difference in the future. The tiny Pacific nation of Tuvalu, some 10,000 people living on six atolls and three reef islands, punched way above its weight at COP15. Bringing a strand of negotiations to a halt, the Tuvaluan representatives led a coalition of small island states and least developed countries to propose what became known as the Tuvalu Copenhagen Protocol: the demand for a legally binding deal on emission levels and for a 1.5 degree Celsius target as the upper limit of tolerable warming – rather than the 2 degrees accepted by most of the rest of the world's nations (Morris, 2009; Sheppard, 2009). Though the proposal was unsuccessful, Tuvalu attracted extensive media coverage and environmental activist support, a status reinforced by the island nation's own plan to trump the developed world by going fully carbon neutral by 2020 (see Clark, 2010c).

Research suggests that low-lying Tuvalu and its neighbour Kiribati will be among the first places to be rendered uninhabitable as anticipated sea level rises occur. This may be inevitable. Because of its 'thermal inertia', water takes longer to heat up and cool down than air does, so that even if greenhouse gas concentrations were to be stabilized at their present level, the earth's oceans would continue to warm and expand for at least another century (Roach, 2005). As Kiribati president Anote Tong put it recently: 'We may be at the point of no return', before adding, 'To plan for the day when you no longer have a country is indeed painful but I think we have to do that' (cited in Marks, 2008; *NZ Herald*, 2008).

Tong's announcement, made at the 2008 UN World Environment Day in Wellington, was intended to put pressure on Australia and New Zealand to accept his people for permanent resettlement. With a population some ten times that of Tuvalu, Kiribati is in a precarious situation. But it's a predicament that's also profoundly problematic for much of the rest of the world. Beyond the immediate need for a future homeland, representatives of nation states like Kiribati and Tuvalu – which have made negligible contributions to atmospheric carbon dioxide levels – know that the charges they make against heavier carbon emitters are effectively unanswerable under present geo-political arrangements. And this is what gives them their gravity. As COP15 made apparent once again, there is as yet no serviceable and binding decision-making mechanism for dealing with the way that the actions of some people in some parts of the world are jeopardizing the existence of others elsewhere. This is an ethical and political fracture line running right through the heart of the globalized modernity we have constructed for ourselves over the last few centuries. It is, we might say, abyssal.

When life-threatening transformations take place in the physical world, the usual priority of critical social thinkers, as we saw in the case of the Indian Ocean Tsunami, is to look for the socio-economic and political factors that place people – unevenly – in the path of danger. This is the inaugural move in an enduring quest for social justice. In the context of global climate change, where the role of historical anthropogenic emissions of greenhouse gas has been demonstrated beyond reasonable doubt, nothing appears more urgent than the need to press forward with this kind of questioning and the action it demands. Though the extent to which global heating contributed to the intensity of Hurricane Katrina remains controversial, media coverage of this disaster has already made a spectacle of the kind of glaring inequities that advocates of environmental justice have been talking about for years. Those who owned or had access to private motor vehicles, those who were thereby likely to have contributed disproportionately to the enhanced greenhouse gas emissions that are transforming global climate, were far more likely to have had a passage to safe ground – while the poor, the carless, those with a lighter carbon footprint, were abandoned to the full force of the hurricane. Only to find themselves wading through the toxic effluent of toppled oil refineries.

And that was all within the borders of the world's wealthiest nation state. Extend and amplify such effects across an even more divided globe and the sheer immensity of the environmental justice issue starts to reveal itself. As the scientific evidence gathers, it looks as though those regions or social formations which have historically contributed the most to greenhouse gas emissions will avoid the most severe impacts of climate change and in some cases may even benefit from warmer temperatures. Those with lower carbon foot-prints, especially in the global south, are far more likely to suffer severely from global heating, while small islands and atolls like Tuvalu or Kiribati face annihilation. Even before we broach the issue of intergenerational equity, this mapping of vulnerability to global heating onto existing global contours of socio-economic inequality presents arguably the greatest challenge for social justice humankind has ever faced.

In this chapter, I look at what Gayatri Spivak refers to as 'the per-haps impossible vision of an ecologically just world' (1999: 382) in the context of human-induced global climate change, and ask what living on an earth with complex dynamics of its own means for the concept of justice. As I intimated in the introduction, justice in rela-tion to climate change carries a paradoxical demand. Apportioning responsibility for climate change requires us to distinguish human impacts from all other 'forcings' of climate. Only from this baseline can we meaningfully commence the task of breaking down the cumulative human imprint into its distinct historical, geographical or socio-economic constituents: the necessary predicate for comput-ing who is liable and what reparations might be made. But as current scientific understandings of the nonlinear trajectories and emergent properties of earth systems suggest, the conclusive disentangling of the various determinants of global climate is a goal that looks set to continue receding.

In particular, it is the notion of the tipping point – the threshold beyond which climate change veers irreversibly into an alternative regime – that plays havoc with the concepts of causality on which conventional definitions of justice depend. Once we concede that there are effects way out of proportion to any cause, and that such wildly disproportionate determinations are inherent to the way cli-mate operates with or without any human input, the very ground upon which an equitable accounting might take place begins to buckle and slide. Dynamical processes come into visibility that potentially exceed the reach of social negotiation and contestability:

that resist any possibility of being done differently or even being known with confidence.

So what are we to make of abrupt climate change? To even partially shift the focus of debate and deliberation away from human influence on climate is to risk consorting with 'climate sceptics'. It is to invite the charge of siding with those who would 'depoliticize' the whole issue of global environmental change. But now that academic science, popular science writing and Hollywood cinema have all warmed to the idea of sudden threshold transitions in climate systems, the issue is unlikely to recede. My gamble, with the usual provisos about decision making under conditions of unknowability, is that we must front up to the past reality and future likelihood of crossing climate thresholds. And that we need to try and dream up some storylines which will help us to nudge the abrupt climate change thesis in the direction of supporting the quest for 'an ecologically just world', rather than relinquishing it to more callous interests.

Taking cues from Jacques Derrida's understanding of the tension between a calculating and a more 'open' sense of justice, I work towards an expanded sense of environmental justice that grapples with events that are too excessive to be accurately accounted for or fully anticipated. I also draw more directly on what I suggested in Chapter 1 was an inspiration behind Derrida's concern with systems open to their outside: Georges Bataille's notion of an economy 'on the scale of the universe'. Almost uniquely among social thinkers, Bataille puts energy at the heart of his theory of terrestrial life, and imagines true human community as an extension of the tumultuous and excessive energy of the sun. He offers provocative pointers to a sociable life that goes beyond the measured and proportionate exchanges we usually associate with fair, orderly social relations in order to front up to the upheavals of the earth itself.

In this way, Bataille sets us thinking in the direction of an exorbitant and 'impossible' environmental justice; one that is not so much threatened by forces beyond human (or even terrestrial) measure, as it is impelled and excited by the violent energies of the cosmos. While all this might sound so excessive as to be beyond any real-world applicability, this may not be the case at all. For already, on the horizon, there are glimpses of an emerging counter-economic retort to the parsimonious and instrumental stratagems that currently prevail at the climate negotiating tables. And not necessarily in the places we might expect.

The universal currency of climate change

There was a time when some ecological radicals looked askance at practices of quantification and calculation, equating them with the very forms of impoverished rationality that they charged with fomenting the environmental crisis in the first place. Then there was a time still further back when Max Weber, formalizing a similar style of cultural critique, took the ascendance of 'rational economic conduct' to task for the disenchantment of the world, anticipating its advance across the modern landscape all the way 'until the last ton of fossilized coal is burnt' (1976 [1930]: 27, 181; Clark and Stevenson, 2003). Today, across the political and cultural spectrum, there is little dissenting from the view that the problem of human-induced climate change demands a prodigious arithmetic: an accounting that fuses the inordinate complexities of modelling the earth's climate with the no-less-daunting auditing of human activity past and present. And there is broad agreement that a frightening amount hinges on how we do these sums. As Tim Flannery puts it: 'Never in the history of humanity has there been a cost-benefit analysis that demands greater scrutiny' (2005: 170).

Critical commentators are now among the most vociferous deployers of figures from the latest scientific and economic forecasts. To give a recent example, here is Mike Davis citing the findings of a study by William Cline of the Petersen Institute for International Economics (see Cline, 2007) on the predicted regional repercussions of climate change on agriculture in the closing decades of this century:

> most climate models project impacts that will uncannily reinforce the present geography of inequality ... Even in the most optimistic simulations, the agricultural systems of Pakistan (a 20% decrease from current farm output predicted) and Northwestern India (a 30% decrease) are likely to be devastated, along with much of the Middle East, the Maghreb, the Sahel belt, Southern Africa, the Caribbean, and Mexico. Twenty-nine developing countries will lose 20% or more of their current farm output to global warming, while agriculture in the already rich north is likely to receive, on average, an 8% boost. (Davis, 2008: unpag.)

The brandishing of such statistics drives home the basic point that global climate change is likely to exacerbate already cruel differentials in the global distribution of opportunity and vulnerability. By another reading, it is a way of taking on the project of modernity

111

according to its own premises – a tactic of turning its most cherished assumptions back upon themselves. For all the challenges to their attainment, the idea that the benefits of modernization should ultimately be available to all and the right to national self-determination are deeply engrained expressions of modernity's universalizing impulse (see Batty and Gray, 1996; Roberts and Parks, 2007: 61–2). The parties around every climate change negotiating table know this, and each knows that the others know this. Which means that however focused climate change debates have been on scientific truth claims, the issue of social justice has never been far away.

Of course, political activists of all stripes are aware of the suppleness of modernity's axioms. Nonetheless, the possibility that future generations might be denied basic opportunities open to present generations, that some nation states may be precluded from following developmental paths previously taken by others, or that the life chances of the populations of some parts of the planet will be seriously infringed upon by the activities of those who live in other places, are options that no serious actor on the global political stage can be seen to condone. 'Avoiding dangerous climate change' and 'levelling the international playing field' with regards to sharing the costs and benefits of climate change deemed tolerable, have taken shape as effectively inseparable aspects of the same problem. Or as Bruno Latour puts it, a previous distinction between representing things and representing people has vanished: scientific controversy has now firmly enmeshed itself with political discussion (2003: 33; 2004b: 71).

Precisely how these twin challenges are to be met, as we might expect, elicits deeply divergent responses. From the Brundtland report's early championing of sustainable development to the Kyoto Protocol's recommendation that industrialized nations take the lead on reducing greenhouse gas emissions while helping late industrializers on to low-carbon development paths, and on to Copenhagen's watery recommitment to international cooperation as a way to help developing countries along low-emission pathways, major initiatives in global environmental governance have sought to reconcile socioeconomic justice with the avoidance of irrevocable climate change. All the while continuing to believe in the possibility of economic growth without end.

At the same time, dissenting voices have consistently underlined the inadequacy or implausibility of such equations. Aubrey Meyer's (2000) principle of contraction and convergence, notably, seeks global equity through drastic reductions in industrialized countries' emissions. Analogously, Andrew Simms' promotion of the concept of ecological debt calls for full redress of the yawning historical inequalities in usage of the planet's energetic and atmospheric resources between the Global North and South (2005; see also Roberts and Parks, 2007: 163–6). Others are already seeking reparations for climate change which is putting land and livelihoods at risk. While abrading their rivals' faith in incessant economic expansion, such radical proposals demonstrate an even stauncher commitment to reconciling the capping of overall greenhouse gas emissions with the smoothing out of the global socio-economic 'playing field'.

More so than any specific political position, it is the tight coupling of the imperative to avoid catastrophe while appearing to pursue justice and equity that is pushing climate change policy in the direction of generalizable units of value. With their common aspiration for universality, modern science, modern economics and modern political–juridical systems have each strived to identify points of reference that would be applicable anywhere, at any time and to anyone. Variously enshrined in periodic tables, genetic codes, gold standards, declarations of human rights and so forth, such codifications of value remained relatively field-specific – each looking for its own grounding, its own guarantee – and yet still partaking in the dream of discovering some kind of 'general equivalence' that would unite all the world's clamouring signs and objects. It was this quest for universal standards and the fantasy of an even deeper unity that postmodern theorists unrepentantly dispatched to the rummage sale of history several decades ago. The end of nature, the profusion of competing value systems, the radical overproduction and promiscuity of signs and objects had all supposedly conspired to shut down the search for a single, coherent law of value (Baudrillard, 1993).

But in the midst of the current quest to avert global climatic chaos, the demand for an overarching system of value is just as brazenly reasserting itself. Only this time the universal signature is being asked to span the spheres of science, economics and the political–legal – reflecting the profound and arguably unprecedented entanglement between the normative call for justice and the practical–cognitive imperative of securing the physical conditions of human survival. A common measure has been sought to cement the bond between the representation of things and people. Blazoned at once favourably over international climate change policy documents and corporate newsletters, and scathingly across the T-shirts of anti-environmentalists, is the blunt pronouncement 'Carbon: the New Currency' (see Victor and House, 2004; Delay, 2007).

Carbon is the basic chemical element of biological life, the geological sediment that fuelled the industrial era, and the main atmospheric pollutant that threatens to destabilize global climate. It is Charles David Keeling's ascending curve of atmospheric carbon dioxide concentration, taken from the Mauna Loa Observatory, that is often credited with the kick-starting contemporary concern over human impact on the earth's atmosphere, while Al Gore's graphic off-the chart 50-year extrapolation of CO_2 levels provided the punchline of the *Inconvenient Truth* movie (Guggenheim, 2006). Today, though it is highly contentious, the figure of a carbon dioxide concentration in the earth's atmosphere of around 500 parts per million by volume (linked to the hope of limiting anthropogenic global mean temperature increase to 2°C) has been widely touted as the threshold beyond which lies 'dangerous climate change' (Stern, 2006). Increasingly, it's also the 'equal right' to consume carbon-based fossil fuels – and thus to make use of the earth's atmosphere as a dump for the waste products of this consumption – that is deployed as a gauge of global social justice.

It is this convergent use of atmospheric carbon dioxide levels as both object of claims for human or sovereign territorial right and as measure of planetary environmental health that underpins the emergence of carbon as a universal currency or signifier of value. This applies even before we consider the controversial conversion of the right to carbon dioxide emissions into a tradable commodity that is now shaping up as the dominant way of mediating between global social justice imperatives and the need to stabilize levels of greenhouse gases. Whether the right to use and emit carbon is legally bestowed, sold, given away, inherited or stolen, what underpins the idea of its universal applicability is the assumption of the fundamental equivalence of units. However we choose to apportion them, a part per million of carbon dioxide in the last Pleistocene glacial is comparable with a part per million of CO_2 in the present, a Chinese ton of carbon equals an American ton, and a particle flaring from a burning forest is commensurate with one emitted from a coal-fired power plant. And that's where the crack in the normative and cognitive edifice of a common carbon currency begins to appear.

What's at issue with the principle of equivalence is pointedly signalled in a contest recently run by UK environmental activist organizations which is aimed at contesting the growing popularity of emissions trading schemes:

Sometimes in well-intentioned attempts to put a price on natural resources, we can miss the bigger picture. So, to connect our politicians with reality before it is too late, we've come up with a question. And, we'd like to know what you think. The New Economics Foundation has teamed up with the Ecologist to run an essay competition. The question is: 'How do you price the extra tonne of carbon that, once burned, tips the balance and triggers potentially catastrophic, irreversible global warming?' (NEF, 2009)

It's a good question. In its wider permutations, this provocation takes us back to Jean Baudrillard's critique of the principle of general equivalence. The idea of a general law of equivalent and exchangeable values, Baudrillard argued, belongs primarily to a civilization that produces objects, images or signs in identical series (1993: 55–7). It is a symbolic order hitched to the material experience of industrial production, and as such is closely associated with the linear accumulation, with the 'indefinite reproducibility' manifest in non-stop, step-by-step advances in economic output, knowledge and any other system of value. But this is the way reality appears, Baudrillard insists, only from within the predicates of a specific phase or order of signs. That does not necessarily make it the way the world works.

As we will shortly see, modern science itself is coming around to the idea that most of the physical world does not operate in ways in which causes are proportionate to effects, in which one more unit of input generates one more unit of output. It points, rather, to a material reality in which tomorrow's emission of a tonne of carbon dioxide might have consequences utterly different from yesterday's tonne: a world which most emphatically does not play by the rules of universal equivalence. To be fair, almost everyone involved in negotiations about climate knows this at some level. It is, after all, what the very admission that there are dangerous levels of climate change is all about; it's what lends the idea of a threshold of a concentration of carbon dioxide in the earth atmosphere its fearful charge. It's also why uncertainty is one of the most frequently used concepts across the whole field of climate research and strategizing.

But the fault line opened by 'non-equivalence' not only fissures its way through the current commitment to carbon markets. It runs through all attempts to equitably distribute carbon usage. And it ploughs on through the very desire to fairly share the costs and benefits of industrial production, to even out the global economic playing field, to attain justice and equity in any social context. Anticipating Baudrillard (and as we shall see, Bataille), Nietszche was attentive to the specific circumstances under which the concept of justice operates. 'Justice (fairness) originates among approximately *equal powers*', he observed, '... the initial character of justice is *barter* ... justice is requital and exchange on the assumption of approximately equal positions of strength' (1994 [1878]: 64, author's italics).

In this sense, whether in law or in economics, a system of justice requires visibility and calculativity: it assumes a context in which there is always already mutual understanding, one in which all participants can assess the outcome of a transaction both before and after it takes place (Diprose, 2002: 28–31). In other words, modern justice presupposes a closed system, one in which nothing is permitted to enter the circuit which is too different or too strange to be weighed up and nothing comes out the other end which was not anticipated or cannot be accounted for. And in this way, justice sustains itself by disavowing or excluding whatever exceeds its predetermined range of acceptable inputs and outputs: it '... exists as such by marking itself off from an "outside" to which it is hostile' (Diprose, 2002: 33).

We have already encountered (in Chapter 3) events which exceeded what the communities or individuals caught up in them could know or process in advance: 'asymmetrical' events that call out for responses involving something other than simply evaluating what afflicted people 'deserve' in return for their suffering. Global climate change, I want to argue, shares important characteristics with these other 'upheavals' in the way that it overflows the 'symmetrical' assumption of 'a social body of equal and harmonious forces' upon which justice depends (see Diprose, 2002: 33). How and why climatic instability exceeds modern conventions of justice requires us to look more closely at the science of climatology, and especially its growing concern with tipping points, thresholds and abrupt transformations.

Thinking across thresholds

In some ways, Ulrich Beck's observation that '(o)urs is the age of the smallest possible cause for the greatest possible destruction' looks more valid than ever (1995: 4). But climatology and other sciences of complexity suggest a much more general point. Because of the very nature of feedback effects in complex systems, the idea that a small stimulus can give rise to a large transformation appears more as an ontological condition than as a characteristic of a particular historical era or mode of technological development. In just a few years, the idea of a tipping point, a juncture beyond which climate lurches into a significantly different state has become one of the key concepts in the scientific, political and popular understanding of environmental change (see Giddens, 2009: 25–7, 108).

While the Intergovernmental Panel on Climate Change remains largely focused on gradual transitions in its official reports, high-profile expert witnesses such as NASA's James Hansen and Gaia theorist James Lovelock have been making provocative claims about the imminence of passing over a threshold into runaway climate change (Lovelock, 2006: 51; Pearce, 2006: 15). While the identification of 500 parts per million atmospheric carbon dioxide levels as the brink of dangerous climate change may be controversial (Hansen and his colleagues suggest 300–350 ppm as a safer upper limit, somewhat below the current level of 387 ppm [Hansen et al., 2008]) , it *has* helped publicize the idea of rapid rather than incremental transformation. But like the other physical upheavals that are the subject of this book, abrupt climate change belongs as much to the past as the future. It lies upstream as well as downstream of where we are at now. And this makes of it both a prospect of shocking and unthinkable dimensions – and a very ordinary aspect of our earth's story.

Climate science tells us that the last 10,000 odd years, covering the interglacial known as the Holocene, has been a period of exceptional climatic stability – a warm and calm anomaly in an otherwise largely glaciated epoch (Burroughs, 2005: 18–19). Move out of this balmy interlude and it's like dropping off a precipice. Between 12,800 and 11,500 years ago, in the midst of a trend towards interglacial warmth, there was a sudden return to ice age conditions, known to paleoclimatologists as the Younger Dryas event (Alley, 2000: 4). As I noted in the introduction, what has struck climatologists about this episode and others like it the speed at which global temperatures transformed: years rather than centuries or millennia. Go back a few thousand years more and this sort of wildly oscillating climate appears as the norm rather than the exception – for hundreds of thousands, perhaps millions, of years.

And this means that almost all the achievements of humankind about which we are familiar and knowledgeable are stamped with anomalousness and provisionality. 'Civilization rose during a remarkable long summer', anthropologist Brian Fagan observes. 'We still have no idea when, or how, that summer will end' (2004: 25). Although the latest data from polar ice cores points to an interglacial longer than our own some 400,000 years ago, the weight of evidence still suggests that we should not count on present conditions persisting. As climatologist Richard Alley sums up: 'The current stable interval is among the longest in the records. Nature is thus likely to end our friendly climate, perhaps quite soon' (2000: 4).

In basic terms, the message from recent geochemical and paleoenvironmental research is that the earth's climate, of its own accord, goes through critical transitions from time to time, at many different spatial and temporal scales (Burroughs, 2001: 1–3). In fact, climate is now understood to be constantly changing at almost every conceivable timescale: there are jitters, judders, short waves, long waves, 'cycles within cycles within cycles' (Macdougall, 2004: 197; Burroughs, 2001: 1). This implicates the field of climatology in the more general turn in the sciences toward the study of complex systems, and in particular with the growing understanding of the non-linear dynamics of systems with more than one 'state' or 'regime' (Clark, 2000, 2005a; Urry, 2005). Through field studies and computer modelling, the sciences of complexity have teased out some of the ways in which complex physical systems, by virtue of their dense internal feedback loops, are capable of absorbing pressures for change whilst maintaining their current state. This means that a major impetus to climate change might lie dormant in the system for centuries, millennia or longer before its impact is manifest. But the other side of this non-linearity is that once a certain threshold is passed, transformation tends to be rapid, unstoppable and irreversible.

After this 'tipping point' is reached, feedback works the other way round, amplifying the impact of stimuli, which can effect a sharp transition into a new regime (Scheffer et al., 2001). Such 'sudden, drastic switches to a contrasting state' have been thoroughly documented in numerous real-world systems, from eutrophying lakes to algal colonization of coral reefs (Scheffer et al., 2001: 591). As Alley puts it, in relation to global climate: 'Sometimes a small "push" has caused the climate to change a little, but other times, a small push has knocked Earth's climate system into a different mode of operation' (2000: 13; see also Broecker, 1987). Though it remains notoriously difficult to identify the approach of a critical threshold, current research suggests that there are early warning signals, such as high-speed 'flickering' between alternative modes, as has been observed at the abrupt end of the Younger Dryas cold period (as well as in contexts as different from the end of a glacial as the onset of a human epileptic seizure) (Scheffer et al., 2009).

As research elaborates on the theme of nonlinear changes in the earth's subsystems, there has been a shift in emphasis away from one almighty climatic upheaval towards a more nuanced understanding of 'tipping elements', which embraces other possibilities, such as small perturbations resulting in major but gradual change (Lenton et al., 2008). But this by no means detracts from the gravity of the quest to identify systems vulnerable to threshold transitions, and to assess their current state and the consequences of their forcing past critical states. Even when the susceptible elements are restricted to those with the potential to shift regimes in the present century, the list is substantial: including Amazon rainforest and Boreal forest die-back, significant changes in the monsoon and in the El Niño Southern Oscillation, the instability of the West Antarctic ice sheet, melting of the Greenland ice sheet and shifts in deep water circulation in the Atlantic. After a major international review of the risks posed by a range of prospective critical thresholds, climatologist Tim Lenton and his colleagues concluded:

> Society may be lulled into a false sense of security by smooth projections of global change. Our synthesis of present knowledge suggests that a variety of tipping elements could reach their critical point within this century under anthropogenic climate change. The greatest threats are tipping the Arctic sea-ice and the Greenland ice sheet, and at least five other elements could surprise us by exhibiting a nearby tipping point. This knowledge should influence climate policy ... (Lenton et al., 2008: 1792)

Delivered in characteristically sober scientific prose, the implications of this message for human populations and other biological life are momentous and mostly terrifying. Under key impacts on the Indian summer monsoon, the report simply states: 'drought, decreased carrying capacity', and for Greenland ice melt: 'sea level rise +2–7m' (Lenton et al., 2008: 1788). These are the kinds of shorthand scenarios which popular science writers are more than willing to flesh out for those who wish to know more about what it might be like to live amid large-scale, rapid and cascading environmental change (see Pearce, 2006; Lynas, 2008).

As Isabelle Stengers and other scholars in the humanities engaging with complexity have shown, the idea of the inherent instability of complex systems has implications for the way we conceive of human agency. But just what these consequences are, in the context of climate change, are by no means unambiguous. The fact that human 'forcing' now appears to have the potential to push vital geophysical subsystems and the overall global climate into a radically different state seems to put human agency at centre stage – to the extent that some physical scientists make the case for a recent transition to a new geological epoch dubbed the 'Anthropocene' (Crutzen, 2002; see also Davis, 2008).

On the other hand, each of the tipping elements explored by Lenton's team and other climate threshold theorists manifest themselves as real and tangible possibilities only because the transitions in question have taken place many times in the earth's past. They are all changes which fit within the normal operational parameters of our planet and its subsystems. So while the focus may now be on systems 'accessible' to human impact, current understandings of the inherent instability of global climate and related physical systems points to a propensity for sudden, momentous change that inheres in physical reality itself, irrespective of human contributions.

By this logic, anthropogenic emissions are merely one trigger among a wealth of possible forcings – and that makes us far from unique or special, however pivotal our contribution might be at this particular juncture. This brings us back to the point made by Stengers earlier – in relation to human-induced global environmental change: 'From the viewpoint of the long history of the Earth itself, this will be one more "contingent event" in a long series' (2000: 145). As some scientists have suggested, global climate might already be 'naturally' close to a tipping point, thus dramatically amplifying the significance of human forcing. There is also the possibility that human impacts have taken climate systems closer to a threshold, for which the final push could turn out to be an unforeseeable nonhuman forcing – such as a large-scale volcanic eruption (Zillman, 2005: 20).

Even this last point comes with complications, for there is a growing scientific consensus that climate change – anthropogenic and otherwise – impacts upon other, 'extreme', geological events. By reorganizing the global distribution of water and ice, changes in climate can significantly alter the loading on the earth's crust, adding to the stresses and strains that are always already present – and thereby increasing the likelihood of volcanoes, earthquakes and submarine landslides (Burroughs, 2001: 117). On the other hand, a big increase in volcanic effluvia in the atmosphere could also counteract global heating, at least temporarily, though in ways which would likely be devastating for human life (McGuire, 2006).

The case I want to make here is not about downplaying human agency. If there is currently a controversy worth dwelling on, it is no longer the one about presence or absence of human imprint on global climate, but the issue of whether anthropogenic forcing is more likely to result in gradual or nonlinear change. My point is that accepting the profound significance of human intervention in earth systems does not equate in any straightforward way with the attribution of values to these inputs or outputs – at least not values that meet the requirements of universal recognition and exchangeability, or 'general equivalence', that the conventions of justice call out for. As sociologist Barbara Adam presciently noted over a decade and a half ago, nonlinear change with regard to climate and other environmental change gives rise to 'a high degree of mismatch between time-frames' (1993: 406). Whether it is a case of significant spatio-temporal delays in the transmission of agency into outcome, or abrupt and runaway consequences of relatively small stimuli, the result is a gaping disproportionality of cause and effect. Asymmetrical causation, in other words.

More generally, because the earth – and all its constitutive physical subsystems – is constantly undergoing its own creative and emergent transformations, the kinds of causality associated with systems or bodies that are assumed to be composed of 'equal and harmonious forces' do not hold well. As the whole ensemble of human and non-human elements effectively form a single complex global system – with its own internal dynamics and emergent properties, conventions of isolating specific causal agents and measuring their contribution to overall change seem destined to remain inescapably fraught. As Silvio Funtowicz and Jerome Ravetz explain: 'Precisely because of the interpenetration of the different dimensions of the emergent complex system that is (in retrospect) the disaster waiting to happen, it can be difficult to assign responsibility or blame for the event' (1994: 577).

So there is a sense in which, strictly speaking, 'the phrase "human-induced" has no scientific meaning' in the context of global climate change (Watson et al., cited in Lohmann, 2005: 213). At the same time, it is the imperative of social and environmental justice that we must indeed commit ourselves to attributions of causality – with every means at our disposal. For without assigning values to cause and effect, we cannot even begin the task of sorting out costs and benefits, and thus reparations for the geopolitically uneven exploitation of the earth's resources. Such is the necessary but impossible point of passage that philosophers call an 'aporia'.

Confronting cataclysm

As Latour aptly observes, modern political philosophy did not shape itself with the governance of sea, sky and climate as its remit (2004b: 204). By the same token, the international institutions assembled over recent decades to administer global 'warming' were not convened with the challenge of rapid or nonlinear climate change in mind. Scientists concerned about climate threshold transitions have their own ideas as to why the major regulatory bodies, such as the Framework Convention on Climate Change, have generally 'underestimated' the possibility of abrupt change. In particular, they have noted that most of the climate models to date have been inclined to represent certain key complex processes in uniform or linear ways, which reduces the sensitivity of simulations to threshold crossings. Researchers have also made the point that the imperative to identify human forcing of climate has steered attention away from the bigger picture of natural causation of abrupt change (Alley et al., 2003).

It is in contexts like this that constructionist social science proves especially helpful. Demeritt (2001) has deftly traced the 'feedback loops' that link the formulation of research questions with the technocratic interests that hold sway in the nascent international regulatory regimes. He suggests that through their ongoing interactions with policy makers, many scientists have been subtly but appreciably encouraged to marshal their inquiries around those aspects of climate change that are most conducive to being managed, with the result that the potential for 'surprises' or extreme events has been systematically played down (2001: 325–6).

A more reflexive understanding of the production and dissemination of expert knowledge, Demeritt proposes, would surely help. But there are situations where 'reflexive discourse' itself moves too quickly to join up what might best be left open and disjunctive, and thus, in Foucault's terms, 'runs the risk of leading the experience of the outside back to the dimension of interiority' (1987: 21). It needs to be stressed here that for those scientists who have taken upon themselves a fidelity to the event of sudden or nonlinear climate change, the experience of feeling subjected to political imperatives can be a frustrating and painful one. We can add that climatologists report that their 'unearthing' of the signatures of abrupt climate change has been a source of both awe and anxiety. As William Calvin sums up: '... whiplash climate changes were easily one of the biggest scientific shocks of the last decade' (2002: 225).

In short, scientists sensitive to the possibility of abrupt climate change rarely have much in common with the 'expert witnesses' whose testimonials are intended to undermine strategies aimed at mitigating anthropogenic climate change. In contrast with 'sceptics', they tend to present claims about the inherent instability of the earth's climatic regimes as a rationale to greatly intensify efforts to avoid crossing climatic thresholds (see Alley, 2000; Lovelock, 2006) – and quite a few of these researchers hold important positions in political advisory bodies. As evidence of past climatic variability accrues and as data about faster-than-expected manifestations of current climate changes rolls in, there is increasing pressure to take what the IPCC refers to as 'low probability, high impact' events seriously. Many scientists and policy makers now agree that as global temperatures rise, the prospect of one or more positive-feedback processes kicking in will shift 'so that it eventually becomes more likely than unlikely to happen'. They also concur that any cost–benefit scenario that excludes full consideration of these nonlinear events is of very limited value (Azar and Lindgren, 2003: 247; see also Tol, 2003).

There are still signs of serious disjuncture, however, when it comes to actually translating concern over abrupt change into prediction or policy. As its title attests, the report sponsored by the US Global Change Research Program *Abrupt Climate Change: Inevitable Surprises* takes the threat of climate tipping points seriously enough to be investigating their possible repercussions. According to its authors:

> there is virtually no research on the economic or ecological impacts of abrupt climate change … Geoscientists are just beginning to accept and adapt to the new paradigm of highly variable climate systems, but this new paradigm has not yet penetrated the impacts on community, particularly in economics and the other social sciences. (Committee on Abrupt Climate Change, 2002: 121)

But it is clear from the report's sketch of potential economic and socio-cultural impacts that even large-scale climatic regime shifts are not necessarily equated with cataclysmic social effects, and do not appear to unduly perturb the kind of managerialism described above by Demeritt (2001). Identifying sectors of the US economy where loss of revenue might be expected as well as laying out areas of opportunity, the document's cost–benefit approach is very much one in which the persistence of familiar economies of production and knowledge goes without question.

We should not underestimate the hold which the idea of equivalence – and the kind of orderly, calculable economy it underpins – has upon the contemporary imagination – at least not if popular culture is any indicator. Though justifiably slated for its hyperbolically inaccurate climate science, the movie *The Day after Tomorrow* (Emmerich, 2004) arguably deserves some credit for popularizing the idea of abrupt climate change. The narrative hinges on an almost overnight advance of full glaciation triggered by a shutdown of the North Atlantic thermohaline. One of the film's more memorable sequences is that of desperate US citizens splashing across the Rio Grande in an illegal attempt to make it into an unglaciated Mexico. As the story winds up, the Mexican government, in negotiation with survivors from the Washington administration, agree to offer asylum to the refugees from the north in return for the annulment of all outstanding debt owed by Mexico to the USA.

Whilst this denouement at least puts the Mexicans in the morally laudable position of honouring a debt whose creditors are in no position whatsoever to enforce its terms, what's remarkable is the film's unwavering faith in the possibility of the immediate reinstatement of an 'economic' logic under cataclysmic conditions. Billions of people have died, entire nations have been expunged, and a large proportion of the planet's living creatures have clearly been extinguished: events for which the global economy, as the storyline indicates, must be held culpable. Yet, it is this very economy which is re-instituted by the debt-for-refuge transaction, mere hours after the catastrophe. Indeed, it is the act of the re-establishing of 'normal economic relations' – that is to say an economy based on equivalent values – that stands as a primordial moment, providing the ray of hope that the values of Western civilization will be preserved and regenerated in the newly glaciated world. Once the 'playing fields' have been levelled by the mutual settling of debts, the orderly, cumulative process of accruing wealth and truth can once more be set in motion.

Effectively, the film begins the process of thinking through what might happen after the unthinkable. It then responds by imagining that a version of the economistic logic by which we are currently attempting to pursue justice and environmental stability (even if it proves totally ineffective in preventing catastrophic change) would still offer the best means of coming to terms with conditions beyond the tipping point. This is much like the findings of the *Abrupt Climate Change: Inevitable Surprises* report, in other words.

The incongruity between potential events and official responses has not gone unnoticed in climate science and policy communities.

Geologist Kenneth Deffeyes offers the retort to technocratic approaches: 'Try writing an environmental impact statement for a continental glacier thousands of feet thick all the way from Hudson's Bay to South of New York City' (2005: 170–1). Likewise, in relation to a switching off of the North Atlantic thermohaline, climatologist William Burroughs announces that 'the economic consequences would be unimaginable' (2001: 273). Even economist William Nordhaus – the pioneer of the application of cost–benefit analysis to climate change – has gone on record saying: 'once we open the door to consider catastrophic changes a whole new debate is engaged' (cited in Meyer, 2000: 54).

As economists Christian Azar and Kristian Lindgren explain, there are still major difficulties when it comes to assigning probabilities to events. Add in the challenge of allocating actual costs to environmental and social catastrophes – which spread across countries with great differentials in income and call for the assignment of dollar values to such non-market eventualities as loss of life or destruction of biodiversity – the result is a situation where 'the uncertainty about the impacts is so large that basically any optimal outcome can be justified' (Azar and Lindgren, 2003: 253).

Demeritt (2001), as we have seen, has pointed out how the likelihood of extreme events of climate transition has been suppressed in the interests of perpetuating more managerialist or technocratic responses. A decade or so down the line, we might now add that scenario planning like the *Abrupt Climate Change* report – which matter-of-factly lays out devastating and more promising prospects side by side can serve to render otherwise shocking possibilities into politically palatable forms, thus defusing their potentially radical implications. On the other hand, it has been argued that imagining 'the world's premature ending in a climatic Armageddon' evacuates the possibility of genuine politics – by deflecting attention to an event horizon that is too far beyond the here-and-now of effective political contestation (Swyngedouw, 2007). But then again, a case has been made that framing of global problems in terms of the imminence of catastrophe also serves to short-circuit due political process, by instilling an atmosphere of emergency in which there is never enough time for collective consultation and negotiation. As Melinda Cooper has argued, such pre-emptive and depoliticizing responses to biological risk are also being deployed in relation to the threat of global climatic catastrophe (2006: 125–6).

The charge of depoliticization is critical thought's most familiar response to practices of which it disapproves. And perhaps also to goings-on in the world in which it is struggling to gain purchase. It is revealing, then, that in various contexts playing up the threat of abrupt climate change *and* playing it down, bringing it forward in time *and* pushing it away, are all just as readily construed as depoliticizing moves. This may be taken as a healthy sign of the vigilance of social and political thought in relation to an important emergent issue. But we need to be careful here, for there is a very real risk that critical social thinkers are sending out ambivalent and unsupportive messages to those climate scientists who are putting their careers, if not their lives, on the line in their commitment to the challenge of nonlinear climate change. Perhaps the point to note here is that it is not only 'vested interests' that strain to develop appropriate responses to the growing likelihood of catastrophic changes in earth systems. Many progressive or radical thinkers are also left in an awkward position when it comes to any kind of fidelity to an event that threatens to undermine the very grounds of the global social justice to which, understandably, their allegiances lie.

Economy and politics at the scale of the universe

The discovery that the earth's climate is much more variable and precarious than previously imagined, I have been arguing, inevitably draws us into confrontation with forces that greatly precede – and exceed – any conceivable measure of human presence on this planet. It is one of the most profound ways in which the asymmetry between the human and the natural that I spoke of in Chapter 1 manifests itself. In the very process of gauging the extent of our impact on the earth, we are reminded that our home planet is quite capable of following its turbulent trajectories with or without us, whereas our persistence in the absence of climatic conditions we have come to depend upon looks decidedly shaky.

So what does it mean for our political engagement with abrupt climate change if the events which now appear on the horizon are but part of a long series, all of which happened before we were modern, many of which happened before we were even human? After science studies, we know there can be no direct and unswerving route from scientific pronouncement on climate change to a political position or programme (though as scientists themselves readily admit to being uncertain about the trajectories climate will take, this is no longer much of a revelation). For Latour, as we have seen, climate change is a hybrid event composed of a range of human, technological and physical components. Global climate is now a real-time experiment whose outcome remains unclear, and in order to take responsibility for this event we must learn to treat our politics too as a collective experiment (2003: 31). It is up to us to work together to decide how and why climate change matters, as part of our collective endeavour to assemble – out of all manner of human and other than human ingredients – the kind of common world we wish to live in. This puts us on a steep 'learning curve' that 'derives its virtue from being at once a productive research program, a dynamic political culture, a prosperous economy, a scrupulous and uneasy morality, and a well-documented procedure' (Latour, 2004b: 206).

As far as I'm aware, Latour has yet to engage with the succession of past climatic transitions whose understanding, climatologists insist, are a key to our future. And while he is always happy to concede that elements within or without our well-ordered collectives will continue to take us by surprise (2004b: 25, 197), there appears to be a limit on just how unsettling these disturbances are permitted to be. As I suggested in Chapter 2, if we take Latour at his word on the ability of nonhumans to assemble worlds (or biospheres, or planets, or solar systems), then we must also credit them with the capacity to break down, break up or otherwise reassemble what they have put together. In this sense, past episodes of abrupt climate change – the earth's 'long series' of catastrophes – can be viewed as manifestations of this flair for autonomous recomposition. Scientists, journalists, activists and cinematographers have already dragged these eventualities through the door and into our collectives. Climatic tipping points and catastrophic global change have ensconced themselves in the assembly. They are officially matters of concern, at once potentially cataclysmic and part of the ordinary history of being human, of being earthly.

Like it or not, the climate change question has prised open the issue of energies, rhythms, periodicities that precede or exceed any human measure. With that recognition, a deep fault line opens up under our conventional definitions of politics, which even its Latourian stretching and folding struggles to accommodate. What if, alongside our more meticulous and measured political considerations, we were to begin with this abyss – with this nature that is to a large degree beyond our 'jurisdiction' and even beyond our comprehension? And what if the very events which critical thought tends to associate with depoliticizing tendencies are actually the most urgent concerns which confront contemporary politics?

While the climatic provocation may be novel, there is nothing new about setting out to analyse and transform human collective life from the standpoint of our implication in a cosmos over which we have next to no influence. As I suggested in Chapter 1, Georges Bataille argued that the only way to understand the predicament of the human and all its achievements and challenges was to think in terms of 'an economy on the scale of the universe'. This means not only that our economic, cultural and political existence is hitched to the extraterrestrial flux of solar energy, but that we are forever in the thrall of forces which are inherently volatile and tumultuous. In response to this insight, Bataille offers us little that is immediately compatible with Latour's carefully crafted socio-political architectures. What he does offer is an exuberant bundle of insights about dwelling well on a planet which periodically revokes the very conditions of secure habitation.

Already at the end of the nineteenth century, as we have seen, Nietzsche had begun to question the idea of human values hitched to notions of equivalence, while also affirming solar energy as the exemplar of an alternative kind of relationship. The sun, Nietzsche argued, defies any model of symmetry or reciprocity: it endlessly bathes the earth in warmth and light, without requiring anything in return (1969 [1883]: 39). In the midst of the next century, Bataille picked up on the idea of the earth and all its creatures receiving an excess of solar energy, and made it the core of his social theory (see Bataille, 1991 [1967]: 28). 'Bataille is hardly the last word on anything', declares Allan Stoekl, 'but he is rare – in fact, unique – among twentieth-century thinkers in that he put energy at the forefront of his thinking of society' (2007: xiii).

What's important about Bataille is not just his 'accounting' for the role of energy in human and other forms of life, but his assertion that the sums would never add up and his dauntless pursuit of the implications of systems that could never be closed. Because the solar flux always rains down more energy than we or other living things require, the main problem of terrestrial existence for Bataille is not so much how to deal with scarcity – as all the theorists of 'restricted economies' have imagined, it is what to do about the excess of energy, and the proliferation of living things and productive forces that it engenders (see 1991: 29). Industrial capitalism, in this regard, is especially problematic in that it has systematically sought to close the loop; to cycle its outputs back into the system as inputs in a constant process of reinvestment and expanded accumulation, which Bataille presciently noted 'has turned the whole world into a colossal powder keg' (1993 [1976]: 428).

Bataille did not explicitly engage with the issue of industrialized humankind tapping into fossilized biomass or otherwise impacting on global climate. What he did understand was that the earth has physical limits, and that wherever growth exceeds these limits there must eventually be some kind of dieback or burn-off. In this sense, Bataille is not as far from environmentalist 'limits to growth' theses as it sometimes appears. There is 'excess', for him, precisely because flows and accumulations over-shoot the very real limits that existing 'bodies' – such as this spherical planet of ours – present to the build-up of energy, life or productive capacities. Where Bataille is at odds with environmentalist discourses of sustainability and with modern economics in general is in his advice on what to do about this over-reaching. And in his recognition that explosive accumulation and bursts of instability inhere in the universe, and not merely in our own mismanagement of available matter and energy.

As we might now say, Bataille is prophet of open and complex systems, systems which do not settle into an equilibrium state. This means that human social life cannot content itself with moderation, with careful and judicious husbanding of its resources. We can confine ourselves neither to the perpetual recycling that radical ecologists dream of, nor to the augmented circularity beloved of modern economists that turns a loop into a spiralling growth curve. If there are resonances throughout Bataille's work with the vitalist notion of vast and generative stream of life, it is just as important to note his insistence that all matter and energy is eventually bound to use itself up in a pointless, non-generative expenditure. The glorious blazing away of stars is not primarily a source of life-giving energy, so much as a pure and pointless expenditure (Pefanis, 1991: 17; Land, 1992: xviii).

Like it or not, humans and other life forms are condemned to partake both in the patient accumulation of matter-energy and in its periodic blow-out. All economies with strategies of stockpiling will sooner or later find themselves obliged to relieve themselves of what they have built up. Bataille did not live to see the frenetic shopping culture that superficially seems to follow his guidance about point-less consumption, but he would have quickly clicked that was more powder in the keg (see Stoekl, 2007: 58, 121). We cannot simply accelerate the cycle that turns consumption into more production. But neither can we resurrect the kind of restraint and hoarding that, as Weber (1976 [1930]) recognized, got us into the accumulation bind in the first place. We have to find new ways to spend.

This is not just a matter of 'production'. If the world does not turn in perfect circles and each soaring curve eventually describes a disaster, then any organized human endeavour will be as prone to irruption and interruption as our strictly 'economic' activities. If all exchanges, obligations and contracts are ultimately set in motion by the non-reciprocable radiance of the sun, then every smooth transaction carries the trace of exorbitance and boundlessness (Land, 1992: 33). Beneath all equivalence, all utility and all certainty is the abyss opened up by the deep surging energies of the cosmos: law, knowledge, every mode of orderly social conduct providing no more than provisional buttressing against elemental upheaval (Stoekl, 2007: 25). While Bataille professes that he has nothing against justice per se, if it is restricted to parity and equanimity it will militate against the recklessness and prodigality required to meet an immoderate cosmos on its own terms (1991: 20). When 'the ground we live on is little other than a field of multiple destructions' (1991: 23), the grand project of levelling the global playing field cannot ignore the recurrence of catastrophe.

Without necessitating any visit to their surface, Gaia theorist James Lovelock figured out that Mercury and Venus were devoid of life simply by observing the dreary equilibrium of their atmospheres (1987: 6–7). So too, without need of the largest cost–benefit analysis ever attempted, Bataille could have told the cost accountants of the current climatic crisis that their sums would never add up, based only on his abiding sense of the far-from-equilibrium energetic state of the earth. Without waiting for Kyoto or Copenhagen to collapse under the weight of their own efforts to enclose, quantify and commodify the carbon cycle, he would most probably have pointed out that radically extending the strategy that had built up all the pressure in the first place was a most unlikely way to open a safety valve.

Catastrophic climate and abyssal generosity

Bataille is as much a poet and a provocateur as a diagnostician. He offers nothing like Latour's attempt to lay out and knit together the core functions of a workable collective, and it's well known that his own stab at assembling the kind of community he desired – with a sacrificial logic at its heart – came to little. Moreover, as Jean

Baudrillard warns, we need to be as wary of the naturalizing of a prodigious and explosive cosmos as Bataille is of the modern economist's (or environmentalist's) tendency to make recourse to a parsimonious and circulatory one (1993: 157–8).

It may be a fine line, but I am arguing that there is a difference between taking a wager on how the world works (and committing oneself to an engagement with the challenges a specific model or ontology raises for social life) and wielding laws of nature as the authorization of specific social arrangements or political stances. Bataille undoubtedly drifts to and fro across this blurry divide, but the gist of his vision of excess is the posing of a problem without the dictation of an answer. We are, after all, free to ignore the build-up of energy and let vast conflagrations catch us unaware. We are equally at leave to unleash our accumulated arsenals in cruel, selfish or suicidal ways – as a theorist writing in the shadow of the cold war nuclear arms race knew only too well. The idea that we might consume or squander a surplus 'generously' is just one of a number of options.

But what a possibility! If Bataille overstates his case, if he stokes up the fiery energies of the universe so as to favour his own obsessions, it is because his idea of a magnanimous, non-utilitarian unloading of wealth has so few precedents in modern Western thought. True gifts, he insists, arrive from beyond the closed circuitry of exchange and calculation, and do not expect a return (1993: 370–1). Such gestures are a continuity of the exorbitant energy of the sun, a perpetuation of the monstrous outpouring of solar energy – on a more intimate scale. '(T)o live', Bataille intones, 'signifies for you not only the flux and the fleeting play of light which are united in you, but the passage of warmth or light from one being to another', to recall a line I cited in Chapter 3 (1988: 94). Paroxysms of generosity go with the flow of the world's tumultuousness, by operating on the same immoderate and discontinuous terrain. They prevent the dangerous amassing of energy or productive potential, not deliberately, but as the fortuitous side-effect of acts worth doing purely for their own sake. In this way – incidentally, secretly, joyfully – the gift subverts the logic of enclosure and accumulation.

Bucking decades of studious evasion of Bataille's potential contribution to environmentalism, Allan Stoekl has recently proposed that we take seriously the idea that a glorious and gratuitous disposal of pent-up riches might offer relief from the current ecological predicament:

Just as in *The Accursed Share*, where the survival of the planet will be the unforeseen, unintended consequence of a gift-giving (energy expenditure) oriented not around a weapons build up but around a squandering (give-away) of wealth, so too in the future we can posit sustainability as the unintended aftereffect of a politics of giving. (2007: 142)

In its own way, this is no more paradoxical than the claim that the modern project of rendering life secure, predictable and transparent paves the way to disaster (an insight that loops together the Frankfurt School, Bataille and Ulrich Beck). And neither is it as alien to contemporary climate change politics as it may first appear.

It is hard to tell at what point the most exacting pursuit of environmental or energetic justice, or the most advanced simulations of terrestrial climate, begin to tip into something other-than-quantifiable. With an eye attuned to Bataille's musing on the limits of knowledge, Kathryn Yusoff speaks of a modelling of global climate so complex and all-encompassing that it begins to reveal excesses of its own: a digital earth that itself functions as an 'ever-evolving model … a continuous organism of change, adjustment, and reconfiguration' (2009: 1013). Gratuitous disorder, that is to say, hatched out of the endeavour to make sense of the world. Elsewhere, if we take a second look at some of the more searching attempts to apportion responsibility and make amends for global climate change, these too seem at risk of edging over a threshold of calculability and dropping into unfathomable depths.

Aubrey Meyer's principle of contraction and convergence, while hinging on the absolute equitability of allocating every person on earth the right to the same quantity of carbon emissions, in practice calls for a dramatic reduction in the non-renewable energy use of the most industrialized populations. Still more extreme is Andrew Simms' conception of climate change as an expression of 'ecological debt' which could only be addressed by way of a settlement between the Global North and South that accounts for all the historical as well as the geographical disparities in energy and resource use. But Simms is not simply asking us to do all the sums, nor insisting on 'the inescapably fraught exercise' of pricing nature (2005: 106). He is trying to tip current ways of conceiving of economic debt on their head: attempting to incite 'a fundamental realignment of who owes whom in the international economy' – and thus justifying a massive global redistribution of wealth (2005: 183). For all their anchoring in a conventional model of justice, what makes such proposals start to resonate with Bataille's dream of a 'modern-day potlatch' on a global scale is that the overcoming of current differentials in wealth is not presented as a prelude for a fully universal resumption of growth (see Stoekl, 2007: 58). It is more in the manner of a once-and-for-all blow-out of Western prosperity: a power down impelled by a sense that the imminence of catastrophic climate change makes a mockery of existing economic axioms.

What's more to the point is that such fantasies of mass, unilateral dissipation of industrial riches are no rare thing amongst environmentally conscious radicals. Indignation over the ecological–economic injustices of the current world order certainly drives a great deal of thought and activism. But whether this deep-seated sense that 'the poor, the weak, the hungry, deserve better' (Wisner, cited in Philo, 2005: 444) actually requires an accurate score-sheet of inequity and disparity is debatable. Tunnel under the reliance on rationalization of ethico-political standpoints, and what so often seems to be coursing beneath is a desire to reach out to those in need that exceeds any requirement of proof, any justification or accounting. Bataille's writing, in other words, may not so much demand a dramatic overhaul of the dreams of green-tinged radical criticism, as give shape and intensity to a will to generosity and discharge that already pervades the genre.

To put it another way, he reminds us that the process of politicization need not necessarily take as its object a state of affairs that is demonstrably already 'political'. Bataille's opening of earthly economies to the dynamics of the universe, the abrupt climate change paradigm's opening of the current climatic condition to the rhythms and pulsing of extra-human earth, do not necessarily threaten the imperative to act in a just way. They may indeed extend the scope of the political. Or point to an 'excess' that perennially animates the more adventurous pursuits of justice.

At least this is what Jacques Derrida (1992b) is suggesting when he offers his own conception of a justice that goes beyond what is owed, calculated or 'right'. Any justice worthy of the name, Derrida argues, cannot simply attend to circumstances that can be contained within the closed circle of simple causality or proven culpability. For this would reduce it to law or to economics. Justice, in the expanded sense, must be able to respond to those events so singular or so surprising that there are no precedents, no regulations in place. It must be ready to come into its own when 'an *irruption* ... punctures the horizon, *interrupting* any performative organisation, any convention, or any context that can be or could be dominated by a conventionality' (Derrida, 2001a: 245, author's italics).

However, a notion of the just which is inherently excessive, which embodies 'a responsibility without limits' (1992b: 19), Derrida concedes, is also dangerous. For even if we are vigilant, the turn to a 'justice' which has at its heart an incalculability, a lack of restraint, a boundless compassion dices with injustice and irresponsibility: 'Left to itself, the incalculable and giving idea of justice is always very close to the bad, even to the worst for it can always be reappropriated by the most perverse calculation' (1992b: 28). Nowhere is this prospect more ominous, more fateful, than in the risk that by foregrounding the innate volatility of the earth's climate we occlude those dimensions of the current crisis that are 'our' own responsibility, and thereby play into the hands of those interests that would undermine the nascent and fragile architectures of transnational climate governance.

Many commentators have noted how easily Bataille's celebration of excess could slip into an apologetic for selfishness or violence (see Habermas, 1987: 235–6; Nancy, 1991: 39), a possibility he himself was aware of, if not always adequately attentive to. But there is certainly a recurring tension in his work between growth and loss, knowledge and non-knowledge, the measurable and the unfathomable – an interminable struggle captured in Edith Wyschogrod's verdict that Bataille's subject was forever 'teetering between … orgy and abstinence' (1990: 145). No less than Bataille's own concern with redistributing global wealth, the 'perhaps impossible vision of an ecologically just world' under the shadow of catastrophic shifts in the earth's climate seems to demand an even more rigorous accounting, in spite of the need to engage with the overwhelming of exchangeable values. Or as Derrida announces: 'incalculable justice *requires* us to calculate'; it summons us to 'negotiate the relation between the calculable and the incalculable' (1992b: 28, author's italics) – in an aporetic logic we have already encountered in Chapter 3.

In relation to the ethicizing and politicizing of abrupt climate changes to come, we are short of guidelines for a workable fusion of the utterly immeasurable and the approximately knowable, though we should not look past the considerable resources that Latour's expanded parliaments offer us. As recent critiques suggest, the most comprehensive attempts so far to calculate and regulate global carbon emissions may have set out from the wrong assumptions, thus courting complete failure while precluding more fair and feasible options (Lohmann, 2005). We should not rule out the possibility that a massive injection of Bataillean generosity earlier in the proceedings may have helped open other options – and might still.

I suggested above that there are promising tendencies toward a more-than-calculable justice in certain strands of Western political ecology and ecologized politics. But the over-industrialized world – 'sick with wealth' as Bataille would have it – may not be the only or best place to start (see Land, 1992: 33). *The Day after Tomorrow* may have denied the people of Mexico a fictional opportunity for unconditional generosity, but real life might yet prove more fruitful. Speaking of the need for 'an excessive response that breaks with the vicious circuit of accounting in the Arctic', Kathryn Yusoff notes the reluctance of the Inuit to concede to an economic logic: citing Aqqaluk Lynge, President of the Inuit Circumpolar Council, Greenland, '(t)he magnitude of the climate change challenge is such that a response of a higher order is needed' (2009: 1026).

Half a world away, the people of Kiribati still await offers of a new land on which to relocate, as the evidence mounts that their islands will become uninhabitable sometime this century. In the study of gift-giving, the Pacific has historically loomed large, with Marcel Mauss (1990 [1950]) notably marshalling available accounts to conclude that the gifting in question set in train relations of reciprocity or counter-giving: rendering them less an alternative to economic relations as a primitive pre-precursor of rational, calculated exchange. It was an argument that once again positioned Europe as the cultural–economic headland and left the Pacific and the rest of the periphery playing catch-up. But in the face of imminent demise, Kiribati has made a gesture for which there can be no reciprocation, an offering which breaks profoundly with the logic of exchange and with the conditionality of the gift.

At a 2006 UN biodiversity conference, the tiny Pacific nation pledged to set aside a huge area of its national waters as a new marine reserve, one which would encompass some of the planet's richest coral reef ecosystems as well as being the only significant stretch of deep ocean under protection (Fogarty, 2008). Later, during an economic downturn in which many other nation states began skimping or reneging on their environmental obligations, Kiribati unexpectedly announced a doubling in the size of the designated zone – bringing the reserve up to 410,500 square kilometres – around the size of California – making it the world's largest maritime protected area. Oceanographer and climatologist James McCarthy described the establishment of the reserve as a 'remarkable gift to the world', while Kiribati president Anote Tong said of the decision: 'It was an opportunity to make that last stand. It was our contribution to humanity' (cited in Whitney, 2008).

Next to the parsimonious and instrumental parleying that predominates in global climate change politics, Kiribati's exorbitant bequeathing of oceanic estate breathes a new logic. The gesture is unlikely to be devoid of self-interest, but there's something deeply provocative about responding to the prospect of territorial loss with an ever bigger territorial give-away: a perpetual endowment that trumps protectionism with abyssal generosity (Clark, 2010c). Bataille, we suspect, would have approved. Though even he may have been surprised to find that one of the most extravagant acts of 'squandering' of our time came from one of the 'poorest' countries on the planet. Or should that read 'least sick with wealth'.

6

Hurricane Katrina and the Origins of Community

Introduction: ground below zero

By way of the curvature of its surface and the tilt of its axis, the earth receives the energy of the sun unevenly. The dissipation of heat away from the tropics to the temperate latitudes is a major determinant of the planet's weather systems, and this flow too is far from even, whipping up winds and storms along the way. At any moment, around a thousand thunderstorms are raging through the tropics, meteorologists tell us, and some of these develop into fully fledged cyclones or hurricanes (Calder, 1997: 112).

In late August, in the midst of the 2005 Atlantic hurricane season, a tropical storm which formed over the south-eastern Bahamas strengthened into a cyclone as it made landfall in Florida. Here it weakened slightly, only to regain intensity as it entered the Gulf of Mexico. Having peaked at sea as a Category 5 hurricane, with maximum sustained winds of 175 miles an hour, Katrina made a second landfall, in Louisiana on Monday 29 August, by which time it had dropped to a 125-mile-an-hour Category 3 (Knabb et al., 2005). It could have been a lot worse. But it was bad enough that it triggered the disaster the people of New Orleans and neighbouring settlements had feared for a long time.

Some 233,000 km^2 of the southern USA was devastated, with the highest death toll of any cyclone in the USA since 1928. Most graphically, 80 per cent of New Orleans was flooded as the levee system was breached in more than 50 places. Dozens of other towns suffered severe damage and around two million people were displaced – making this the largest diaspora in modern American history (Bankoff, 2006; Crowley, 2006). Many of these people have not returned home, and they may never do so. 'Katrina', as one commentator put it, 'is about the sudden and complete loss of all that home means – safety, respite, privacy, comfort, and security' (Crowley, 2006: 155). Or, we might say, about the decimation of community.

'The gravest and most painful testimony of the modern world', writes philosopher Jean-Luc Nancy, '… is the testimony of the dissolution, the dislocation, or the conflagration of community' (1991: 1). The Tsunami, as we saw in Chapter 3, partially or completely obliterated many communities around the Indian Ocean. For all that acute social disparities played their part in exposure to the physical forces unleashed on Boxing Day 2004, there is not the same sense of betrayal of the most vulnerable that is the disgrace of Katrina. There was the time and the physical means to evacuate the entire population of New Orleans. But large numbers of the poor, the elderly and the incapacitated were left behind while others loaded up and drove to safety. If other social variables could not always be divined in mediated images, global audiences could certainly gauge for themselves the stark racial division between the abandoned and the safely relocated. Just as they could watch, in real time, the interminable spectacle of official relief failing to reach Katrina's worst-hit victims.

At least in part because the drowned cities and countryside of the Gulf Coast portend life in an age of rising sea levels and increasingly extreme weather events, Katrina's shockwaves continue to resonate. 'Katrina may yet be to 21st century America as the Lisbon earthquake was to the Enlightenment', Alex de Waal muses, 'a moment for profound self-examination' (2006: unpag.). And, perhaps, not just for America. Over the intervening years, this reflection has proceeded in ways which have drawn disaster studies' concern with the intersection of social underprivilege with physical vulnerability deeper into the heartlands of critical social thought. As sociologist Michael Eric Dyson observes: 'in New Orleans, the higher, safer ground has always been occupied by richer, whiter folk, while the lower, more dangerous ground, has always been the province of poorer people' (2006: 79). If this is a predicament with parallels in many places, it is also one for which Katrina has now supplied an iconic imagery.

When the social determination of suffering reaches the intensity it did in New Orleans, before, during and after the storm, it is tempting to push the elemental dimensions of the disaster into the background. But Dyson resists the either/or option of physical and social causation, and instead gestures towards a more dynamic relationality – one in which natural extremes do not simply happen to vulnerable communities but are themselves deeply engrained in the very process of communal formation. 'Black folk have built communities in the most hostile conditions imaginable', he asserts. 'They have beat back both natural and man-made disasters to stake bold claims of citizenship and common humanity' (2006: 75).

In Chapter 3, we touched on the argument, a staple of critical disaster studies, that human susceptibility to variable environmental conditions is profoundly and often tragically configured by pre-existing socio-economic and political inequities. Without rebuking this vital insight and all the life-changing critical and practical work it informs, I will be following Dyson's lead and radically extending the encounter between communities and geophysical instability. Worlds have been swirling, shifting, shuddering, since long before human beings made their appearance – which suggests that as collective beings, we exist downstream as well as upstream of the challenge of elemental processes. In keeping with what I have been arguing about the fundamental non-symmetry of the natural and the human realms, I want to explore the proposition that natural extremes or 'disasters' are not simply visited upon pre-constituted communities, but are themselves imperatives for the very process of communal or social formation.

I made the point in the last chapter that the physical world works in ways which exceed the assumptions of reciprocity and equivalence upon which modern conventions of justice hinge. We need an expanded sense of 'justice', I suggested, that does not wait on the symmetry of a mutual exchange in order to create new openings conducive to the earth's own symmetry-shattering outbursts. This is more than an abstract ideal. As we saw in the case of the Indian Ocean Tsunami, as we witnessed again in the aftermath of Haiti, as we may glimpse in some recent rejoinders to global climate change, the upheavals of the earth are a scene in which singular acts of compassion and care take place – often performed by those who have the least to give. In this chapter, I push this further, suggesting that on our turbulent planet such extraordinary gestures may in fact be quite ordinary (though no less remarkable and wondrous) responses to the equally ordinary ungrounding of the ground, to the ongoing and inevitable un-worlding of worlds. In this sense, the challenges of an innately unstable nature may be one of the most basic and primordial incitements for coming together with others.

'Community', as Nancy would have it, 'is *what happens to us* – question, waiting, event, imperative – *in the wake of* society' (1991: 11, author's italics). But what appears in the backwash of the social is also what was happening all along – the bonds that are made moment by moment, being-with-others as a process rather than a predicate or an outcome. In the midst of the cataclysm that was and is Katrina, people were forced to improvise, to take rescue and provisioning and care into their own hands. That improvisation – with all its raw exposures and rough edges – *is* community, I want to argue. Katrina is a complex event with many lessons, but one we should not overlook – amid more glaring admonitions is that the imperative for being-together is not only the needs and demands of others, not just the abject failure of social or technological infrastructures, but the precarious physicality of our planet. The response to Katrina, in this sense, offers insights not only about how communities respond to the loss of their supporting terrain, but how the rumbling of the earth, repeated over and over again, has never ceased to be an impetus for the very emergence of communal being.

Historicizing the hurricane

The town of New Orleans, intentionally sited at the confluence of three waterways, has grappled with the agency of floodwater and storm from its inception (Cutter, 2006). 'In 1718', writes Mike Tidwell, 'the year the French colonists first settled along that crescent-shaped bend of the Mississippi River, heavy rains sent river water pouring into the settlement, flooding crude homes made of cypress, moss, and clay' (2006: 7–8). The modest levies constructed by the settlers (or rather, by their slaves) in response to this episode were themselves overwhelmed by muddy Mississippi water the following year (Tidwell, 2006: 9; Protevi, 2009: 166). Hence, the embankments were raised – inadvertently setting in motion the cycle of incessantly rising water and sinking land.

With the expansion of New Orleans into surrounding marshlands, water had to be constantly pumped out to keep new developments from regressing to swamp. This has resulted in subsidence as the alluvial soils compact, a gradual sinking of the city aggravated by the fact that flood control measures interrupted the natural process of lying down new sediment (Bakker, 2005). At the same time, upstream damming and the canalization of the Mississippi River – to improve shipping access for the oil industry – has led to a dramatic reduction in the depositing of sediments in the Louisiana Delta. It is estimated that since the 1930s, over a million acres of coastal wetlands and barrier islands have been lost, removing the buffer zone which formerly helped absorb storm surges. Stripped of these once densely verdant speed bumps, the raised and broadened lower Mississippi now offers heavy weather an inviting passage inland that locals refer to as 'the hurricane highway' (Bakker, 2005; Tidwell, 2006).

In the years just prior to Katrina, the potentially catastrophic consequences of this unhappy dialectic of human development and natural elements had been obvious to Tidwell's respondents – Cajun fishermen with an intimate working knowledge of the Gulf Coast – as it seems to have been, with varying degrees of conviction, to many of the region's inhabitants, including state and federal policy makers, advocacy groups, hydro-engineers and physical scientists (Tidwell, 2006: 4). Anxiety over the possible effect of a high-force hurricane direct hit on New Orleans has been on the rise since the storm surges of Hurricane Betsy overflowed the city's levees in 1965, intensifying after force 5 Hurricane Camille wrought havoc along the Mississippi state coastline four years later (Wisner, 2005). But the sense of living in the shadow of catastrophe goes back a lot further, at least as far as the Great Mississippi Flood of 1927.

Following exceptionally heavy rains in the summer of 1926, the Mississippi breached its banks early in the new year, causing flooding across nine states and displacing some 700,000 people (Barry, 1997). Where the Great Flood left its stain was not only in loss of life and extensive destruction of property, but also in its conspicuous mapping of natural disaster onto social inequality. Levees were infamously dynamited in an (unnecessary) attempt to save the 'better' quarters of New Orleans by sacrificing low-lying and mostly poor black districts to the floodwaters, while the aftermath of the deluge saw the internment of hundreds of thousands of homeless black people in forced labour camps (Barry, 1997: 313–14; Dyson, 2006; Oliver-Smith, 2006).

In the collection *After the Storm: Black Intellectuals Explore the Meaning of Hurricane Katrina* (2006), historian Clement Alexander Price reviews the complex history of encounters between African Americans and destructive physical events such as the Galveston flood of 1900 and Great Mississippi Flood. Price's sharp attunement to the disproportionate vulnerability of poor black communities to environmental extremes prompts his call 'to reconsider how the pervasiveness of natural disasters influenced the way modern and contemporary black life unfolded' (2006: 73). In a similar vein, Michael Eric Dyson (2006) points to the lasting repercussions of early twentieth-century catastrophes for southern black communities. As well as reminding us of the way that white power-holders capitalized on the social chaos and dislocation after the Great Flood of 1927 to coerce the black poor into unremunerated reconstruction work, Dyson explores the role of these oppressive experiences in the accelerating migration of black people to the northern cities.

While Price and Dyson provide a valuable historicizing of the injustice manifest by Katrina, it is notable that both writers manage to stress the racialized political and socio-economic dimensions of recurrent catastrophes without any corresponding demotion of the role of physical variables. Dyson both acknowledges the excessiveness of natural forces and pays tribute to the capacity of under-resourced and abandoned people to answer the imperatives of these world-shattering events. Likewise, when Price advocates that 'the unpredictability of nature's wrath should be factored into our perception of the American past', he is at once calling for an excavation of the 'enduring fault lines of race, class, and generation', and counselling us to take full account of the more literal fissuring of volatile earth processes (2006: 73, 71).

Drawing insights from the relational materialities literature into a productive encounter with the work of Giorgio Agamben's notion of Homo sacer, Bruce Braun and James McCarthy (2005) have identified some of the concrete ways that the socio-political practices articulate with a broader topology of objects, materials and elements. They claim that what happened to those left behind in New Orleans is a glaring example of a particular kind of abandonment that Agamben argues is characteristic of the exercise of power in the contemporary world. That is, certain categories of people found themselves denied the rights or protections to which they are entitled while at the same time being brutally subjected to the disciplinary functions of the law: they were at once left to suffer or die and forcibly prevented from the actions by which they could have saved themselves or relieved their suffering (Braun and McCarthy, 2005: 807).

But prompted by Katrina to recognize that 'the body politic and individuals' inclusion in it are defined in very large part by relationships with the more-than-human world we inhabit', Braun and McCarthy propose that the notion of abandoned *humans* needs to be developed to take in an expanded field of human and nonhuman elements (2005: 804). Extending Agamben's cruel paradox of inclusion crossed with exclusion, they present New Orleans' afflicted populations as being caught up in life-threatening consociations with extreme weather, pathogens, pollutants and failing infrastructure, even as they are excluded from life-supporting networks that should have connected them with food, medicine, transportation, shelter and information.

The point Braun and McCarthy make is not simply that such complex material entanglements are visited upon certain categories of social being, but that socio-political orderings and individual bodies are actually forged out of the articulations of heterogeneous elements. John Protevi (2009) makes a similar point, but goes still further, summoning up the kind of autonomous and asymmetrical forces of nature that I have been talking about, in order to compose a backstory of Katrina's Louisiana that weaves together potent elemental forces of solar energy, fluvial processes, the biology of sugar cane and the human energies channelled by slavery.

What needs to be historicized, Protevi is telling us in ways which chime with Dyson and Price, is not just the social ingredients of the particular situation, but the full contingent of physical processes that converge to make a region, a place, a people what they are. As Gilles Deleuze once put it, in a commentary on Michel Foucault's conception of power: 'human forces ... have to combine with other forces: an overall form arises from this combination, but everything depends on the nature of the other forces with which the human forces become linked' (1995: 117). As its more searching commentaries acknowledge, Katrina's perfect storm is calling for new kinds of stories to interrogate these cruel combinations of human and more-than-human energies and processes.

It's important to remember that for Foucault and Deleuze, the directing and channelling capacities of power are always enabling as well as restricting. But just as vitally, we need to recall Levinas's very different conception of power: the hold that one who is suffering or debilitated may have over those who capabilities remain at least relatively undiminished. As Dyson's comment about African Americans crafting communities in the midst of nature's chaos intimates, it is not only dominant orders that combine with disparate elements, not just the powerful who make history out of the materials and the energies of the other-than-human. Being together with others in ways that involve a constitutive exposure or vulnerability, I am arguing, also entails articulations with forces far beyond the human. And not merely in a manner that involves the using or tapping of these forces, but also in ways that apprehend such forcefulness in and through its resurgent exteriority as an excitation, an impetus, an imperative.

In the beginning

Before I address some of the ways that the people of New Orleans and the Gulf Coast forged new forms of 'being-with' out of the recent catastrophe of Katrina, I want to push Dyson's notion of the engendering of community out of 'hostile conditions' back still further. Back, with the help of Michel Serres, beyond any possible recourse to empirical verification and historical narrativization. In *The Natural Contract* (1995), Serres offers an imaginary account of 'what happened in the beginning': a tale that sets out from a flood and tells of the formation of the social or the communal in response to this event.

It is not just the deluge that makes Serres's story valuable, it's the sheer fact of his willingness to speculate about origins. These days, it's much more common critical practice to flush out primordial stories in order to expose their malignant effects than it is to try and compose alternatives. The favourite inaugural story to target is the one that infers an original state of unity, plenitude and oneness with nature (a version of which we have already encountered in Derrida's critique of Husserl in Chapter 1). For a long time, such 'metaphysical' thinking blatantly or furtively informed prevailing notions of community, lending a sense that all true communities have sprung forth from the infinitely receding depths of a native soil. The corollary of this vision is that the members of such a community are bound together by shared rootedness, their unbroken lineage tying them 'organically' to a portion of the earth – and thus justifying their dominion over this territory at the expense of all-comers.

It hardly needs to be added that this sort of thinking is anathema to contemporary social and philosophical thought, to the point where it is near obligatory to set out one's distaste for it and distance from it (see Bauman, 2000: 184; Beck, 2000: 80–1). Communities, we are now used to hearing, are composite entities. Whether they avow it or not, all communities are to some degree open, unstable and heterogeneous, and given that they manifest a differential play that goes all the way back, there can be no legitimate recourse to a solid, anchoring ground.

A good half century of critical deracination of collective existence from soil or bedrock has ensured that primordial stories have gone out of fashion, precisely because going all the way back generally entails a terminus in the state of nature. And that's why Serres' mythical tale is a rare gem. Against the grain, he does indeed return to nature as the original scene of the emergence of human collective existence. Only his is not the fixed, timeless and harmonious nature of the old metaphysics. It is a nature that surges and recedes, that overflows and undermines.

'Floods', Serres contends, 'take the world back to disorder, to primal chaos, to time zero, right back to nature in the sense of things about to be born, in a nascent state' (1995: 51). Setting the scene in the alluvial delta, he speculates how the receding of a periodic inundation is the incitement for the establishment of order: an ordering which takes the form of measuring and marking out freshly deposited land so that it can be distributed amongst those who will set to work farming it. This inscription, this enactment of a border, Serres announces, is the first law on earth. Wherever it occurs – on the floodplain, around an oasis, in a forest clearing – it is this de-cision which inaugurates a bond between all those concerned. Through the process of distinguishing culture from nature – in agreeing how to make the cut and accepting this jurisdiction – the collectivity defines and formalizes its own existence. The same 'cord' which cordons off and measures out a realm of cultivation also ropes us together into a new accord:

> Thus was concluded a social contract – will we ever be sure of this? – out of which politics and laws were born. This contract may be a mythic or abstract notion or event, but it is fundamental and indispensable to understanding how the obligations that bind us to one another were born (Serres, 1995: 53).

What stands out in this account is not so much the link between the demarcation of ourselves from nature and the commitment to the basic covenant of the 'social'. Political philosophers have a long tradition of imagining that it is the enactment of some kind of contract – albeit a virtual one – that marks our shift out of a 'state of nature' and into the condition of socialized existence. As Serres himself stresses, what makes his primordial scene distinctive is his insistence that the flood – or any other natural upheaval – is a recurring one. Our collective carving out of a civilized and contractual realm is not a once and for all achievement. It is something we have to persist with, a performance repeated each time the unruly forces of nature reassert themselves. The trouble with the standard social contract story and all successive social or historical narratives that imagine a decisive break with nature, Serres argues, is that once separation has been achieved, the 'social' is henceforth imagined to be autonomous, self-mobilizing, unmoored from any earthly directive: 'From the time the pact was signed, it is as if the group that had signed it, casting off from the world, were no longer rooted in anything but its own history' (1995: 34).

Through the flood story, Serres reminds his critical compatriots that their extirpation of a particular metaphysics of nature does not simply endorse the idea of human collective existence as an open and endless play of its own internal forces. If society or community is to be prised out of its self-enclosure, this move demands – rather than prohibits – a further opening to the elemental forces that underpin human life, an opening that is ongoing and unending. Far from unbinding the social from the natural, this means that we are com-pelled to reconsider the question of a social ordering or communal formation that responds to the imperatives of the earth. This is not a call to re-embed the social in a stable substrate, but a stipulation that social and communal life always was and always will be responsive to the rumbling of the earth, to the periodic ungrounding of its ground.

Reckless abandon

For Serres then, there is no community that is not enabled, haunted and from time to time commanded by 'hostile conditions'. That we must take such conditions as an imperative for the renewal of collec-tive bonds has been powerfully restated in the aftermath of Katrina. The problem of how devastated ground – especially in zones that remain significantly evacuated – is to be reapportioned and resettled is a fraught one. There is justifiable suspicion that the administration responsible for reconstructing New Orleans is discriminating against the re-establishment of minoritized evacuees – prompting charges that a systematic 'ethnic cleansing' of the city is taking place (Bakker, 2005: 797–8).

Refusing such stratagems, David Dante Troutt's plea for the 'remaking of our social contract' in the wake of Katrina (2006: 23) resonates with many other voices in demanding that decisions over the city's future and resources for rebuilding it should be shared equitably among all of New Orleans' disparate and dispersed popu-lace. But it is one thing to envisage a new social contract several years after the event, when the immediate problems of surviving the storm have long subsided. It is a very different thing to imagine that 'contractuality', however loosely defined, offers a guiding light in the midst of swirling confusion and collapse. This raises questions about the timing of the process of re-formulating the social, and where it sits amid other priorities.

While Serres's flood fable does admirable work in revitalizing the issue of the material 'ungrounding' of community, the passage from the disintegrative mayhem of the deluge to the consensual gathering around a new political–legal infrastructure – for all the necessary simplification of his tale – seems overly hasty. And altogether too painless. If an earthly convulsion such as flooding genuinely returns the world to chaos then there will be dispossessed and traumatized people. As we saw in the case of the Indian Ocean Tsunami, the immediate need of the victims of an upheaval or disaster is support, a handhold that offers a modicum of stability in a world stripped of its sense and solidity. In the media coverage of New Orleans, during the seemingly endless interval before organized relief arrived in the city, many of us found ourselves watching the spectacle of survivors struggling on without any visible means of support – doing whatever they had to do to survive and to help others survive. We watched them struggling against rather than with the authorities who could have been offering them assistance.

Over the intervening years, these mass-mediated images have been supplemented by detailed accounts of the 'ground-level' experience of enduring Katrina, including personal stories and testimonies, archival material, journalistic reconstruction and more poetic or fictionalized interpretations. While tales of survival under duress may be a genre with its own dramatic conventions, different events come with their own singular blend of props, settings, storylines and emotional registers. Unsurprisingly, much of the 'literature' of Katrina evokes the gritty improvisatory talents of under-resourced people confronting overwhelming physical forces: an affirmation of self help most often set against a bleaker background of abandonment by higher powers.

Among the most iconic stories is that of the commandeering of a school bus by 20-year-old Jabbar Gibson, who drove some 70 evacuees to Houston. It's a tale given added bite by reports of his subsequent clash with the authorities (for driving without a Louisiana heavy vehicle licence) and the backdrop of hundreds of buses which could have taken people to safety being locked up and left to the floodwaters (Bryant and Gaza, 2005; Solnit, 2005b, unpag.). No less resonant is the story of the 'Cajun navy', the ad-hoc flotilla of vessels piloted by local hunters and fisherfolk that gathered by word-of-mouth and converged on New Orleans, rescuing over 4000 stranded survivors (Tidwell, 2006; Stephenson and Bonabeau, 2007). Similarly, the actions of the US Coast Guard have been widely praised. One of very few federal agencies to move into action without waiting for authorization, the Gulf Coast contingent quickly adapted to the challenge of working in an urban environment, reputedly rescuing more people from the submerged streets of New Orleans in a few days than it had in its previous half century of open-water operations (Wachtendorf and Kendra, 2006; Stephenson and Bonabeau, 2007).

Stories from 'ground below zero' feature ordinary people rescuing themselves and their neighbours, continuing to do their jobs amid collapsing infrastructure, going on requisitioning missions for vital supplies, and cobbling together supply chains and support networks. A recurring theme is the value of local knowledge: intuitively carrying an axe in the hasty retreat to the attic, knowing where to find supplies and high ground, figuring out who would be most in need of urgent assistance (Gibson, 2006; Tidwell, 2006: 20). Other resounding tropes include the improvisation of repertoires or equipment in the heat of the moment; the suspension of familiar divisions of class or race or neighbourhood; and the disregard for regulation, protocol and authority structures. But most of all, as John Protevi rightly insists, these are tales of care and compassion:

> the stories of the thousands and thousands and thousands of the brave and loving people of New Orleans who refused to leave their old, their sick, their young, their helpless, and who walked miles through the floods to safety, pushing wheelchairs and floating the sick on 'looted' air mattresses. Yes, we saw images of helpless poor people waiting to be rescued at the Superdome and the Convention Centre, but we should never forget that they rescued themselves prior to that, through heroic solidarity, through what we should not be afraid to call "love". (2009: 177)

The evil twin of these hopeful and heroic tales are the now familiar accounts of official incompetence, negligence and downright brutality: the abject failure to evacuate the most vulnerable; the use of force by police and private security to prevent pedestrian evacuation (most infamously on the Gretna Bridge); the prohibiting of survivors from accessing emergency provisions; the detainment of large groups of evacuees in places with inadequate supplies or sanitation and even without shelter; and the abandonment of prisoners to rising floodwaters (Solnit, 2005b; Russell-Brown, 2006; Protevi, 2009). At the crux of most of these stories is the insistence of authorities at every level to put command and control before care, a prioritization exemplified by the head of the Louisiana National Guard's Joint Task Force. Even before his arrival in the disaster zone, Brigadier General Gary Jones announced: 'This place is going to look like Little Somalia. We're going to go out and take this city back. This will be a combat operation to get this city under control' (cited in Solnit, 2005b: unpag.).

While it is widely accepted that centralized organizations will fall short of reaching all who need help during a large-scale disaster, they need not fail as spectacularly as city, state and federal authorities did during Katrina. A new generation of management theorists, attuned to the 'emergent properties' that a well-oiled organization ought to manifest during 'rapidly evolving situations' point to the possibility of rules being over-ridden, routines revised and new strategies invented (Stephenson and Bonabeau, 2007). Of course, agencies tasked with responding to complex emergencies know this. They know it so well that sticking to programmes that are blatantly foundering is a feat in itself. In the words of Rebecca Solnit: 'Failure at this level requires sustained effort' (2005b: unpag.).

But there may be more at stake than institutional structure and strategy. As Harvey Molotch contends, what is also needed, and what was conspicuously absent in the majority of official responses to Katrina, is the affective jolt that emboldens the suspension of normal practice and boosts innovation and risk taking: the 'kind of *panic of empathy* that trumps organizational habit and individual postures' (2006, unpag., my italics). What Molotch's felicitous phrase conjures is precisely the exceeding of considered and calculating responses that I have been speaking about in previous chapters. This is the sort of sensuous receptivity to the plight of others that does not oppose reasoned or deliberated action but is the very condition of a just and effective engagement with an inherently immoderate situation. The idea of a 'panic of empathy' evokes the wave of embodied intensity that seems to have galvanized successful self-help efforts by survivors, at the same time as it permits even the most hulking bureaucracy a streak of raw susceptibility to pain and distress.

Down by law

Contrary to some over-eager readings of Levinas, however, it is quite possible to gaze into the eyes of suffering and then to return to one's usual repertoire. 'We can turn away from faces as we can turn away from the surfaces of things', as Alphonso Lingis reminds us (1998b: 132). Turning away is easier when strong, negative images pre-exist the encounter in question to such a degree that they channel the affective intensities of exposure and proximity. Many of those in positions of authority appear to have had such entrenched impressions of lawlessness and depravity among the minoritized populations of New Orleans that incoming information during Katrina was readily slotted into a template of abject social breakdown. Accusations of mass looting, rioting, murder, even child rape and cannibalism were widely circulated in the media, most of which later turned out to lie somewhere between gross exaggeration and total fabrication. But they had already served a purpose: helping to recast a humanitarian crisis and a failure of civic responsibility into a law and order issue.

This tension between a responsiveness that hinges on susceptibility and a reaction that can countenance only the reassertion of control invites us to follow Jean-Luc Nancy's lead in asking what is at stake in committing ourselves to the identity of 'the social'. A vision of social disintegration that sets a premium on the re-establishment of order assumes an existing reference point, a pre-conceived image of what society is or what it stands for. This returns us to the issue of Serres's prioritizing of consensus in the immediate aftermath of the flood. As Nancy would have it, there is a flaw in the logic of the social contract, one that Rousseau himself was aware of. It demands of community that it imagines itself as a complete and integrated entity, in order that it brings itself into existence (2000: 24). In other words, to become a contractually bonded totality, a society must be able to present itself – to itself – *before it exists*. The trouble with this fast-forwarding to common being or self-identity, Nancy argues, is that it cannot do justice to the singularity or uniqueness of the situated encounters in which people come together in the first place – or what he refers to as '*the plural singular of origins*' (2000: 26, author's italics). Instead, it prioritizes an imaginary end point over the ongoing and concrete processes which may or may not eventually generate something in common. (There is a similar logic here to Latour's critique of the way the deployment of such readymade conceptual wholes as society or nature comes at the expense of showing how they are actually composed.)

As I argued in Chapter 3, the effect of a sudden loss of elemental support is likely to be traumatic, an estrangement from one's own sense of self, not to mention each other. This is why for Levinas, and analogously, for Nancy, the encounter with another who is in some way bereft is inevitably a meeting across a divide: a coming together across a core of irreducible difference (Nancy, 2000: 5). Shattered people do not instantly form wholes by joining forces with others, even with those who are relatively 'together'. What must come first, ahead of any kind of commitment to a 'substantial identity' of the social, is the sharing of the *'lack of an identity'* (Nancy, 1991: xxxviii, author's italics). By this reasoning, any togetherness which emerges in response to an extreme event would initially involve no more or less than a constellation of singular contacts: unique bonds forged out of difference within proximity – thus obviating any overarching presentation *of* itself *to* itself. In other words, the disaster will incite being-in-common, rather than revealing or cementing common being. Or as Derrida puts it: '... before any contract, ... the other's coming as the singularity that is always other' (1992b: 25).

What Nancy's affirmation of being-in-common over common being points up is the danger of investing in images of the social – society as its own spectacle – at the expense of the unpresentable multitude of encounters and openings that reinvent collective exist-ence moment by moment (2000: 65). The lesson we might take from the shamefulness of the official response to Katrina is that the will towards the self-presentation of the social as a unified entity has as its no-less pernicious flipside the enthralment with the spectacle of society in disintegration – the image of the all-out conflict zone whose overwhelming demand is for the reinstitution of law and order at any cost. So strong is this imperative that it can preclude the *panic of empathy* – overriding the plea of survivors of traumatic events for what Nancy refers to as 'com-passion' – 'the contact of being with one another in this turmoil' (2000: xiii).

It is not just a matter of championing impulsiveness and disre-gard for the law over orderly and rule-bound conduct. Following a logic which we have already encountered in his thoughts on the co-implication of deliberated action and an unconditional opening to others, Derrida (1992b) teases out a more complex relation between improvisation and upholding convention. He proposes that responsibility in times of crisis requires respect for the spirit of the law, even in the midst of our compulsion to suspend or rein-vent the rules. Rules are needed because there is always more than one other calling for attention – because 'in actual social existence, these multiple claims must be adjudicated' (Wyschogrod, 1998: 237). This means that an act of transgressing the law should ideally work in and through an ongoing respect for that order or pro-gramme from which it is exempting itself. In this sense, knowing what is 'right', and suspending this knowledge in response to a sin-gular address, are tangled-up imperatives of the same predicament, co-constitutive demands of the one moment. And this suggests a much more complex temporization than a simple prioritization of spontaneity over procedure. In this way, in keeping with his cautioning over the risks attending an 'excessive' concept of justice, Derrida warns that the deferral of regulation – no less than the refusal to bend the rules – inevitably carries the risk of violence (1992b: 23; Wyschogrod, 1998: 248).

That does not, however, imply a need to defer to the spirit of laws or conventions or programmes whose intention clearly departs from the adjudication of disparate and competing needs. In this regard, the condemnation by Braun and McCarthy and others of the exercise of particular forms of political–legal power during the crisis of Katrina remains vital and trenchant. A form of state power which applies the full force of the law to bodies which are already raw and exposed by way of being stripped of the safeguards of citizenship, even before they have been abandoned to elemental forces, would seem to exempt itself from the respect owed to institutionalized justice. A situation where thousands of people are left without food and water yet surrounded by police, are told to 'fend for themselves' then threatened with incarceration or death for 'looting' (Braun and McCarthy, 2005: 803), is one in which the misfit between social ordering practices and the basic requirements of enduring earth processes borders on the pathological. Clearly in this context, any insistence on the need to leave an opening for improvisatory conduct – whether in institutionalized or popular settings – comes up against the demand to address the injustice sedimented into legal–political structures: that programmatic partiality which, during Katrina, determined that a whole range of basic survival tactics were pre-emptively condemned before they could even be tried out.

But it is not only state powers and their arms of enforcement that refuse to amend substantive images of the social world and corresponding repertoires in times of crisis. Critical thinkers too, as we have seen, tend to arrive at the scene of an event with their own identifications of the social – which may be no less obdurate than those they wish to contest. It is hardly surprising that many political and social critics, mostly but not only from abroad, saw reflected in the debacle of Katrina everything that they most despised about the last superpower, or at least its then-current administration. Here, in audio-visual immediacy, was the evidence of a society deeply divided by race and class, a culture too centred on self-interest and individualism to care for its disadvantaged, a state so intent on imposing its authority overseas that it had neglected its own most vulnerable people (see Bakker, 2005: 799; Oliver-Smith, 2006).

Yet such commitments and fidelities, even when underscored by profound solidarity for the least advantaged, can come with their own pre-emptions; their own imperviousness to the possibilities inhering in momentary and flickering gestures of being with and for others. There was another side of the response to Katrina that does not sit comfortably with some of the best-rehearsed condemnations of contemporary American society, one that was especially difficult for domestic critical thinkers to ignore. As we saw in the aftermath of the Tsunami, the first and often the most effective aid came from within the afflicted regions, or from neighbouring settlements or states. Likewise, Katrina triggered perhaps the most massive outpouring of public donation, volunteering and hospitality that the United States has ever seen. Whatever our preconceptions about the current state of social cohesion in the Deep South or elsewhere in America, care and compassion does not appear to have been in short supply.

Improvising community

While there are few American writers as incisive on the subject of social injustice as Mike Davis, his interventions on Katrina are most memorable for his tribute to the grassroots conviviality it inspired. In an article co-authored with Anthony Fontenot, Davis (2006) speaks at first hand of his visit to Ville Platte, an impoverished Cajun and black Creole community in southern Louisiana. It was the people of this town, along with boat-owners from neighbouring settlements, who banded together to form the 'Cajun Navy'. With a median income less than half the national average, and with no federal aid or Red Cross contribution, 'the folks of Ville Platte' went on to provide food, shelter and support to more than 5,000 displaced people, who they referred to tellingly, not as refugees or evacuees, but as 'company'. Davis characteristically teases out the political implications of this gesture and the situation that incited it, but he is just as comfortable speaking simply of 'an act of love in a time of danger' (Davis and Fontenot, 2006: 121).

Ville Platte was far from exceptional. Because the devastation from Katrina was so widespread, there was a shortage of neighbours in a fit state to offer assistance, and much of the support which was offered to evacuees and the help which arrived in the disaster zones came from far afield. This was facilitated by a series of online databases and bulletin boards set up by groups of infotech-savvy volunteers, some of whom drew on experience gained from working on the tsunamihelp blog and wiki. Organizational theorists have applauded the hastily hatched networks like hurricanehousing and katrinahelp as exemplary of the kind of emergent collaborative structures – or what they like to term 'swarm intelligence' – that have proved to be so effective in situations where there is limited institutional support and widespread infrastructural failure (Stephenson and Bonabeau, 2007). But the idea of 'intelligence' misses something important about the motivation of this 'panic' of networking, just as it fails to do justice to the hundreds of thousands of offers that brought these websites to life. As one posting on the New Orleans Metblog put it, in the midst of the crisis:

> obviously anyone way outside who has never been a part of it couldn't possibly understand what you're going through. But I think you're probably going to have to make allowances for a new breed: people who woke up and sensed something about the place they had to be a part of: a sort of inexplicable yearning solidarity vaguely akin, but greater than, falling in love. Some of us want to indefinitely 'hep yew' because we want to help ourselves, or at least our own hearts reflected on the rising waters.[1]

Municipal authorities offered shelter, schools and universities across numerous states reserved places for displaced people, businesses set up job placements or donated supplies, workers volunteered their labour and skills (Crowley, 2006; de Waal, 2006). Most of all, people opened their homes. In their own words:[2]

> I have an extra bedroom and couches that I would be honored to let someone use. Please email *Kathy Ross*

> My wife and I have 2 spare bedrooms available for Katrina victims. We want to help any way we can. Nothing is expected and nothing will be accepted. We all need help some time or another. Please let us help. – wpsmith@cabletvonline.net

> lets get you back on your feet! Temp. shelter and work for flood victims. call 509-438-4266 or 541-481-3747 ask for Josh

> I AM A SINGLE 30 YEAR OLD WOMEN WITH A 2 YEAR OLD DAUGHTER AND I DON'T HAVE MUCH BUT I VCAN OFFER A PLACE TO LIVE FOOD COMPUTER USAGE A WARM PLACE TO SLEEP PRIVATE BATHING AND A SHOULDER TO CRY ON. I AM OFFERING HOUSING TO ANY SINGLE WOMEN AND CHILD EDERLY AND OR A COUPLE. I AM AN AFRICAN AMERICAN WOMAN BUT IT DOESNT MATTER. EMAIL ME AT (msdeanneg@yahoo.com) call 24hrs 713-271-1595

And so on, screenful after screenful: the invitation to 'company' adding up to over 200,000 beds offered to strangers in homes across the nation (see Clark, 2006). To some critical commentators, these are feel-good humanitarian efforts: individualized acts of charity that paper over the deeply-incised structural divisions that set Katrina's catastrophe in train. To others, more positively, such self help is evidence of a civil society ever ready to burgeon and flourish in the void left by failing structures of authority, revealing at once the potential of free association and the fragility of the existing political order (Solnit, 2005b).

Empathizing with the latter reading, I want to add a more primordial, more ontological twist. This kind of opening to estranged others *is community itself*. The compassion shown in this multitude of gestures, in the words of Nancy, is 'nothing other than the passion of and for community' (1991: 34). It is what Bataille, Levinas, Blanchot, Nancy, Agamben, Wyschogrod, Lingis and fellow theorists of 'the other community' have spoken of, with both sophistication and a sort of beautiful naivety, as the originary impetus to social existence. It is the desire to be together with others with whom we do not yet share anything in common, a passion that is also a kind of passivity, a receptiveness in the face of need or loss or just for its own sake. What Lingis (1994) refers to as 'the community of those with nothing in common' and Agamben (2005) terms 'the coming community' is not just a distant hope. Its intimations show up in the interstices of state power, wherever people congregate in advance of any affirmation of a group identity; wherever 'community is mediated not by any condition of belonging ... but by belonging itself' (Agamben, 2005: 84). Such is Villa Platte's 'company', we might say, or the busload of neighbours and strangers who self-appointed bus driver Jabbar Gibson described simply as 'my people' (cited in Protevi, 2009: 177).

There are of course many reports of towns or districts placing severe restrictions on evacuee settlement, including some which barred the passage of people fleeing the hurricane itself (Russell-Brown, 2006). As time went on, news filtered in of an initial amicability in many places turning sour, as the pressure of playing host to disorientated and often traumatized visitors took its toll (Ogletree, 2006; Sullivan, 2006). A crisis is by definition a pivotal moment, and it is hardly surprising that the excitement of throwing one's door open to the survivors of nature's fury is difficult if not impossible to sustain. Ordinariness descends. Some people return home, some try to return home but fail, others simply stay on in accommodation or employment or places they would not have otherwise chosen. Acts of love in a time of danger give way to mere tolerance, or impatience or animosity.

The resurgent weight of the mundane that accompanies any disaster or forced displacement suggests a need for caution over the exalting of the instant of an opening to an other, or the decision taken in the heat of the moment. Nancy's insistence that the world turns on each singularity offers hope in the midst of the worst, yet it also invites counter-question about what becomes of this promise when the gravity of the predictable and the quotidian reasserts itself. It summons forth the evidence of years of scholarship and frontline experience which presents the stubborn fact that privileged, already well-connected individuals and groups generally recover more quickly from disaster than those who have less resources and fewer or more tenuous social ties (Hurlbert et al., 2006). It doesn't take a load of research to work out which strata of the New Orleans populace stayed bailed up in the trailer parks of Baker, Baton Rouge and Houston.

We know that most often when the world begins to turn again, it spins on a familiar axis. But I want to hold on to the idea that the disaster is an incitement to new alliances, practices, repertoires – and that the most important improvisation is community itself.

The moments when one stranded family reaches out to another, when an armada of small boats assembles, when spare rooms are offered in a distant state, these unrehearsed offerings are the very inauguration of sociable life: they are 'community ... bodied forth in its preoriginary structure as hospitality', as Edith Wyschogrod puts it (1998: 240). Like the gifts we looked at in Chapter 3, such gestures are always falling short, missing the mark, not effecting closure. This is inevitable, because community itself is never complete. It is constantly being interrupted or 'unworked' (Nancy, 1991: 38–40).

What Nancy takes from Bataille is the idea of a community that is not itself a work, that is not primarily about utility or exchange, but is set in motion by the very interruption of work or goal-oriented activity. Whereas community was once construed as having sprung forth from the earth, as we saw earlier, this vision has to some degree been superseded by a more 'modern' tendency to envisage communities arising out of work, production or a common 'project' (Wyschogrod, 1998: 233–4). For Bataille, both these options are damned by their closed circuitry, their hinging on the known and the calculable. In keeping with his resistance to any notion of the world that revolves on the expectation of a return, Bataille hungers for a community forged in response to the incitements of an outside, one that declines the dutiful traffic of reciprocity in favour of the radical asymmetry of a gratuitous opening (Nancy, 1991: Ch. 1). His is a community, as Nancy affirms, that begins to forge itself in advance of any shared understanding that what is given will eventually be repaid. One in which 'nothing is expected and nothing will be accepted', we might say.

And yet, as the post on katrinahelp continued: 'We all need help some time or another'. There is an inkling here that roles might be reversed, that the host might yet become a guest, the giver a recipient (see Dikeç, 2002). And indeed, when the equally ferocious Hurricane Rita followed hard on the heels of Katrina, evacuees in Texas found themselves quite suddenly contemplating a reversal of fortune.

Weird ... how the refugees are now becoming the helpers and the helpers are now becoming the refugees.
Here in Dallas, we're seeing Houston/Galveston folks now streaming in. Best course of action, seems to me, is for those of us who had to get out of New Orleans to now find a way to help the new arrivals. We've got some recent experience and, frankly, plenty of time to kill anyway. Besides – we share an affinity for rice, I-10, skanky water and iffy football teams ... We'll be looking for you. Good luck in your travels.[3]

From the point of view of the recently dispossessed, if feels as though there is something reassuring in this first whiff of reciprocity. It is as if the possibility of a return, the hint of an emerging 'economy' of care and support, is less a fall from the grace of pure gratuity and more a foretaste of sustainability – the promise of a community that might endure beyond the moment of its opening embrace. As Derrida would have it: 'That I am also essentially the other's other, and that I know I am, is the evidence of a strange symmetry whose trace appears nowhere in Levinas's descriptions' (1978: 128). It is an observation with relevance for any theorization of sociality that wishes to body forth from the singularity of an unexpectant offering to an other, for it is suggestive that mutuality or multi-directionality is not just a chance event on a far horizon but a potentiality that inheres in the very heart of a hospitable welcome. In the preoriginary stirrings of community, then, all participating bodies might not have access to a complete image of the common being of the social, but they may well figure out that the support gained from an other today could be passed on to other others in times to come, that 'what goes around comes around'.

In this way, the radical exteriority constitutive of the 'other community' might be somewhat more enmeshed in the internal machinations of its more deliberative or rational counterpart than is usually acknowledged (see Wyschogrod, 1998: 244). Nancy reminds us that Bataille himself was well aware that gratuitousness alone could not sustain the communal impulse: that he found cause to revisit the 'themes of justice and equality', recognizing that 'without these themes, regardless of the way one chooses to transcribe them, the communitarian enterprise can only be a farce' (Nancy, 1991: 20).

Just as the suspension of the law requires the safeguard of a respect for the law in general, and the impulsive act of generosity requires understanding and judgement to be effective, so too can it be argued that an unconditional hospitality calls forth certain conditions of its own. It does so for a number of reasons: because of the risk of unfairness to the many others that attends an unrestrained welcome to a single other, because of the need for hosts to protect and conserve the conditions of their own hospitality, because the guest too desires the right and honour of being a host. Thus, there is an imperative for the 'other community', the 'open community' to develop its own regulations, its own expectations, its own economy: 'without which *The* unconditional law of hospitality would be in danger of remaining a pious and irresponsible desire, without form and without potency, and of even being perverted at any moment' (Derrida, 2001b: 22–3; see also Dikeç et al., 2009).

If singularities are to merge into sociality, if surges and ripples of affect are to congeal into relatively enduring arrangements, they need to be able to summon up conditions, structures, systems. At the same time, as Molotch has reminded us, even long-established social organizations can loosen their cogs with a surge of empathy – and function all the more effectively for it. Indeed, formal institutions may well be continuously dependent on the generosity of their 'functionaries', however hard it may be to account for the hidden transfers of good will and affective energy at their core. For as Genevieve Vaughan insists, 'unilateral gift-giving is one of the load-bearing structures of society and not just wishful thinking or good intention transformed into its opposite' (2002: 98). If an event like Hurricane Katrina or the Indian Ocean Tsunami exposes the structured injustices and restricted channelings of power that unevenly determine vulnerability and resilience, I have been arguing, they also reveal the as-yet-unstructured or loosely grooved gestures of care and support that are the preoriginary impulse of communal existence.

Just as power works on and through bodies, so too do these primordial expressions of being-together manifest themselves in flows and offerings between material bodies, in the warm relay of abundance between one body and another (see Diprose, 2002; Vaughan, 2002). But the ever-present tendency of unruly earth processes to pressure and pummel bodies also reminds us that this corporeal permeability carries with it the traces of a further opening: the inescapable perviousness of living bodies to their material surroundings. And that in turn implies that communities are not simply pre-existing formations that find themselves obliged to respond to visitations of environmental stress and extremity, but that such challenges and promptings are written into sociable life even before a community is capable of recognizing itself as such.

Communing with the outside

As I suggested earlier, the opening of the political to the other-than-human is too important to be restricted to the critique of predominating configurations of power. It is not only in the dominant 'diagrams' of power that 'everything depends on the nature of the other forces with which the human forces become linked'. This insight applies no less to the hopeful side of Agamben's ethico-political thought and all the thinking around 'the other community' with which it converses.

The idea of a community that assembles not around a common identity but around its exposure to an unassimilated 'exteriority' shared by Agamben, Nancy and others also needs to be thought of as constitutively situated and enmeshed with a more-than-human world. For it is the raw and the processed physicality of the earth – howling wind, surging waters, failing levees – that unravels pre-existing bonds and propels exposed beings into each other's paths – and in this way re-enacts an originary imperative to being-in-common. And this is where theories of the other community need Serres's primordial story: not the convening around a contract, but the idea of the ungrounding of the ground as the impetus to communing with others. We need to remember that solar energy was bathing the earth, a vast river was overflowing and cyclones were whipping themselves up over the ocean long before there was a New Orleans or a Ville Platte. The point is not that the stumbling, chaotic, cobbling together of community in the midst of Katrina changes everything or anything. It is that whatever new bonds or ties were improvised in the heat of this event are reminders that vital aspects of the being of community emerge in response to the imperatives of the earth, that they have always done so and will continue to do so.

Much of the thinking of community in terms of a constitutive openness already gestures beyond the human. When Nancy speaks of being 'exposed to the exposure of the other' (1991: 31), it is more than a matter of witnessing a susceptibility to the violence or unsociability of the social. It is also about making contact, through our own reception to their bodily trials with a whole universe of impinging forces and elements. 'It is not so much the world of humanity as it is the world of the nonhuman to which humanity is exposed and which humanity, in turn, exposes', as Nancy professes (2000: 18). Here too, we must give credit to Bataille for forging the direct link between the permeability of one body to another, and the perviousness of these bodies to a forceful and tumultuous cosmos. For him, as we saw in the previous chapter, gifts of warmth and abundance that flow between living bodies are perpetuations of the sun's gifting of terrestrial life with excessive energy: a unilateral giving at a bodily level that recapitulates the radical asymmetry of solar exorbitance (Bataille, 1988 [1954]: 94; Stoekl, 2007: 93, 148). In this way, for Bataille, community is a resonance, a rippling after-affect, of an outburst that is not even of this earth – which behoves us to think always in terms of a communal ethos and a social economy that operates 'at the scale of the universe'.

Of contemporary theorists, it is Alphonso Lingis who has gone farthest in the elaboration of this idea of community as an opening to others that is also, inescapably, a window to the worldly events these others have lived through. In the chapter before last, we saw how Lingis made a case for the formative importance of our sensuous and somatic responsiveness to the imperatives that issue forth from the physical world. But this phenomenal experience is also mediated through our rapport with fellow beings, human and otherwise. Through the reception of the other, we also make contact with threats and allures of an insistent materiality: 'The face of the other is the place where the elemental surfaces to make demands' (Lingis, 1994: 132).

For Lingis, our answering to others whom we confront and do not turn away from is inevitably an encounter with all the physical forces they have endured, the extremes they have weathered, the illnesses they have stomached, the elements that have nourished or buffeted them. Whether or not we are attuned to it, when we face an other, what appears before us (and what appears of us before them) is 'a face made of carbon compounds, dust that shall return to dust, a face made of earth and air, made of warmth and blood, made of light and shadow' (Lingis, 1994: 11–12). The exhaustion we see in their eyes, the tension or tiredness in their body, the marks of injury or exposure, all serve to draw us more deeply into the life of the one before us. 'This perception extends on behind the substance enclosed with these surfaces, to the depth of the world behind it – envisions the road the other has travelled, the obstacles he has cleared, the heat of the sun he is fleeing' (Lingis, 1994: 23).

What Lingis has sketched out is an ontology of human being-together in which the bodies who are present are vehicles of an eventful, and often testing, physico-material history. With echoes of Levinas, he proposes that every community, every event of being-in-common is 'allied against the rumble of the world' (1994: 12). Each opening of one body to another brings into play an inherent inter-corporeal susceptibility – with all the risks and possibilities this entails. In so doing, it inevitably articulates a further opening of these bodies to the more extended volatility of the earthly environment. Every body carries its memory – psychically, somatically, socially – of past experience of the instability of the ground: the trace, we might say, of Serres's earth returned to chaos or Levinas's sudden loss of a supportive substrate. Whether these marks are raw and recent and etched on the surface or whether they are buried, hidden and irre-cuperable, they connect us – through the make-shifting of our com-munities – to the upheavals of the earth.

When floods or other convulsions take away the certainty of the world, what the ones who have lost their footing seek first is not the self-consciousness of a contract – the figuration of common past and future – so much as stability, a ground to stand on: ' The fatigue, the vertigo, and the homelessness in his or her body appeals for the force of terrestrial support from those whose earthbound bodies have the sense of this earth and this terrain to give' (Lingis, 1994: 128–9). The appeal that is answered by the welcome of Ville Platte, the appear-ance of a rescue vessel, A WARM PLACE TO SLEEP AND A SHOULDER TO CRY ON. If the one who is in need is not offered this support, or it is withdrawn: 'she will prefer to work out the ways and the operations on her own, by trial and error' (Lingis, 1994: 129). She will take sustenance from a flooded supermarket, they will sling together a raft, he will borrow an abandoned school bus.

Whenever earth processes test our tolerance, there is trial and there is error: we can see this in the desperate inventiveness of those who are scrabbling for survival, in the occasional bouts of organiza-tional rule-bending, in the ongoing improvisation that is community itself. Improvising is always done with the materials, the connections, the bodies at hand. Serres's scenario of a flood which demands a wholly fresh start clearly overstates the case: however severe the deluge, we never start afresh from the purity of a total effacement or the innocence of a re-levelled playing field.

But neither can we expect the laws, policies and practices that were generated in times of relative quiescence to acquit themselves adequately when the world convulses. This may well be a particularly acute problem in Western modernity, thanks to a propensity to process intimations of vulnerability like the Lisbon earthquake into assertions of strength and self-sufficiency. As de Waal puts it 'Modern western societies invest heavily in denying the inevitability of disaster' (2006: unpag.). Like modern political philosophy, modern jurisprudence and everyday social regulatory practices, to paraphrase Latour (2004b: 204), did not constitute themselves with the governance of natural catastrophes in mind. Today, after more than half a century of concerted re-education by earth scientists about the inherent dynamism of planetary and cosmic systems, we still seem to insist on being taken by surprise by the physical world's perfectly ordinary rhythms and realignments.

Perhaps those of us who, as Serres charges, have cultivated a peculiar distance from the periodicities and singularities of the earth might yet have something to learn from the way people in other times and places have ridden out inconstancies in the elements they relied upon. There is something to learn from the way others have learnt, over time, to live with uncertainty and change. Perhaps we have already been taking advantage of what others have learned about coping with environmental variability and extremity without acknowledging it. Or even being aware of it. In the next chapter, I delve into the *longue durée* of surviving, even thriving amid volatile physical forces, and look at what is at stake in the trial and error of responding to change over the long term.

Notes

1   Posted by Gassho, 18 September, 2005. Available at http://neworleans.metblogs.com/archives/2005/09/so.phtml (accessed 26/09/2005).

2   Downloaded from http://katrinahelp.info/wiki/index.php/Housing_Offered (accessed 30/09/2005).

3   Posted by Craig Giesecke, 20 September, 2005: available at http://neworleans.metblogs.com/archives/2005/09/so.phtml (accessed 26/09/2005).

7

'Burning for the Other':
Colonial Encounters on a Planet of Fire

Introduction: big country in flames

When the sunset was a deep and angry red, my parents would tell us it was because, over the sea, the big country was on fire. My brothers and I climbed the cliffs on the west coast, eager young eyes hoping for a glimpse of smoke and flame, but saw only the blue horizon. Sometimes, when there was a strong westerly, ash fell from the sky. We felt sorry for the people whose country had fierce, unstoppable fires. Sorry, but also excited and a little envious.

Australia has been ablaze once again – the 2009 fires in Victoria, one of the worst natural disasters the country has endured. Once more, there were images of homes, farms and towns laid to waste. Small figures were set against the inferno: volunteer firefighters, some of whom had already lost their own homes, some still unaware of the fate of their own families and neighbours. Wildfire has a way of picking through a settlement, turning some homes into smoking ruins, leaving others untouched – bringing a community together, searing a dividing line through it. The 'loss of a stable ground', the shorthand I have been using for the impact of a physical upheaval, scarcely does justice to a force that sucks the very air away, that turns the solidity of a shelter into an excuse for heightened fury. Even the idea of an inherent human vulnerability, a constitutive exposure, barely begins to speak of what flames can do to living bodies, their fearsome literalizing of Levinas's 'denuding beyond the skin' (1998a [1974]: 49).

There is talk of human-induced global warming exacerbating the heat waves that parched the bush, though many settler Australians have already learnt that the sun-burned country they love is also is a pyrophytic land, a continent in which fire is as much a part of life as sunshine, drought and animals that bite. A pronounced seasonal distribution of sunlight, dryness and rain, a flora that alternately burgeons and bakes, brings south-eastern

Australia together with California and the Mediterranean Basin, as the earth's most fire-prone regions. These terrains may be extreme, but they are not exceptional. Nearly all landscapes with vegetative cover will burn, naturally, sooner or later. And just about every stretch of land that will burn of its own accord has also been burned – for thousands, sometimes tens or hundreds of thousands of years – by its human inhabitants. Australia may be a fire country, but this is also a fire planet.

Earthquakes, tsunamis, floods, I have been arguing, are each experienced by those caught or pushed into their paths as extraordinary and climactic occurrences. They are life-threatening and life-changing. But each of these events is also extremely ordinary in geophysical terms, part of the planet's ongoing, offbeat rhythms – as normal as tidal ebb and flow, the beat of a heart, the turn of the seasons. Looking at the propensity of the earth's vegetated environments to burn helps push this question of the 'normal chaos' of the elements further. All communities live with and through fire. But some more intensely, more intimately than others. What is a natural disaster for one group of people – the most devastating event they can imagine – is for others everyday work and play.

In the last chapter, we saw how responsiveness to the periodic instability and extremity of earth processes might be seen as an originary impulse to the formation of community. Communities, as Nancy and others have argued, are not fully or even primarily generated out of what individuals have in common, but emerge out of the event of people coming together in their difference, with such more readily recognizable characteristics as reciprocity, exchange, shared goals or values as 'emergent properties' that arise later. By this logic, the rumbling of the earth is an ancient and unending imperative for human communing, not simply testing existing communities but reactivating, again and again, a primordial impulse for being together with others. This makes of fire a complex and ambivalent 'object', at once an environmental hazard capable of leaving individuals or groups lost and bereft, and the cosy hub – the campfire, the hearth – around which togetherness or being-in-common is re-enacted.

More than this, for most of the time we have been human, fire has been our pre-eminent means of modifying the environment, of opening up pathways, of rendering the earth more fruitful, more homely, less hazardous. So important is fire, or has fire been, across most of the earth's terrestrial surfaces, that it is perhaps only in Europe that we could imagine a 'biopolitics' that was not first and foremost a 'pyropolitics' – centred on the regulation, manipulation and enhancement of fire. Or is what we have come to call biopolitics, already, covertly, a set of practices concerning the governance of what can be burned, how, where and by whom? Much of the management of human populations, of energy, of life itself in which the modern west has engaged itself, both at home and abroad, I argue, has been premised on the drive to contain or channel fire. Then again, the very fact that Europeans and other migrant populations have been able to compose so much of the terrestrial earth as a space of mobility and settlement speaks of the capacity of other people to manage fire, to alter landscapes, to render environments 'hospitable'.

In this chapter, drawing on the work of fire theorist Stephen Pyne, I explore the issue of learning to live with the rhythms and extremes of the earth. Amid the tragedy of the Indian Ocean Tsunami there were salutary stories about individuals, groups or communities evading the worst of the waves because they recognized the warning signs: hopeful tales pushing against the current of widespread failure to read the signals and respond accordingly. In the case of Katrina, I touched upon the idea that local know-how may have been helpful in coping with the chaos after the levees broke. But this is just skimming the surface next to the knowledge about living and working with fire that has accrued over generations in many parts of the world. Fire, unlike earthquakes, hurricanes or tsunamis can be cut down to size, corralled, tamed. A sense of the importance of working with fire, of its role in shaping environments, raises questions about what we might owe those collective bodies that come before us, those who opened up and secured the ground on which we live or through which we travel. Levinas (1998a: 50) has spoken of 'burning for the Other' with regard to an unruly desire to reach across the rifts that separate one from another. Histories of fire tell us that others have been burning for us, quite literally, all over the planet and for a very long time.

Encountering fire

The faces that stare out from images of the recent Victorian bushfires look battered, drained, defeated. They are also overwhelmingly white. Fires like these have been tormenting settlers for a long time. Essayist and poet Mary Gilmore, who spent her childhood in rural New South Wales in the 1860s and 1870s, documented the constant threat of wildfire – both natural and accidently sparked by her own people – observing how it played out in the context of relations between her settler community and the local Wiradjuri people. "'Send for the blacks!'", she recalls, 'was the first cry on every settlement when a fire started' (1934: 152; see also Main, 2004).[1] Before adding:

> it was the natives who taught our first settlers to get bushes and beat out a conflagration. My grandparents used to tell of how new immigrants when they first came to the country, unaccustomed to the danger in the wild country, would start fires and let them run heedless of the result; and then stand panic-stricken at having loosed something they could not control. And they would go on to relate how the natives would run for bushes, put them into the immigrants' hands, and show them how to beat back the flame as it licked up the grass. Indeed it was a constant wonder, when I was little, how easily the blacks would check a fire before it grew too big for close handling ... . (1934: 152)

Reporting in 1840, Lieutenant Stokes of the *Beagle* was surprised to see Australian Aborigines 'engaged in kindling, moderating, and directing the destructive element, which under their care seems almost to change its nature, acquiring, as it were, complete docility, instead of the ungovernable fury we are accustomed to ascribe to it' (cited in Pyne, 1998: unpag; see also Hallam, 1979: 33). Many other early accounts join with Stokes in affirming the indigenous peoples' ease and dexterity with fire, though it is rarer to see an explicit contrast drawn with settler practices. Gilmore, however, is an astute observer of different bodily dispositions and their place within a broader economy of managing natural forces:

> The white man used large bushes and tired himself out with their weight and by heavy blows; the blacks took small bushes and used little and light action. The white expended the energy of panic; the blacks acted in familiarity, as knowing how and what to do. They used arm action only, where the white man used his whole body. Where, as a last resort, the white man lit a roaring and continuous fire-break, the aboriginal set the lubras[2] to make tiny flares, each separate, each put out in turn, and all lit roughly in line ... The aboriginals said that not only must fire be met by fire, but that it could only be fought while still not too hot ... when it became so hot that it burnt and exhausted men, it had to be met from a distance. They also said that a big fire as a fire-break was as dangerous as a big fire itself, as the wind might change and bring it back on the watchers ... . (1934: 152–3)

Once again, it appears that Beck's claim that '(o)urs is the age of the smallest possible cause for the greatest possible destruction'

(1995: 4) invites a much wider application. To encounter wildfire is to be reminded that this is a runaway planet, not just a runaway epoch (see Goudsblom, 1992: 1). Along with the recognition that we did not have to wait on modernity to be confronted by densely connected and delicately poised systems, stories of fire and its human deployment also prompt us to reconsider the historicizations of risk now on offer.

The idea that prior to the manufactured hazards of the industrial era, people faced a nature 'animated by demons' (Beck, 1995: 76) or driven by the 'ineffable intentions of the Deity' (Giddens, 1990: 30) simply will not do. Far from facing a world of hazards over which they had no influence or control, fire historian Stephen Pyne insists that the highly skilled use of fire 'allowed the Aborigine to move a continent' (1997a: 31). This is an acknowledgement that is by no means new (see Jones, 1969). In his *Recollections of Squatting in Victoria* in the 1840s and 1850s, settler Edward Curr weighed up the overall significance of intentional fire use, which led him to doubt 'whether any section of the human race has exercised a greater influence on the physical condition of any large portion of the globe than the wandering savages of Australia' (1965 [1883]: 88).

The question we might better ask is why the demonization of fire amongst those who call themselves modern? As well as an insight into indigenous practices, Gilmore's account gives us a glimpse of a mode of European bodily comportment: a particular disposition of forces and corporeal capacities, caught in the moment of its unravelling. As we will see, this has much to do with the decisive climatic and biological differences between north-western Europe and south-eastern Australia. But it also says a lot about a set of socio-cultural transformations that took place in an early modernizing Europe, changes that had vital implications for the use and the conception of fire.

At the same time that urban populations were being subjected to new disciplinary and regulatory practices, rural traditions of burning fallow were also undergoing restriction and containment. Dismissed as wasteful and unruly, free ranging fire was cast out of the landscape. And with it went a host of ancient customary practices of managing open cast blazes (Pyne, 1997b: 162–8, 2001: 145–6). The object of 'a *general prohibition*' in everyday life, fire ceased to be of interest even to science, as Gaston Bachelard noted (1987: 11, 2). And thereafter, Johann Goudsblom adds, it dropped from the agenda of social science (1992: 3). When émigré Europeans in another hemisphere eventually found themselves face to face with elemental forces beyond their measure, there was little alternative but to turn to other collective bodies if disaster was to be averted.

Disaster, of course, could not always be averted, and local expertise was not always available or heeded. The recent spate of bushfires that Australians now refer to as Black Saturday bring back memories of Black Friday – the blazes that took their name from 13 January 1939 but raged across the state of Victoria for a week – taking numerous lives, immolating dozens of settlements and destroying millions of acres of forest. The devastation cast a pall of dread and anxiety over white Australia, initiating a rethinking of the role of fire that eventually ushered in the era of prescribed burning (Pyne, 1991: 309–14; Griffiths, 2001: Ch. 10).

More than this, the holocaust seemed to have sparked a new sensitivity towards temporality among a settler society that had scarcely seen out a century and a half on their new continent. As head of the Royal Commission into the fires, Judge Leonard Stretton said of those caught up in the flames of Black Friday: 'They had not lived long enough' (cited in Griffiths, 2001: vii). Tom Griffiths teases out the full import of this deceptively simple pronouncement:

> The judge ... was not commenting on the youthfulness of the dead; he was lamenting the environmental knowledge of both victims and survivors. He was pitying the innocence of European immigrants in a land whose natural rhythms they did not understand. He was depicting the fragility and brevity of a human lifetime in a forest where life cycles and fire regimes had the periodicity and ferocity of centuries. He was indicting a whole society. (2001: vii)

In accentuating the briefness of European tenure on the land, Victoria's week of hellfire and all subsequent infernos also gesture at the feat of those who have made a home of the planet's driest inhabited continent for tens of thousands of years. But there is more at stake here than a simple contrast between Australian Aboriginal wisdom and white settler ingenuousness, more to be done than merely setting traditional capacities to 'go with the flow' of nature's forces against modern intransigence and rigidity. A simple celebration of Aboriginal achievements in managing fire-prone environments – awe-inspiring though they may be – obscures as much as it highlights, if it does not ask how, under what conditions, and at what cost, such expertise has been acquired. We may not ever know exactly how many of their own 'Black Fridays', 'Red Tuesdays' and 'Ash Wednesdays' Australia's first human inhabitants had to endure in the course of learning to live and work with fire. But those of us who have appropriated or inherited 'fire countries' need to ask such questions. As, perhaps, should all current inhabitants of this 'fire planet'.

Ancient fire histories may be deeply interred, but they are not entirely inaccessible. On the basis of charcoal and pollen sediments from parkland around Sydney, paleoecologists Manu Black and Scott Mooney have recently pieced together evidence of a past episode in which climatic conditions and associated fire regimes underwent a sudden shift. What appears as a dramatic spike in the graph of charcoal deposits is indicative of a rapid increase in the prevalence and intensity of fire in south-eastern Australia around 5,700 years ago (2007: 47). This signature of irrupting wildfire shows up at the same time not only in comparable records from other sites in Australia, but right around the Pacific Basin.

These convergent traces have been interpreted as the footprint of the El Niño Southern Oscillation, the planet-girdling ocean atmosphere system that serves to dissipate the solar warmth received by the equatorial Pacific Ocean to cooler latitudes. Paleoclimatologists believe that ENSO passed through a critical threshold some 57 centuries ago, its irregular rhythms of drought and dampness suddenly intensifying at this juncture (Black and Mooney, 2007; Caviedes, 2001: 256). What Black and Mooney's charcoal sediments offer is a frightening intimation of the impact of this transition at ground level: wildfire of a scale and ferocity that could only have come as a shock to those who had experienced thousands of years of much less intense El Niño events – even if, like the Aboriginal people of the Sydney basin, they had already been working with fire for many millennia.

But the charcoal and pollen record hints at further changes, no less noteworthy. For some 2,500 years after the turning point, fire more or less maintains its new intensity, flaring, waning, flaring again. And then, around 3,000 years ago, there is a marked tailing off. There is no evidence of an accompanying shift in the ENSO regime, however. Nor does it appear that fire ceases to be a significant force in the landscape. It is just that big fierce fires seem to have given way to smaller and more numerous low-intensity burns. Black and Mooney's explanation is tentative, but intriguing. They suggest that by this stage Aboriginal land management using a strategy of intentional and controlled burning had developed to the point where it could mitigate the intensities of El Niño's deadly wet – dry fluctuations – and pre-empt the risk of vast and deadly conflagrations (2007: 50).

The evidence is sketchy, and entangled with other variables – such as increasing Aboriginal population density. But what we may be seeing in the charcoal record are the vital signs of 2–3,000 years of improvisation and experimentation by human collectives in response to the effects of a major climatic change. These indices cannot tell us about the experience of an abrupt climatic shift – what it would have been like to be confronted by a sudden change in a local fire regime. They do not spell out the human impact of these momentous transitions, or the personal and social cost of learning to live with them. But what we may be seeing in the ash cores is a trace of the background story to the indigenous pyrotechnical skills that so impressed Stokes, Gilmore and other late arrivals in Australia: an intimation that the price of ease and familiarity with 'the destructive element' was an almost unthinkably extended effort, the putting of bodies on the line over countless generations. All of which, with the privilege of hindsight, we might see encapsulated in Gilmore's account of the passing of bushes and torches – the paraphernalia of working with fire – from one people to another (Clark, 2010b).

Fire planet, fire species

In recent years, there have been major outbreaks of wildfire not only in Australia, but in Russia, Spain, Greece, Croatia, Kenya, the Yukon and California. In many cases, the shock with which people living in or near woodlands have confronted burning forests invites comparison with the failure of so many contemporary coastal dwellers to accustom themselves to the possibility of seismically generated waves. In the quest for explanations of these fires, there is increasing reference to heat waves or drought bearing the signature of global warming, and even more frequent charges of arson or identification of such accidental ignitions as faulty power lines or sparks from industrial machinery. Attributing culpability, in this way, comes up against much the same problem of isolating causes from within a dense network of interacting variables that we looked at with regard to climate change in Chapter 5. It is not just that the tiniest input can spark a massive, runaway event, but that the event itself is utterly indifferent as to whether its trigger is anthropogenic or natural; a careless cigarette or a fork of lightning.

What most reported explanations still share is the assumption that forest fire is an abnormality, and is thus both undesirable and avoidable. Stephen Pyne and many of his compatriot pyro-technicians think otherwise. Reviewing such monstrous blazes as Australia's Ash Wednesday of 1983, Yellowstone National Park in 1988 and Sweden's Gotland fires of 1992, Pyne proposes that a unifying thread is the counter-productive effect of strategies of fire prevention (1997a: 320; see also Jones, 1969; Franklin, 2006). The idea that fire could be completely banished from wooded landscapes – institutionalized in policies of total fire exclusion, he argues, led to the long-term build-up of combustible biomass. Eventually, the amassing of flammable material brought forests to a critical point where fire was at once inevitable and guaranteed to be of an extreme intensity.

Though I am unaware of any explicit link with the work of Georges Bataille in Pyne's writing, the resonance is clear. Bataille's own profuse references to fire may be mostly metaphorical, but his logic that resisting any 'immolation' of constantly accumulating matter-energy would eventually lead to a 'conflagration' invites an objective reading. We need to recall that there was an empirical core to this reasoning. Bataille had a clear sense that more solar energy bathed the earth than plants require to grow, demanding some kind of die-off to make room for new life: an expression of his reconceptualization of earthly economies 'at the scale of the universe' that drew upon Vernadsky's then novel theorization of the biosphere. It's worth adding that Vernadsky himself was so attuned to the interplay of the sun's energy and terrestrial vegetation that he referred to plant life as 'green fire' (cited in Sagan and Schneider, 2007: 231).

Like Bataille and Vernadsky, and unlike the forensic forest fire investigators who sift through the ashes looking for discrete causes of ignition, Pyne engages with wild fire as part of a 'general economy' – at the scale of the earth as a whole, in all its perennial openness to the energy of the solar system. As the opening passages of *World Fire* (1997a: 3) spell out, for the chemical reaction that is fire to occur there must be combustible material, free oxygen and a means of ignition. Elsewhere in our solar system, Saturn's moon Titan has fuel – in the form of methane, Mars has traces of oxygen, Jupiter has the spark of lightning. But only our planet has all three essential components in a workable combination. With analogies to the theorem of an integrative and self-regulating biosphere pioneered by Vernadsky, Pyne stresses that it is life itself which generated the conditions that render the earth uniquely conducive to fire.

Marine phytoplankton first produced oxygen as a by-product of photosynthesis, the vascular plants which colonized the earth's landmasses some 400 million years ago supplied the carbon fuels and helped stabilize atmospheric oxygen levels, and it is the inorganic physics of lightning and volcanism which provide the ignition (Pyne, 1997b: 16–17, 2001: 3–6). But the proportions have to be right. Experimental evidence suggests that with an atmospheric composition of less than 12 per cent, free oxygen fire smoulders and fails to flare – over 25 per cent and the whole planet would go up in one almighty fireball. Higher oxygen content does not necessarily translate directly into more fire, but seems to be mediated by available fuels. The co-evolution of fire and life, Pyne argues, helps to maintain oxygen levels and fuel loads in a range which is sustainable: fire and vegetation working together to keep the planet poised between respiration and conflagration. Thus, 'if fire could not exist without fuel, neither would fuels – the planet's vegetative cover – exist without the evolutionary and ecological presence of fire. Each has directly shaped the other' (Pyne, 2001: 10).

Across the earth's continental surfaces, wherever there is vegetation under an open sky, Pyne continues, there is the possibility of fire: 'virtually every environment can burn, and most eventually do' (1997b: 17). Fire opens densely forested land to sunlight, it purges ecosystems of pests and pathogens, strips away acidic humus, cloaks the ground in fertile ash. By accelerating the circulation of nutrients, flames can jolt an ecosystem to new levels of productivity and stimulate biological diversification (Pyne, 1997b: 233, 250, 1998: 9). In this way – as disturbance and catalyst – fire plays a hand in the evolution of life, setting a challenge to living things, selecting for form and conduct that is favourable to further firing.

Most terrestrial species have found ways of accommodating to occasional fire, and many have cast their lot in with frequent fire. Amongst all the pyrophiliacs, in Pyne's account, one species has been exceptionally successful in accelerating the feedback loop that favours free-burning fire. By capturing and propagating naturally occurring fire, and later, by generating new fire, humans sped up the selection of fire-tolerant vegetation, extending the scope and the frequency of fire – and in the process they dramatically expanded their own range (Pyne, 2001: 25). From the adoption of fire tending, over a million years ago, through the move to fire starting some 100,000 years ago, fire use has effectively emerged as the biological niche of our species. If this is a fire planet, Pyne boldly pronounces, then we are fire creatures. 'The prevalence of humans is largely attributable to their control over fire; and the distribution and characteristics of fire have become profoundly dependent on humans', he concludes (1997a: 4; see also Goudsblom, 1992: Ch. 1, 194–5).

Pyne's narrative is intentionally pyro-centric, and it is up to his audience – if we want to reverse the loss of intellectual interest in fire noted by Bachelard – to decide how far we will accompany him. The point I want to take from his account, with full conviction, is that the deep historical embroilment of our species in free-ranging fire has made of our fire use not simply a habit, or a role, but a responsibility. By virtue of the ways that the human application of fire has shaped the dynamic interplay of the organic and inorganic elements of this planet, Pyne argues, any abdication from the deployment of fire has serious consequences. '(I)t has been an ecological and moral duty of hominids since the days of *Homo erectus* to actively manage fire', he counsels. 'Because anthropogenic fire is a symbiosis between humans and the earth, the decision not to burn can be as ecologically fatal as promiscuous burning' (1997a: 253). Aboriginal fire scholar Marcia Langton makes a similar argument, more pointedly applied to her own country. For white settler Australians not to confront the issue of Aboriginal land management practices, to not front up to the possibility of a 'co-dependent relationship between human and non-human species resulting from burning practices,' for Langton constitutes a kind of wilful ignorance or 'studious' forgetting (1998: 53).

To try and remove fire from an environment or ecosystem adapted to it, Langton, Pyne and other experts insist, is to dramatically transform the conditions under which a whole array of species lives. It is, in nearly all cases, to impact negatively rather than positively on the quality and quantity of biological life. It is also to render our own lives less secure. One thing that hominid fire attendants probably worked out fairly early on was that by encouraging a large number of small or moderate fires they earned themselves protection against less frequent but larger and fiercer fires (Pyne, 1997a: 303). It is the signature of this strategy that Black and Mooney seem to have unearthed in the charcoal record from around Sydney, and it is a tactic that is still used in many parts of the world today.

But there is more at stake than the instrumental logic of hazard reduction, as signalled by Pyne's claim that fire use is a moral obligation. With regard to Australian Aboriginal fire regimes, the longest known continuous tradition of intentional fire use, Head and Hughes observe: 'while much research has focused on economic objectives and the ecological outcomes of fire use, there has also been recognition that fire was widely used to achieve the social objective of fulfilling responsibilities to country' (cited in Langton, 1998: 40). The Ngarinman people, of Australia's Northern Territories, characteristically contrast 'quiet' country, which has been tended with fire, with 'wild' or uncared-for country. 'Quiet country is country in which those who know how to read the signs see human action of the most responsible sort', writes Deborah Bird Rose (cited in Langton, 1998: 40–1; see also Franklin, 2006: 564). And this is a responsibility, Langton insists, that is intimately tied up with an ethos of sharing natural habitats with others, including other-than-human beings (1999: 173).

The trials of fire

Debate about the environmental impacts of fire use by the earliest inhabitants of Australia and the Americas gets heated, especially when the issue of the extinction of large animals is on the agenda. Whatever sealed the fate of Pleistocene megafauna (evidence currently sides more with climate change), the question about whether indigenous peoples have been ecologically destructive or benign can obscure a more intriguing and more ethically searching issue. That is: the question of how – under what conditions and at what cost – early colonizing populations learned to live in new and challenging environments. As Marcia Langton points out, the original settlers of Australia would have come from wetter tropical regions, lands that offered little experience relevant to coping with the fierce wildfires they encountered in their new home (1999: 169). And so they were compelled to take chances, to improvise, to experiment.

In Chapter 2, we touched on the idea that a certain experimental attitude had escaped the confines of the laboratory. As Bruno Latour argues, in conversation with Ulrich Beck, issues like global climate change and emergent diseases associated with novel agricultural practices signal a broader contextualizing of experimentality: 'The problem is that while we know how to conduct a scientific experiment in the narrow confines of a laboratory, we have no idea how to pursue collective experiments in the confusing atmosphere of a whole culture' (2003: 31). But who exactly are 'we'? What we may need here is an injection of Latour's own scepticism about the uniqueness of our so-called modernity – for a sense of the *longue durée* of fire management is suggestive of a necessarily experimental attitude. It points to an immense succession of field trails that greatly precedes any confinement to the laboratory. Indeed, as Pyne argues, fire ecology has never made it as a laboratory science (2001: 15).

Fire is a recalcitrant object of lab science because every fire season is different and every fire is unique. Each new season and each individual burning brings together its own combination of weather, topography, ignition and, most importantly, available fuel. Fuel loads themselves are the outcome of an intricate interplay of soil and climate; of insects, diseases and organic decomposers; of storms and other weather events; and of the fires that have gone before (Pyne, 1998: 33). 'Real fires do not occur in strict cycles', Pyne intones, '… they burn in eccentric rhythms. They integrate not only seasonal and phenological cycles, but events that are unexpected, stochastic, irrepeatable, and irreversible' (1998: 30). Because the conditions under which fire occurs are constantly changing, fire too is essentially changeable.

Climate, as we have seen, is a vastly complex and dynamic system. As a mediator between the forces of biological life and climate, open-cast fire partakes of this almost unthinkable complexity. And this means that systems of fire – like the elemental forces they bring together – have rhythms, patterns, periodicities of their own. Fire has its self-organized critical points, its thresholds, its runaway episodes, its own emergent properties. Western scientists admit to finding it immensely difficult to identify the moment at which a real-world physical system is ready to pass over a threshold into a new regime or state. But this is precisely the kind of knowledge that technicians in the field – 'nomad scientists' if you will – gradually build up over generations of working with the heterogeneous and irregularly distributed elements of their environments.

Careful burning, as skilled pyro-technicans and those who have worked with them attest, is a matter of judging the bulk, moisture content and specific combustible qualities of available fuels, weighing up wind speed and direction, anticipating forthcoming turns in the weather, and from such assessments and an immensity of other small calculations, making decisions about the best time for firing and the most suitable type of fire for the conditions. As Deleuze and Guattari famously expounded in *A Thousand Plateaus* (1987: 369–73), the key to this kind of knowledge is becoming attuned to the moments in which physical systems pass through transitional points. In a field of shifting forces, variable energies and inconsistent aggregates of matter, mastery is out of the question: it must be a matter of working with, rather than against the transmutational properties of the physical world. Thus, '(o)ne is obliged to follow when one is in search of the "singularities" of a matter, or rather of a material' (Deleuze and Guattari, 1987: 372). Because know-how is context-dependent, and the context is constantly re-configuring itself, knowledge resists codification into invariable rules or abstract principles. The skill of a timely intervention must be acquired tacitly, through careful and patient experimentation. But changing conditions mean this experimentation is never-ending: working with fire and other 'flows' is inevitably a trial and error process, a learning that is never complete.

Provincializing European fire

Though a certain kind of Western 'state' science features in Deleuze and Guattari's account as the vehicle of another kind of knowing and doing – law-like, generalizable, context-independent – their intention was never simply to set up a binary division between the West and the rest of the world (1987: 363–9). Europe too has its traditions of vernacular experimentation, and Western science draws upon other traditions of engaging with matter in the field. The history of European fire and its encounters with a world of other fires is interesting in this regard, not just for its reminder of the past importance of 'nomadic' practices, but also because of its intimations that even abstract principles bear the trace of their own particular physical context.

As Pyne (1997b) recounts with fervour, there was a time, a long time, in which intentionally set fire played just as vital a role in European land management as it did on other inhabited landmasses. Customary burning practices ranged from the landnam or *svedjebruk* of the Scandavian boreal to the torching of the Mediterranean littoral, from the firing of heath and moors of the British Isles to the Slavic variant of swidden known as *zalezh*. These were all variants of shifting cultivation, in which cropping and animal foraging briefly took advantage of the ash-enriched soil before moving on to freshly fired clearings. Then, gradually, as tillage and grazing intensified, a new system evolved in temperate Europe in which pastoralists and cultivators stayed put, while the fields themselves rotated (Pyne, 2001: 96).

The key to this tightening of the circuits of agricultural production was not simply the alternation of different kinds of farming – with varying demands on the soil – but the regular resting of plots:

the system known as fallow. But if fixed field rotation meant less fire, it most certainly did not mean no fire. For as Pyne insists, fallow was not simply land abandoned to weedy and woody regrowth. It was essentially land in which vegetation was left to accumulate for the very purpose of feeding fire: to stoke the flames that fertilized the field for the next round of sowing and reaping (2001: 71–2). In this way, free-burning fire may have become increasingly contained and disciplined, but it remained a vital part of rural folk culture, cherished for its role in the regeneration of land and life.

This was, however, not how it appeared to a new breed of agricultural experts, raised in cities and tutored in urban academies. For the new metropolitan intelligentsia and officialdom, fire was experienced primarily as an expression of social unrest or breakdown, a mark of excess and disorder (Pyne, 1997b: 162, 2001: 83, 145–6). It is no coincidence that the notion of curfew, as a means of keeping tabs on the populace, is derived from *couvre feu*, covering or dousing a fire (Pyne, 2001: 109; Goudsblom, 1992: 69). At the same time that urban populations were being subjected to new regulatory practices, enlightenment agronomists were busily stamping out rural folk traditions of burning fallow. Just as unruly urbanites were being induced to channel and augment their bodily energies (Foucault, 1991 [1975]), Europe's peasant farmers were compelled to quell their fires and desist from fallow – so as to tighten and amplify the energetic circuits of agricultural production.

According to the rationale which Bataille dissects so powerfully, fire came to stand for a squandering of resources. Enthralled by a Newtonian universe of celestial bodies rotating in orderly and predictable orbits, Enlightenment agronomists set about closing the loops of agricultural production (see Fernández-Galiano, 2000: 37–8). If the practice of fallow came to appear as a glitch in the strict cyclicality of Nature's economy, fallow that went up in smoke was an unconscionable waste. Henceforth, those products of the earth which could not usefully be consumed were to be ploughed back, reinvested in the interest of increasing soil fertility and expanding output (Pyne, 1997b: 162–8, 2001: 145–6). In this way, across Europe, customary practices of working with fire as a means of modulating variable flows of warmth, moisture and biomass were gradually attenuated and extinguished, a loss which forms the distant backcloth to the encounter of white settlers with Australian fire that I spoke of earlier in the chapter.

The story, needless to say, is more complex than this. By the sixteenth and seventeenth centuries, Western Europeans were experiencing fuel shortages, timber scarcity and soil erosion, and the threat of famine and poverty-induced disease was never far away. Those who sought to rationalize agriculture were more than just Enlightenment ideologues, they were responding to real material challenges (Pyne, 1997b: 163). But the irony was that traditional field rotation – with the firing of fallow driving the renewal of soil fertility – already constituted a fairly tight circuit of its own, albeit one open to the 'general economy' of the solar flux. It was a circle torn apart by the attempt to prohibit burning, a rupture that exacerbated rather than solved the pressures on the ecology of rural Europe. Reducing fallow and banishing fire, Pyne argues, had deleterious effects on biodiversity and on agro-ecosystems more generally: 'Without regular firing the land became decadent, biodiversity shrank, and wildfires raged more intensely' (1997b: 171). This profound ecological shift would have been even more immediately unsustainable but for a series of developments that substituted for the flows of energy and biomass that were short-circuited by agricultural 'rationalization'. These developments were to transform not only the ecology and economies of Europe, but those of the globe in its entirety.

What occurred under the guise of a tightening of the energetic circuit of agriculture was in fact a radical opening into new and previously untapped sources of energy. At first, this supplement was drawn from Europe's overseas colonies: as biotic surplus extracted from distant 'outfields' subsidized the European infield. But the most momentous subsidy was to come from tapping into that 'fallow' that lay beneath the earth's surface: the mass of sequestered fuel provided by the fossilized remains of past biological life. Effectively, fallow and its firing was exiled from enlightened agriculture, and its place was taken by hydro-carbons appropriated not only from other places, but from other times – pumped into the agricultural ecosystem in the form of fertilizers, pesticides, herbicides and the exertions of the internal combustion engine (Pyne, 1997b: 164). Fire, as Pyne hastens to remind us, remained integral; it is just that free-burning fire had been displaced by another kind of burning, which gave every impression of being contained, predictable and orderly: a type of fuel and a sort of fire which was to allow for the tightly coiled cycle of agricultural production to open into an ever-increasing spiral of reinvestment and increased output. This, then, is the backstory for the issue of anthropogenic climate change we encountered in Chapter 3.

Before we come to the consequences of these innovations for the wider world, there is one more point to note about the energetic transformation of Europe. Though some of its peoples may have taken the lead on global fire suppression, this should not be taken to mean that Europe is in any sense representative of the planet as a whole. Pyne's argument is that European 'pyrophobia' is far more than a cultural affectation: it is a techno-cultural phenomenon made feasible by a set of quite specific biophysical and meteorological conditions (1997b: 3–6). The case that Pyne makes insistently throughout his numerous tomes on fire is that Europe, like most other regions, has its own unique fire ecology. But some places are more unique than others. One of the special features of the north-western promontory of Eurasia is the absence of a natural fire season. Most of temperate Europe lacks that alternation of wet and dry periods that is the condition of wildfire elsewhere: its well-dispersed rainfall and chronic sogginess rendering this region 'an anomalously fire-free patch of Earth' (Pyne, 2001: 168). This meant that anthropogenic fire has been *even more vital* there than in most other places.

After the receding of the last of the Pleistocene glaciations, some 8–10,000 years ago, most of Europe was colonized by dense shade forest, presenting a formidable obstacle to human habitation. It was only by way of the introduction of fire, through the long slow prising open of this dark canopy by the blazes kindled by generations of shifting cultivators that more sedentary agriculture became an option (Pyne, 1997c: 20, 2001: 95). But when the old forest was gone, what remained were rich, freshly churned, post-glacial soils which could support farming at an intensity that few other regions would tolerate. Temperate Europe was effectively converted into a mosaic of garden plots. It was this peculiar density of cultivation, coupled with the lack of a definite fire season and a paucity of natural fire, that made it possible to put the squeeze on fire: 'encourag(ing) the belief that fire was, in principle, a strictly human agency, that it was a convenient tool but not an essential process' (Pyne, 1997b: 4).

In short, Europe north of the Mediterranean was amenable to a degree of control and containment of fire that was exceptional on a world scale (Pyne, 1997b: 156, 2001: 81–2). This specificity was to have profound consequences when self-assured emissaries from metropolitan Europe set about imprinting their own ideas of biotic production and energy use across the wildly variable expanses of our planet.

Exporting fire exclusion

As Europeans began their global dispersal around half a millennia ago, they took with them conceptions of fire and techniques of fire use that came into frequent collision with local conditions and long-established regimes of burning. Settlers from some parts of Europe introduced their own traditions of shifting cultivation along the mobile and tumultuous contact zones that came to be known as 'frontiers'. Other migrants discovered passions for broadcast burning for which they had no living memory or experience (Pyne, 2001: Ch 8). Some had even been banished to the colonies for the very crime of continuing to burn in disregard for the outlawing of fire in their own rural homelands, only to find themselves consigned to regions immeasurably more fire prone than those from which they had been expelled (Pyne, 1997b: 359).

The results were mixed, but usually messy, and sometimes cata-strophic, entangled as they so often were with the decimation of prior inhabitants and the disruption or cessation of existing modes of fire management. But not all impacts were fatal or final. If the rough guide to colonization generally affirmed one's own practices of burning while disparaging the fire of 'the native', at ground level the shocks and rigours of a strange environment called for improv-isation (Pyne, 1997b: 464–5, 472, 2001: 144). This often included the kind of desperate embrace of indigenous practices that Mary Gilmore documented in rural New South Wales, which in places eventually gave rise to hybridizations of traditional and introduced fire. Beyond the flaming frontier of the North American and Australasian settler colonies, as rural life bedded into more seden-tary patterns, free-ranging fire in all of its guises came to be seen as more of a threat than an agent. Here, in a recapitulation of Europe's own suppressive drive, fire was subjected to increasing levels of discipline and containment, if it was to be tolerated at all (Pyne, 1997c: 24).

In regions which proved resistant to European-style farming and white settlement, colonizing powers found other ways of imposing their own order on the landscape. Reserving tracts of land that had been left vacant by the demise of their previous inhabitants or prised out of the hands of long-term occupants emerged as a leading strat-egy for the 'improvement' of Asia, Africa and the wilder reaches of the settler colonies. The impetus for creating forest or wildlife reserves came from a mix of concerns, including anxiety over the impact of deforestation and other forms of environmental degradation in

Europe, and the experience of the ecologically catastrophic effects of previous colonial land use practices (Pyne, 1997c: 25). More than this, however, the reserve or park can be seen as the imperial manifestation of the 'enlightened' drive to tighten up the circuits of biological productivity; to convert all forms of waste into spiralling biotic wealth. And needless to say, along with all the other restrictions on customary land use by indigenous people, traditional practices of burning were vigorously suppressed (Pyne, 1997b: 422; Kull, 2002: 940). As Christian Kull explains:

> Many colonial leaders were biased against burning by their urban or temperate backgrounds, by elitist anti-indigenous views, or by their desire to replace extensive, fire-based forms of farming and ranching with intensive, more productive systems characterized by permanent fields, fodder production, and haying. (2002: 932)

As in the case of the exorcizing of fire from Europe, the abolition of flame from forests, veld or savanna was as much to do with disciplining a potentially unruly peasantry as it was about conserving biomass and accumulating nutrients (Pyne, 1997c: 28–9). But even when imperial foresters were willing to deploy all the social and technological power at their disposal, fire persisted. Fires broke out because these were biotas that were evolved to burn, and they broke out with particular frequency where there remained local people with traditional knowledge. It has often been noted that incendiarism or 'folk arson' is a common and obvious form of resistance for those whose customary practices of gathering, cropping, grazing and hunting have been reclassified as criminal acts (Pyne, 1997b: 423). What Kull observes in Madagascar applies pretty much anywhere that grassroots pyro-technicians chafe against abolitionist officialdom:

> peasants take advantage of the complex nature of fire in order to continue burning and escape punishment. They burn at night or out-of-sight, letting fire do its own work. They use time-delay ignition techniques. They let escaped authorized blazes run their course. They allow fires to escape 'accidentally'. Finally, they piggyback one fire on another, lighting additional fires ahead of a wildfire to get some burning done but avoid blame. (2002: 942)

While it may be true that burning often increases during times of social unrest, Kull adds, we need to be cautious about ascribing explicitly political motives to such acts. Taking advantage of distraction to do what is deemed necessary may be more appropriately designated as 'straightforward livelihood practice' obliged to go clandestine (2002: 949). This is care for the land, we might say, gone undercover.

Even after former colonies attained independence, prohibitions on free-burning fire have frequently been upheld by local administrations under the sway of Western training, international development agencies and, increasingly, transboundary environmental legislation (Pyne, 2001: 152–4; Tacconi and Ruchiat, 2006: 73). As Luca Tacconi and Yayat Ruchiat observe of one recent headline example:

> the zero-burning policy endorsed by the regional Agreement on Transboundary Haze Pollution ... perpetuates the Indonesian government's exclusive focus on fire suppression and crisis management instead of fire management, which is a continuation of failed colonial legislation ... . (2006: 77)

'Experts' from Europe, or their proxies from European settler societies, remain the global guiding lights on fire suppression. This leaves largely unreconstructed the colonial predicament in which, as Pyne puts it, the most pyrophobic people on the planet set the terms and conditions to the keepers of the most pyrophytic biota (1997b: 495, 2001: 153). 'The U.N.'s Food and Agriculture Organization', he wryly observes, '... has dispatched Germans, Finns, and French to Mauritania, Nepal, and Patagonia to advise on forestry and fire, but has not sponsored Senegalese and Filipinos to help reintroduce fire to Sweden and Austria' (1997a: 319).

Blazing the trail

There are limits, however, to the persistence of hopelessly inappropriate social constructions of nature. Even during the colonial period, there were times when forestry and agricultural officials were compelled to acknowledge the impracticality and impossibility of zero-burning policies (Laris and Wardell, 2006: 276–7). Again and again, the hands-off approach to wooded or otherwise 'wild' land that was intended to stave off ecological degradation turned out to exacerbate it. Fire suppression both stimulated the efflorescence of undesirable biological life – in the form of disease, pests and weeds, and contributed to the reduction or disappearance of species that were held in higher regard. And predictably, what traditional fire-tenders had long known became increasingly hard for abolitionists to ignore: the often fatal logic that banning small fires was the best possible way of promoting massive conflagrations (Pyne, 1997c: 30; Tacconi and Ruchiat, 2006: 76).

Many international experts in the Western mould now find themselves conceding to the necessity of letting wildfire do its work, though there is still a strong sense that fire is a necessary evil rather than an essential and desirable element (Pyne, 1997a: 166). At the same time, across many regions, the sheer persistence of folk and indigenous pyrotechnicians has kept alive the option of selective burning. There is now a significant body of fire scholars and ecosystem managers who appreciate the value of such traditions – especially for living and working in the most fire-prone environments. After intensive research in the savanna landscapes of West Africa, for example, Paul Laris and Andrew Wardell conclude that: 'A reasonable first step in developing a new policy would be to replace the old view, rooted in colonial thinking ... with a new one rooted in indigenous practice and supported by landscape ecology and cooperative management strategies' (2006: 286; see also Kull, 2002; Tacconi and Ruchiat, 2006). Such a turn opens the possibility of new forms of exchange and compromise between Western fire science and localized knowledge, a process led appropriately by Australia – as recently documented, in all its complexity and muddled promise, by Helen Verran (2002).

With the growing recognition that the termination of longstanding burning practices has many derogatory effects on valued landforms and life forms also comes a new – or renewed – appreciation of the benefits that have accrued over time from the skilled deployment of fire. There is a long and geographically dispersed record of European explorers in far-flung regions stumbling across terrain that seemed beguilingly reminiscent of favoured landscapes back home (Clark, 2005c). When sixteenth-century English voyagers to Guiana encountered open grasslands 'with divers copses scattered heere and there', in the words of Walter Raleigh, they were reminded of 'forrest or parke in England' (cited in Raffles, 2002: 106). Two centuries later, as James Cook coasted the Illawarra region of what became New South Wales, artist Sydney Parkinson would note that 'the trees, quite free from underwood, appeared like plantations in gentlemans park' (cited in Smith, 1989: 179). What appealed intuitively to the roving European eye was a combination of woodland – thinned, penetrable, cleared of under-story and grassland – open, verdant, beckoning for grazing animals (Sauer, 1963: 47–8; Pyne, 1998: 133).

Such fortuitous 'natural endowments' often served as a lure for return visits and more permanent arrangements; while the accounts that put these hospitable environments on the map almost always reveal ignorance of the role of intentional burning in their shaping, in much the same way as they overlook the role of fire in the crafting of the referent 'parks' at the European end of the journey.

When settlers followed explorers into already inhabited lands, the significance of this 'trail-blazing' took on a new whole cast. As Sylvia Hallam observes in the Australian context 'The progress of exploration and settlement had depended and continued to depend on indigenous knowledge, use and development of the country and its resources – "native wells", "native paths", clearance and vegetation patterns dependent on Aboriginal firing' (1979: 66). Pyne makes an analogous argument for North America, noting that settlers migrated along grassland corridors opened by Indian fire, that they appropriated prairies moulded by indigenous incendiarism, logged forests in which the most valuable trees had been selected by intentional fire, and learned techniques for controlling and surviving fires from neighbouring Native Americans (1982: 82, 100, 124; 1997b: 466).

Whether 'aboriginal' burning actually created temperate grasslands, or whether it has more modestly shaped and sustained clearings that have been forged primarily by the interaction of climate, vegetation and lightning-sparked wildfires, are the subject of intensive debate amongst fire scholars (see Sauer, 1963: 47–8; Vale, 2002). But the difficulty of distinguishing anthropogenic impacts from other-than-human forces is itself revealing, both in the general sense that it implicates human activity in a broader horizon of dynamic physical processes, and in the more specific way that it opens up the issue of the role of disturbance as a vital feature of many landscapes. Over recent decades, the whole question of whether forest or grassland is the natural form of vegetative cover in many regions has been thoroughly shaken up by the interrogation of the notion of climax ecologies and by the growing appreciation that various forms of upheaval are a vital and generative characteristic of ecosystems (Botkin, 1990).

New approaches argue that ongoing disturbances – such as fire, storm or disease – often give rise to landscapes that are heterogeneous in terms of their age and composition of vegetation. Such patch or mosaic patterns are generally more resilient than spatially or temporally homogenous ecosystems when further stressful events occur (White and Pickett, 1985). They also tend to contain more biological diversity, on account of the fact that they are rich in boundaries or 'edges' between different kinds of ecosystems (Laris and Wardell, 2006: 272).

This perspective casts new light on traditional burning practices. Given that wildfire is now known to be the dominant mode of perturbation in most grasslands and many woodlands, it is becoming increasingly apparent to ecologists that many folk or indigenous burning practices deliberately enhance the patch or mosaic effect, thereby increasing the heterogeneity of vegetation and proliferating biologically diverse edges (Jones, 1969; Kohen, 1995: 113, 132; Russell-Smith et al., 1997: 174–5; Vale, 2002). As Laris and Wardell conclude: 'mosaic burning has been deemed so critical to ecosystem management that land managers in several savanna environments are working to reintroduce it' (2006: 272–3).

There is growing evidence that in numerous species-rich terrestrial ecosystems, such as rainforest and savanna, much of the range of vegetation is attributable to human influence, with fire being the prevalent stimulus. This leads on to the more general claim that anthropogenic fire use has made a significant contribution to what is now termed, in environmentalist discourses, 'global biodiversity' (Pyne, 1997a: 64, 246). Together with the growing appreciation of the value of traditional pyrotechnics in ameliorating potential holocausts and opening access to otherwise impenetrable landscapes, new understandings of fire's capacity to enhance biological richness does more than simply undermine Western imperialism's fire-suppressionist canon. It also promotes a new respect for the trans-generational landscaping ventures of long-term inhabitants. As a voice from white settler Australia, Tom Griffiths is far from alone in speaking of 'owing a debt to Aborigines' (2001: 26–7).

There is more than one way in which to express indebtedness to the lives and labours of 'first people's', however, and they are by no means equally appealing to politically progressive ears. Writing in 1848, emigration advocate Joseph Byrne roundly acknowledges the valuable contribution Aboriginal Australians and their incendiary skills made to a landscape which came to serve the needs of white settlers. As he expounds:

> ... the fires of the dark child of the forest have cleared the soil, the hills and the valleys of the superabundant scrub and timber that covered the country and presented a bar to its occupation. Now, prepared by the hands of the lowest race in the scale of humanity ... the soil of these extensive regions is ready to receive the virgin impressions of civilised man ... . (cited in Hallam, 1979: 76)

If we need any reminder beyond Byrne's brazenly racialized narrative of progress, the brute fact that most of the lands I have been talking about were taken, without permission and with force, injects a potent moral–political imperative to the issue of indebtedness. The title of Hallam's groundbreaking account of one fire-prone region announces this unabashedly: *Fire and Hearth: A Study of Aboriginal Usage and European Usurpation in South-Western Australia* (1979). The fraught and ongoing process of decolonization and the interminable struggles for indigenous rights and restitution in settler colonies speak of the immensity of the challenge of dealing with the legacy of the seizure of lands and resources from those with prior claim. Much of the critical rethinking of fire history I have been drawing upon directly or indirectly engages on this ethico-political terrain. What many of the new generation of fire theorists seem to be insisting – in conversation with indigenous fire scholars and practitioners – is that the commandeering of fire should be right up there on the political agenda with the appropriation of forests, plains, waterways, cultural objects and built environments. In the light of both its socio-cultural and ecological consequences, the widespread banishing of fire, as Langton, Yibbaruk, Pyne, Krull and many others would have it, calls for immediate and profound redress.

For those of us raised in so-called 'settler' societies, the extent of the debt we owe prior claimants on the lands we inhabit can take on a palpable weight – though in many ways it is just as much an issue for all those who have benefited from the bounty stripped from the colonial 'outfield'. Claims have been made, as we saw in Chapter 5, that the West owes a vast 'ecological debt' to the less-developed world for its cornering of a disproportionate share of the earth's resources – including fossilized energy, raw materials and the capacity of the atmosphere to absorb energetic waste products. The issue of the Western appropriation of foreign fire, and its seizure of fire-shaped landscapes, brings a vital supplement to this ethical accounting. But it is not simply a matter of adding vegetation consumed by fire – and the resultant greenhouse gas emissions – to the unfair share of sequestered carbon already expended by the early industrializing nations: for this is a logic that leads, yet again, to the imposition of restrictions on the use of fire.

While burning down forests and permanently replacing them with pastoral or arable land is a different matter, the periodic and cyclical application of fire to vegetation as a form of land management should by no means be compounded with 'mining' fossilized carbon. Such an equation elides the crucial difference between a restricted sense of economy, and the vision of a general economy of terrestrial life open to the ongoing energetic flux of the solar system. It confuses 'through-flow' of energy with the use of a standing reserve, conflating a form of 'consummation' of past growth that is sooner or later inevitable with one that imagines that there can be endless growth or perpetual conservation. In brief, it mistakes keeping forests free *from* fires for keeping forests free *for* fires.

'Burning for the Other'

Open-cast fire rails against containment within the closed circuits of a restricted economy, just as it resists conversion into a laboratory science. Even the technical terms 'controlled' or 'prescribed' burning seem to miss something important about the use of fire in the field: the fitful interplay of life, weather, solar energy demanding more of those who would brandish flame than the pursuit of mastery or the following of prescriptions. It calls for constant re-writing of the rules, for improvisation, for taking chances.

This sort of learning by trying out possibilities sometimes goes by the name of 'play'. Gaston Bachelard speaks of the importance of an early and formative prohibition on playing with fire in the raising of children: a repression 'which leave(s) little room for the acquiring of an unprejudiced knowledge' (1987: 11). But injunctions against playing with fire experienced by European children, particularly in urban environments, should not be generalized (Goudsblom, 1992: 41, 191). It has been noted that Australian Aboriginal children raised in contexts where aspects of traditional ways of life persist learn their respect for fire through playing with it. Dean Yibarbuk speaks of children from a very early age 'learning by experience and experimentation' how to use fire for a whole range of purposes 'under a watchful but relaxed eye' of parents and family (1998: 2). To which Wali Fejo (1994) adds that he and many other Aboriginals carry the bodily scars with them from their childhood encounters with fire.

But the scars may run deeper than individual bodies. Because the elements that come together to make a fire are constantly changing, often in inherently unpredictable ways, free-range burning never ceases to be experimental, and by the same token never ceases to be risky. Wherever it is deployed, human fire, like any fire, retains its capacity to be less or more or other than what is required (Pyne, 2001: 83, 2004: 109–110, 191). As Pyne punctuates his account of customary burning practices in North America: 'Even under ideal circumstances, accidents occurred: signal fires escaped and camp-fires spread ... Burned corpses on the prairie were far from rare' (1982: 79).

We have just witnessed the suffering and loss visited upon the current inhabitants of south-east Australia. And that's in spite of satellite weather forecasting, industrial fire-fighting apparatuses and high-speed escape vehicles. It is up to us to try and imagine what it would have been like for Australia's earliest colonists to have encountered their first particularly vicious fire season. Or to speculate about the lived experience of passing through the climate tipping point that Black and Mooney have identified, with its sudden, intense firestorms: a transition that is likely to have unravelled – in just a few short seasons – the accumulated wisdom of thousands of years of working with an alternative fire regime. It's a cruel trial that would have been repeated on inhabited islands and continents all around the Pacific Basin at that time.

Human populations tend to be mobile. When they move, they may well find themselves encountering new fire regimes: configurations of heat and fuel and weather for which their existing skills are no longer appropriate. Or they may stay put, and find that the world around them has changed. Climate, as we saw in Chapter 3, is constantly changing at different temporal and spatial scales: rhythms which are tightly coupled with transformations in the distributions and densities of biological life. All of this means that sooner or later, any human collective is likely to be confronted with environmental conditions that exceed all previous experience. If the deployment of fire is always a matter of trial and error – then there are going to be moments, junctures, episodes when the chance of erring is high – and when the cost of error is extreme.

Bodies that can register the finest gradations of fuel loading, the rustling presence of animal life, the hint of shifting wind are also bodies that are vulnerable to racing flame, to scorched earth, hunger and thirst. To experiment with fire is to put one's body on the line, even to risk one's whole community. But when an environment is experimenting with its inhabitants, when it is testing them with hitherto unknown elemental variations or extremes, this is a wager that may be unavoidable. Working with fire, one does not have to be a recent arrival to experience the 'fragility and brevity of a human life time'. And this is why the romanticizing of indigenous 'oneness with nature' commits just as much of an injustice as indicting first peoples for their initial or occasional ecological stumblings. However much we may be impressed by the ease and dexterity with which Australian Aboriginals or Malagasy or Terra del Fuegans handle 'the destructive element', to conceive of bodies or collectives that simply go with the flow of nature is to lighten the weight of our ecological 'indebtedness' to those who have gone before us. It is to make less of what we might come to see as an offering: the vast, immeasurable, unreciprocable gift of a ground on which to stand.

In a strikingly literal sense, the efforts of the Waradiji to teach white settlers how to deal with wildfire embodies Bataille's definition of generosity as 'the passage of warmth or light from one being to another' (1988: 94). If it is indeed the case that every true gift – by virtue of the trace of the unknown that it brings into the circuit of the familiar – comes with an element of danger, then it may well be that fire is the primordial form of the fraught offering.

Anthropological evidence suggests that most human groups have been reluctant to lend or give away fire to strangers (Pyne, 1997b: 28, 2001: 121). This is hardly surprising, given the risk that follows from putting a potentially runaway force in the hands of those who may be unaccustomed to local terrain and conditions. But as Johann Goudsblom speculates, once strangers had gathered around a domestic fire long enough to be trusted, it may well have been the gesture of mutual lending or sharing of fire that cemented the bond between different groups (1992: 40). It was an exchange of fire, in other words, that manifested the shift from a unilateral opening to a relation of reciprocity.

What has also been shared, willingly or not, are the landscapes forged by fire: the pathways and clearings, the fertility of the soil and richness of life, the security of reduced fuel loads. This too is Bataille's 'passage of warmth and light': the use of fire to moderate the effects of the surging energies that shape landform and life form; to smooth out the jagged extremes of drought, storm, heatwave, and the exuberance of biological life; to render inhospitable environments into hospitable, cared for, caring terrains. This is not just a question of the debt owed by those who have appropriated fire-managed landscapes in colonial contexts, though these are contexts where indebtedness presents itself with particular poignancy. It is a matter of the work that has been done – by fire and other means – to open up and tend *all* the terrains that current generations live in, move across, or otherwise benefit from. It is about recognizing that almost all terrestrial inhabitation is subtended by the achievements of often silent and mostly departed predecessors whose bodily efforts offer us 'a gift of the possibility of a common world' (Diprose, 2002: 141).

As we saw in Chapter 5, there are categories of injustice or inequity which can be made visible, added up, recompensed. This applies, certainly, to aspects of the forcible appropriation of previously inhabited lands, as it does to facets of the global climate change problem. There are, furthermore, forms of 'ecological debt' reaching into the past for which approximate values might be given: this much coal consumed, that much carbon dioxide emitted, and so on. But there are also forms of indebtedness to others which are too deeply interred to ever make present, involving intensities of bodily and communal investment for which there is no conceivable recompense: gifts which have made an immense difference to the lives of those who come after, but which are destined to remain 'immemorial, unrepresentable, invisible' (Levinas, 1998a: 11).

In the last chapter, I spoke of the way that a sense of community can emerge out of the experience of being together with others with whom at the outset we do not necessarily have anything in common. And we speculated about the role of the raw uncertainty of the physical world as an impetus for this togetherness. What the long history of managing volatile environments hints at is that, even before this originary 'thrown-togetherness' of bodies, there are connections, obligations, liabilities that come down to us from those who are no longer present, those with whom we can never be together. As Catherine Chalier puts it: 'The history of every creature stands in relation to that anteriority or that absence, it bears witness to them, in spite of itself and often unbeknownst to itself' (2002: 119). If it is Bataille who helps us conceive of a generosity which binds the bodies in question to the blazing excesses of the earth and cosmos, it is Levinas who guides us into the shadowy underworld of profound, immeasurable and undischargeable obligations to those who have preceded us. 'To be responsible is always to have to answer for a situation that was in place before I came on the scene', as Lingis sums up (1998a: xx). 'Responsibility is a bond between my present and what came to pass before it'.

This is a responsibility that takes account not only of what we have done – or what it can be proven we have done – but also of who we are, how we became who we are (Gatens and Lloyd, 1999: 81; Chalier, 2002: 123; Massey, 2004: 9–10). The debt that Levinas has in mind is one that accompanies us from our very inception (1998a: 87). Whether we are aware of it or not, it is what our body, any body, owes to the bodies that have come before us, for it is they who enable my 'being at home', they who have imparted me with the 'well-trampled places' which provide my everyday support (Levinas, 1969: 138).

Not just well-trampled places. Well-*lit* places: Levinas spoke of 'burning for the Other' as a way to express the intensity of our desire to be with and to be for others. As at so many other moments in this book, I find myself burrowing beneath the figure of speech to dislodge a physico–material referent; the residue of a dynamic earthly encounter that lends its depth-charge to cultural–linguistic play. If an exposure and response to the address of others is the primordial impulse to community, that opening is always in some way implicated in ways of coping with the variability of the physical world, in the ongoing engagement with the rumbling or the roaring of the earth. Whether it is a matter of 'caring' for an environment so that it is safe and hospitable for its human and nonhuman dwellers, or whether it is an invitation to share the warmth of a fire or hearth, there is no being-together with others that is not always already an accommodation with a volatile materiality. And that is long before we ever get the chance to sit down to negotiate which nonhumans we will admit to our collectivity. But Latour has it spot on in his insistence that our humanity, our communities and our bodies are an amalgam of more-than-human ingredients. Though if he had hailed from some place other than Eurasia's soggy western promontory, he might well have gone on to note that fire has always played a special part in the transmutation and fusion of these vital elements and their annealing into a workable whole.

Before it is the energetic and symbolic focus of a gathering in, fire is first a means of grappling with an exteriority, with the problems and provocations of a world beyond us. There are many places where a negotiable path, a safe trail, is one that has been fired, carefully, repeatedly, sometimes desperately. A trail that others have blazed for us. Most of these others are long gone, and there is nothing we can offer in return. But what we can begin to do is to bear witness to this indebtedness, its depth, its pervasiveness, its often painful intensity. To feel grateful for the hospitable environments we have inherited. And perhaps to use this gratitude as a point of departure when we address those forms of debt and injustice which we can do something about.

Notes

1 I am indebted to George Main's superb 'Red Steers and White Death' (2004) for pointing me to Gilmore's writings.
2 A settler term for Aboriginal women, now considered offensive.

8

Extending Hospitality:
Global Mobility and Journeys in Deep Time

Introduction: hope after Haiti

We drink from wells others have dug, follow trails others have blazed, settle into landscapes others have shaped. We feed on life forms millions of years in the making, inhale an atmosphere excreted by countless other organisms. Others both human and nonhuman have, step by step, fabricated the worlds we depend upon, realities to which we add our own amendments and surcharges. But these worlds can also withdraw their support – gradually or suddenly, temporarily or permanently. They take turns we do not foresee, push us further than we are prepared to go. Those who have come before us, those whose welltrodden paths we walk, whose bodies and behaviour we inherit, have also had their tolerance tested by the elements they relied upon, in more ways than we can ever know. We follow not only their successful moves, but also their hesitation, their stumbling or their overreaching. And even their disappearance.

In this chapter, I gather together themes already broached around the issue of how to live sociably on an unpredictable planet; how to live as well as possible in a cosmos not designed for our comfort or even our continuity. We know the stakes are high. Whatever can be gleaned from our predecessors and their capacity to make it across shaky ground, this is a planet that we are pressuring as never before. Our task, as Wolfgang Sachs summed it up some years ago 'is the search for civilizations that are capable of extending hospitality to twice as many people on the planet as today without ruining the biosphere for successive generations' (1999: xi). To this unthinkably demanding assignment we must add that, at the very moment we are coming to terms with the extent of our impact on the earth's life support systems, we are also learning just how much uncertainty inheres in these systems themselves. This means that we need to be at once attuned to the prospect of human-induced global climate change drastically diminishing the availability of land to live on along with its capacity to nourish us – and to the likelihood of equally devastating surprises of the planet's own doing.

Across the surface of the earth, populations are clustered on precarious terrain, and many of the most vulnerable places have seen massive in-migration and growth over the last half century. Today, over 630 million people live within 30 feet of sea level, and this is where two-thirds of the world's cities with populations over 5 million are sited. The span over which many conurbations have sprung from small towns or villages is a blink in geological time, offering nothing close to a significant sampling of the physical variability their locations are subject to, and providing their inhabitants with only a fraction of the experience they may require to have the chance of living well over the longer term. What Mike Davis has to say about Southern California, as he knows all too well, applies equally or more so to human settlements throughout the world:

> If the average human lifetime is defined biblically as 62 years, then native Californian cultures spent at least 142 lifetimes nourishing an intimate knowledge of the environment as a dynamic system. In contrast, Anglo-Americans have occupied the region for little more than two and a half lifetimes. Most of the major water, flood control, sewage, energy, communications, and transport infrastructures are less than one lifetime old. These spans are too short to serve as reliable proxies for ecological time or to sample the possibilities of future environmental stress. (1998: 35–6)

At least California *has* infrastructure. We have recently witnessed what happens when a major seismic event follows a devastating cyclone season in a country where the majority of the population already lacks basic amenities and where disaster preparedness is minimal. For all its shocking consequences, Haiti's earthquake was an ordinary adjustment on a relatively minor fault line, the result of a re-alignment after some 250 years of inching movement by the Caribbean plate. Once more, in spite of rapid international mobilization, we have seen how so much of the burden of first response fell on neighbours and fellow citizens. And once again, we've glimpsed the incredible forbearance and resourcefulness of ordinary people under the most horrific circumstances (blighted only by the global media's grating insistence on describing emergency requisitioning and desperate improvisation as 'looting').

Unfortunately, after the US military took control of relief operations, there again appears to have been a prioritizing of 'securitization' as the immediate task. Alongside the imposition of 'order' on the traumatized population of Port-au-Prince and neighbouring towns, American forces were also intent on maintaining their own homeland security. 'As well as providing emergency supplies and medical aid', we were informed, 'the USS Carl Vinson, along with a ring of other navy and coast guard vessels, is acting as a deterrent to Haitians who might be driven to make the 681 mile sea crossing to Miami' (Waterfield, 2010; see also Hallward, 2010). This strategy turns out to be an activation of 'Operation Vigilant Sentry', a contingency plan set up by the Bush administration to thwart any future 'threat' to the US mainland from migrants fleeing natural disaster or political unrest in the Caribbean (Sutton, 2007). In what appears to be a riposte to the US stance, President Abdoulaye Wade of the small West African state of Senegal offered an open door and plots of land for any dispossessed Haitians who sought a new home (Waterfield, 2010). Though, at the time of writing it is too soon to gauge the full intent and meaning of this gesture – as an adventure in hospitality, it at least offered a speculative counterpoint to the militarization of Haiti's tragedy.

Wolfgang Sachs' choice of 'hospitality' as our perhaps unreachable goal is a revealing one. He might have settled for equity or rights or just plain basic needs. Without foreclosing on any of these worthy ambitions, 'hospitality' announces something more. It is suggestive of a welcome, an offering, a provisioning that is based foremost on a felt sense of what others require, irrespective of whether it is owed or deserved. One that, like Senegal's recent offer, need not await any request. For Sachs, as for many other theorists who take the demands of hospitality to heart, it is a concept – and a calling – that breaks with an 'economic' logic. To offer hospitality is to give without expectation of a return. It is to respond to the needs of those who appear before us asymmetrically – which is to say, with no assurance of a reciprocal arrangement. While such a gesture might indeed set a cycle of exchanges in motion, as hospitality's more ardent theorists and practitioners like to point out, it does not demand that the circle is already in place. It is an opening gambit, a new beginning – albeit one that may be inspired and enabled by what has gone before.

Tying together some threads teased out earlier, I make a case for 'extending hospitality' so that it takes into its orbit not only those people who arrive at our borders from some other place, but also those who have been caught up, like the people of Haiti, in an event that is as much temporal as spatial. I want to consider what's at stake in welcoming not merely those 'others' who move 'horizontally' across our planet's uppermost strata, but all those who have had to ride out the mobilizations of the earth itself – without necessarily going any place else.

Just as there are momentous 'boundaries' or checkpoints which people traversing geo-political space must navigate, so too are there life-changing transitional points or thresholds in the state of the physical earth, as we have seen: staging posts through which even those who wish to stay in place must negotiate from time to time. What form might a cosmopolitanism take, I ask, that took these 'vertical' spatio-temporal junctures in earth history – and all their impression on the vulnerable bodies that pass through them – as seriously as it took the horizontal mobilities and flows that too narrowly define what we have come to call 'globalization'?

What might it mean for the way we encounter others in the contemporary world if we could attune ourselves to the imperatives of an earth which 'constantly carries out a movement of deterritorialization on the spot'? What difference might it make when we sit down at the negotiating tables to thrash out the rules and regulations of a shared world if we could envisage that every body present bears the marks of a vast and hazardous voyage through deep time? Or to put it another way, what would happen to 'the perhaps impossible vision of an ecologically just world' if we were to recognize that we arrive at this task only after an improbable journey – a course that has already taken all of us on so many wild swerves away from the straight line of justice and out of the circles of orderly exchange?

Space, time and mobility

At an earlier moment in our modernity, Immanuel Kant penned the famous *Toward Perpetual Peace* (1996 [1795]) , a proposal for the institution of a single globally recognized set of laws of hospitality which would guarantee the security of those moving across nation-state borders. If the intention was to overcome some of the limits imposed by the division of the earth's surface by national boundaries, his scheme also bolstered the importance of sovereign states, by elevating them into the pre-eminent unit through which mobility and residence was to be administered. If the intervening centuries have proved receptive to many of the details of Kant's ideal, they have also provided plentiful reasons to doubt his faith in the state as the requisite vehicle for enacting a 'cosmopolitan' sensibility. Sovereign states have come to be singled out by critical commentators as the progenitors of the very intolerance Kant would have had them prevent: the project of unifying and strengthening the state being charged with the production of whole categories of officially unrecognized or unwanted people (Dillon, 1999; Dikeç et al., 2009).

As Michael Hardt and Antonio Negri put it: 'the nation-state is a machine that produces Others' (2001: 114). In this way, the critique of the belief that communities are rooted in soil extends to the 'imagined community' of the nation state, with many theorists noting the strife that arises from binding national identity and belonging to the enduring occupation of a fixed territory. It has often been noted that the containment of human difference within the hard-edged boundaries of a state will inevitably exclude some who wish to belong and force others into unwanted compliance. By a similar logic, many critical thinkers affirm the positive effects of dismantling divisive borders and allowing for the unrestrained intermingling of embodied subjects. As we saw in earlier chapters, the idea that change and difference emerge through the coming together of heterogeneous 'beings' has been a pervasive theme in social and philosophical thought over recent decades. Not only in relational materialist thought, but in postcolonial theory, feminist theory, queer theory and other politically progressive fields, a sustained assault on 'essentialist' thinking has been closely tied to the valorizing of mobility, encounter and intermixture.

It is now routine to assert that identities are made rather than given, that they are malleable rather than fixed, and that they take shape through engagements with others rather than by way of filiation to any original form. Such affirmations of the 'fluidity' of identity are frequently expressed in spatial tropes: openness is favoured over closure, inclusion over exclusion, mobility over stasis (see Barnett, 2005: 6–7), to the point where it makes sense to speak of 'the radical contingencies of space and identity' in a single breath (Shapiro, 1999: 80). In this context, the event of leaving home and the process of moving across borders tend to assume a special significance. 'Migration' comes to be viewed not only as the ever more frequent process of physically relocating to another place, but as a figure for any kind of thought or experience that frees itself from inherited limits and strictures. 'Such a generalisation of the meaning of migration', Sara Ahmed observes, 'allows it to be celebrated as transgressive and liberating departure from living-as-usual …' (2000: 80; see also Cheah, 1998: 298).

This sense that the global political order we have inherited is a significant contributor to the 'manufacture of estrangement' is perhaps the prime impetus behind the revitalization of the concept of cosmopolitanism over recent decades. The pathologies of the nation state, with its constitutive practices of regulated inclusion and exclusion, have incited a quest for 'spaces of hospitality' in which others might be welcomed, sheltered, cared for – even when their papers are not in order. But however much this renewed questioning of the territorial imperatives of the nation state and the search for more accommodating political dispositions is a welcome one, we need to be careful that the enthrallment with a sort of 'horizontal' movement and relationality does not preclude other kinds of relating (see Barnett, 2004, 2005; Dikeç et al., 2009). As Ahmed points out, hitching a certain kind of spatial mobility to all that we would most wish to affirm about our humanness is an investment with effects of its own (2000: 80–94). It comes with certain assumptions about 'home', about 'borders' or 'boundaries', and about 'staying put' and these too require interrogation.

If critical concern and hope is bound up with horizontal or lateral movement, we have to ask, what does this imply for those who choose to stay in one place? What does it say about those who respond to challenges or opportunities by 'holding their ground'? In particular, we need to be vigilant about the continuing tendency, intentional or otherwise, to counterpose the motility and mutability of human beings with the obduracy of the ground they are seen to be moving across: the contrast of ideally free socio-cultural agents with the imputed fixity of the soil or the bedrock from which they have apparently liberated themselves (see Cheah, 1998; Clark, 2002). To put it another way, if the radical contingencies of human spatial location are set against the intransigence of geological or biophysical strata, what does this infer about those people who see their own lives as closely connected to the earth and all its ongoing processes?

This is an issue raised recently by philosopher Gayatri Chakravorty Spivak, a theorist who is herself no stranger to the thematic of human mobility and encounters across difference. Our fascination with new modes of transglobal migrancy, Spivak counsels, should not be allowed to eclipse the experience of peoples who have dwelled otherwise on the earth. 'The figure of the New Immigrant has a radical limit: those who have stayed in place for more than thirty thousand years. We need not value this limit for itself', she adds, 'but we must take it into account … Let this stand as the name of the other of the question of diaspora' (1999: 402). Displaying a similar scepticism towards an 'over-excited celebration of openness, movement and flight', geographer Doreen Massey, conversing with Catherine Nash, prompts, us not to overlook 'the potential validity, in political terms, of some of the pulls towards settledness and even closure in the context of the social construction of the identity of place ...' (2005b: 172–3).

One of the reasons why it is important to Spivak to address the figures of an 'immensely slow temporizing' is that this move reprises the question of the physical subtending of human existence (1999: 402). If not necessarily in ways which bring all the contributory factors fully to light, stretching our consideration of human dwelling across centuries or millennia prompts us to engage with those strata often overlooked in the course of tracking horizontal movements across the earth's surface. It compels us to think of social life in terms of its implication in biological and geological processes – to attend to the borderlands where '"history" moves into "geology"' (1999: p. 69 footnote 86). In entering this transitional zone, we also glimpse the threshold of our capacity for effective action, the very limits of the human ability to '*make* history in a deliberate way' (Spivak, 1995: 171).

Massey too makes a case for thinking through place in terms of a whole range of forces operating at temporal scales from the everyday and the seasonal all the way through to the 'really *longue durée*' of geological processes like plate tectonics. In this way, she opens up the prospect of nonhuman agencies that are not only mixed up with our own world-making efforts, but which assert themselves as the dominant force. Massey does not shy away from the challenges that follow from this. She recognizes that such a stretching of our sphere of interest and engagement to take account of the long-wave rhythmicity of earth processes exposes our critical projects to 'contrasting temporalities (that) pose real problems for politics' (2005a: 356).

In their own ways, both Spivak and Massey dissociate themselves from a genre of accounts of a global nomadism that unequivocally affirm the 'irrepressible desire for free movement' (see Hardt and Negri, 2001: 213). However, in working up the tension between migrancy and settledness, they may actually be more in line with Gilles Deleuze and Felix Guattari's own characterization of the nomad than those theorists who take this figure as the exemplar of a will to unimpeded flight across the face of the earth. It's worth recalling Deleuze and Guattari's insistence that nomadism is not to be defined by horizontal mobilization, but by a willingness to stay put. Thus 'the nomad is not at all the same as the migrant .... he occupies, inhabits, holds ... space; that is his territorial principle' (1987: 380–1). In contrast to 'migrants', nomads are prepared to ride out the instabilities and transformations of their environment, to hang on and do the dirty, dangerous work of coping with the variability of the elemental forces around them:

> Whereas the migrant leaves behind a milieu that has become amorphous or hostile, the nomad is the one who does not depart, does not want to depart, who clings to the smooth space left by the receding forest, where the steppe or the desert advances, and who invents nomadism as a response to this challenge. (Deleuze and Guattari, 1987: 381)

What's important here is that it's the earth itself that does the moving, the transforming, the breaking away from its existing patterns and arrangements ('deterritorializing' or 'destratifying' in Deleuzoguattarian speak) just as much as it is the human agent who dwells upon it. The nomadic response is by no means conservative. It is, of necessity, engaged and experimental. Nomads are 'ambulant'. Their defining aptitude, as we saw in the last chapter, is to be able to go with a flow, to recognize and track crucial transitions in the systemicity of the physical world. But if this is a kind of mobilization, it is as much a journey that involves temporizing as it is one that negotiates or composes space. The Aboriginal occupation of Australia that Spivak alludes to, stretching over tens of thousands of years, may be an extreme case, given that it encompasses the height of the last glaciation and the shift into the present warmer interglacial. But as we have seen, a range of contemporary 'environmental' issues are now demanding that we stretch our imaginations over timescales of this and greater magnitudes.

Multiple rhythms, discordant temporalities

Massey's reference to the 'longue durée' is a reminder that deep time has not fully escaped the agenda of social and cultural thought. Historian Fernand Braudel famously counselled the humanities and social sciences to look beyond the clamour of contemporary or recent events – 'the tempestuous borders of the short time span' – and address the 'deep-seated' conditions in which these events unfold (1980 [1969]: 37–8). This meant taking into account human relationships with the physical environment. Seas and waterways, vegetation and animal populations, climate and geology are all credited with playing a constitutive, persistent and inescapable role in human affairs (Braudel, 1980: 31, 1995 [1949]: 20). When Braudel defines the *longue durée*, whether his concern is with human or nonhuman processes, he consistently emphasizes its extreme slowness. Long-term history obeys a 'slower tempo', it 'borders on the motionless' and is 'sheltered from all accidents, crises, and sudden breaks' (1980: 33, 45). Only short-term history, the conventional focus of historians and social scientists, is characterized by 'brief, rapid, nervous fluctuations' (1980: 27). This is the world of 'events', and hence the time span that is 'the most dangerous' (1995: 21).

If the quest to expand the humanistic imagination to embrace the depths of time is a welcome one, how Braudel actually interprets the earth processes he brings into relief is rather less promising. His assumption that big, deep forces move only gradually precludes the possibility of the longer *durée* irrupting into the present, ruling out any chance that it might be the clash of different velocities or durations that breaks the flow of social life. In a related way, Spivak's 'immensely slow temporizing' only gives us part of the story. What we need to address are Massey's 'contrasting temporalities': the potential for radically disjointed experiences which result from the more typically human-scaled passage of time coming up against high consequence physical processes that can take anywhere from seconds to eons to do their work. It is precisely these kinds of disjunctures that Robert Frodeman wishes to bring into view. 'Earthquakes, floods, hurricanes, and droughts', he proposes, 'are places where deep time erupts into more familiar temporal rhythms' (2003: 125).

In *Basin and Range*, the book credited with introducing the term 'deep time', geologist John McPhee evokes the irregular tempo of a north American mountain range: 'These mountains do not rise like bread. They sit still for a long time and build up tension, and then suddenly jump' (1980: 48). Likewise, anthropologist Julie Cruikshank, describing the dominant geomorphic forces in the landscape of coastal Alaska and the Yukon, observes that glaciers 'may advance without warning after years of stability, sometimes several kilometres' (2005: 6). Similar stop-start dynamics – where spells of slight or gradual change alternate with brief spans of much more rapid reorganization have been cropping up throughout preceding chapters, from the periodicities of New Zealand's Alpine Fault to the locking and releasing of tectonic plates at the subduction zone off Sumatra, from the see-sawing of abrupt climate change to the sudden shift of fire regimes.

If there is one theorist in the humanities who deserves credit for drawing such rhythms into the realms of critical inquiry, it is Michel Serres. Again and again, he returns us to multiple temporalities – the longwave, the shortwave, the regular, the surging, the discontinuous – in which human life is immersed. Speaking of climate, Serres reminds us: 'our lives depend on this mobile atmospheric system, which is constant but fairly stable, deterministic and stochastic, moving quasi-periodically with rhythms and response times that vary colossally' (1995: 27). Alongside the more regular cadences of the weather, he constantly keeps an eye on 'meteora' – the singular or chance events that punctuate the predictable (Serres, 2001: 67–8). And with a special passion, Serres exhorts us to look beyond the drastically abbreviated time frames characteristic of our modernity, and reacquaint ourselves with the long-term rhythmicity of the earth (1995: 29–30). His nearest counterpart within the social sciences is Barbara Adam – who stands out for her insistence that social thinkers must take account of the full range of rhythms – from the neural to the cosmic, 'from the imperceptibly fast to the unimaginably slow' – that orchestrate our earthly existence (1990: 165). Drawing our attention in particular to the implication of the pulsing of life with the tempos of its physical environment, she points to synchronicities, entrainments, attunements – but also to pauses, ruptures, discontinuities, catastrophes:

> A symphony of rhythms and temporalities thus underpins our development as humans and as living organisms. It marks us as creatures of this earth, as beings that are constituted by a double temporality: rhythmically structured within and embedded in the rhythmic organisation of the cosmos. (Adam, 1998: 13)

As disaster studies, environmental studies and development studies each reveal in their own way, these varying temporalities have life-changing consequences. We have seen that the El Niño Southern Oscillation has been implicated in changing patterns of fire in the Pacific Basin around 5,700 years ago. Its more familiar pulsing at intervals shuffled anywhere between two and seven years continues to play a major part in the irregular rhythms of rainfall and drought across much of the southern hemisphere and equatorial regions. Beyond this short-term frequency, now relatively well-understood, climate scientists speculate about larger-scale periodicities that could range between decades, centuries or even millennia (Davis, 2001: 234).

There is gathering evidence that the recent drought in Australia, seven or eight consecutive years of 'deficit rainfall', may be due to a rather ordinary multi-decadal shift corresponding to one of these longer-wave ENSO cycles (Lester, 2006). So devastating are its effects, however, that the decline in the nation's grain production is now considered to have been a significant factor in the escalation of staple food prices on the international market, with questions being raised about the long-term viability of numerous small and some larger urban centres across the continent (Ayre, 2007; Clark, 2008). As water management expert Mike Young sums up: 'What we seem to have done is ... built Australia on the assumption that it was going to be wetter, and we haven't been prepared to make the change back to a much drier regime' (cited in Vidal, 2006).

This is not just a problem for Australia, nor just for arid and semi-arid regions more generally. The closer we look at longer-term rhythms – like the blip of warmer weather in Europe's Middle Ages that impacted catastrophically on civilizations in drier regions or the saw-toothed oscillations that preceded the Holocene – the more it appears that we have done a vast amount of 'building' on doubtful assumptions. This applies not only to the sudden surge of urbanization over the last half century, not only to the frenetic temporal sliver that is our modernity, but to the entirety of human settled life, and beyond. Whether it's a matter of identifying future seismic events, deciphering climatic cycles, or understanding the surges and lapses of biological life, the stakes for human life are high – even before we heed Sachs' prompt about escalating global populations.

In this context, care must be taken so that an atmosphere of urgency does not serve to depoliticize potentially contentious issues (see Braun, 2007; Swyngedouw, 2007). But so too do we need to be very wary that critical appraisals of the physical science's tendency towards 'mononaturalism' – the positing of a single objective reality – do not undermine vital attempts to understand terrestrial dynamics that rely on an integrated planet-scaled vision. As I have been intimating throughout this book, there are situations in which the demand that science slows down and lays open each step of its constitutive world-comprehending activities to painstaking collective assessment may not be the top priority. There are junctures when a deep ontological commitment to a particular model of physical processes may be called for, even moments when a 'panic of empathy' with the nearest available explanation might suffice.

Improvisation, danger and loss

There is an assumption in some branches of the social study of science that a coherent, integrative model of physical processes necessarily comes at the expense of alternative ways of knowing and doing the world. This view, however, may have at least as much to do with the special privilege afforded to 'contestation' or agonistic modes of relating in certain strands of critical thought (see Barnett, 2004), as it does to actual or potential encounters between contemporary physical science and other traditions of engaging with dynamic materialities. Now that scientists routinely acknowledge the problems in identifying the point at which complex physical systems are likely to change their state, there is every reason for productive engagement with those who have practical, 'hands-on' expertise in dealing with changeable environments or ecosystems. Indeed, this is the conversation that Deleuze and Guattari anticipate in their nuanced juxtaposition of 'nomad' and 'state' science in *A Thousand Plateaus*. Combining a flare for nonlinear dynamics with a speculative ethnography of artisans, pastoralists and other 'traditional' material practitioners, they generate a set of conjectural insights about how to live amid elemental processes that will forever defy full predictive understanding (Deleuze and Guattari, 1987: 369–73). This is what ensures that their concept of the 'nomad' is much more than a simple celebration of human mobility.

Science studies offer useful reminders of the salience of tacit knowledge in scientific research: captivating us with tales of the way experienced researchers '... walking the outcrop or working in the lab ... quietly absorb a thousand small signs that lie beneath every law like generalization' (Frodeman, 2003: 35). But there is also the matter of such lawlike generalizations playing a reduced role in fields that scientists themselves are increasingly willing to see as characterized by sensitivity to initial conditions, singularities, emergent properties and other non-linear dynamics. Resonating with Deleuze and Guattari's account of nomad science, we have seen how Stephen Pyne couples observations about the 'stochastic, irrepeatable, and irreversible' properties of fire with a deep appreciation of the skills of traditional pyrotechnicians in dealing with intrinsically non-generalizable conditions. Serres marshals his favourite examples of the peasant farmer and the experienced sailor with similar intent. He reminds us of the value of a working knowledge of the weather and other rhythmical earth processes – a knowing and doing made even more precious when it channels collective memories of longer-wave variabilities (1995: 28–9). And in juxtaposing the ability of the peasant or the sailor to weather the storms of capricious environments with the new sciences of chaos, turbulence and complexity, Serres is also making a vital point about the compatibility of these lineages. As Isabelle Stengers sums up, with generous echoes of both Serres and Deleuze/Guattari:

> When we learn the 'respect' that physical theory imposes on us with regard to nature, we must also learn to respect other intellectual approaches, whether they be the traditional approaches of seafarers and peasants, or approaches created by other sciences. We must learn no longer to judge the population of knowledges, practices, and cultures produced by human societies, but to interbreed with them, establishing novel communications that enable us to deal with the unprecedented demands of our era. (1997: 57)

But if there are to be new reprochements and cross-fertilizations between science and traditional practice, they cannot simply be additive or amalgamating – for the knowledges in question come with their own ontological cracks, their own anguished incompleteness and non-self-consistency. As Deleuze and Guattari were well aware, even if they found ways to evade its most nihilating implications, an earth rife with destratifications never ceases to endanger the skilled material operators who tap its volatile seams (1987: 149, 503). The point that Pyne, Langton and others make about the intrinsic risks of even the most expert deployment of free-range fire resonates with other recent work which lies at the intersection of ethnography and environmental history. Writing about the Aboriginal peoples of northern coastal Australia, anthropologist Nonie Sharp (2002) vouches for their rich, deep and complex understanding of seaways and marine life. And yet, she poignantly notes, this knowledge can never smooth out all the irregularities of the maritime environment. 'People do not live simply in harmony with the sea, because cross-currents accompany its rhythms', she explains. 'At times the sea rages. Its movements, rhythms and patterns vary with winds and tides and the movements of celestial bodies' (2002: 81). The subjects of her study, Sharp concludes, are 'sea hunters for whom the violence of death is commonplace' (2002: 60).

In a related way, Julie Cruikshank familiarizes us with the stories and the material practices through which North Pacific Coast Tlingit and Athapaskan people negotiate their heavily glaciated surroundings. Knowledge which comes from direct engagement with environmental instability finds expression in 'layered memories ... accumulated through centuries of oral tradition' (Cruikshank, 2005: 24). But Cruikshank makes it plain that lifetimes of learning cannot alleviate the hazards of co-habiting with masses of mobile ice, especially during periods of climatic and geological transition: 'travel through transforming landscapes is a recurring theme in inland glacier stories. Living with the risks associated with the behaviour of surging glaciers is another – unexpected advances, violent surges, catastrophic floods, and accompanying weather variations' (2005: 40). Not only are communities buffeted and lives lost, Cruikshank recounts, but some events are so catastrophic that the very traces of human habitation are erased (2005: 131, 140–1).

As well as providing a counterpoint to the 'semi–stillness' of Braudel's *longue durée*, these studies should go a long way toward dispelling any lingering romanticization of 'indigenes' as living in perfect harmony with their environment or hewing to a temporality of repetitious cycles (see Sharp, 2002: 60; Cruikshank, 2005: 257). Time makes a difference. Just as events do not turn in perfect circles, neither is memory or knowledge simply accumulated in linear time. It may be the case, in a rough and general way, that the longer a people can hold their ground – the more time they spend in a place, a region, or a physical system – the greater the range of environmental variation they are likely to have experienced, and thus the better the odds that they will have learned to co-exist with this variability. This is Mike Davis's point about indigenous Californians vis-à-vis later arrivals. But equally important is the probability that long-term inhabitants will at some point be subjected to singular or concatenating events that exceed received knowledge and cultural memory. And that they will therefore find themselves compelled to respond in new, unlearned, untested ways, like the Australian Aborigines confronted by the intensification of the El Niño effect in Black and Mooney's study. Speaking of episodes of a climatic change that have befallen our species in the past, evolutionary psychologist William Calvin surmises that the shifts were often '… so large and so quick that a single generation gets caught, forced to innovate *on the spot*' (2002: 17, my italics). This is time in all its jarring multiplicity: not a circle or a curve or even an agitated line but a potentially deadly clash of divergent temporalities.

As the evidence of past bouts of abrupt climate change accrues, an impression is forming of just how dramatic the disjuncture between human-scaled rhythms and longer-frequency geo-climatic fluctuation can be. Paleoclimatic data suggests that, while temperature changes were more pronounced closer to the poles, the sudden flip into a cooler regime would have had severe impacts right across the planet, resulting in drastically declining rainfall, fierce winds and dust storms, vast forest fires and collapsing animal populations (Calvin, 2002; Burroughs, 2005). Time and time again, early humans or hominids would have had to face the rapid onset of such conditions, far enough apart to rule out any continuity of experience or memory. As Calvin puts it: 'one unlucky generation ... suddenly had to improvise amidst crashing populations and burning ecosystems' (2002: 4).

It is at junctures like this that 'experimentation' becomes at once more urgent and more deadly – and decisiveness may need to take precedence over deliberation. But this is not only the case at the level of planetary transformation. As we have seen, there are rhythms, vacillations, tipping points at every spatial and temporal scale, with the implication that the need to improvise under conditions of high uncertainty is in no way exceptional. To put it bluntly, this means that all environmental knowledge is hard won, provisional and fallible. What Stephen Pyne has to say at the conclusion of his survey of the human use of free-range fire could well be said of all our ongoing engagements with a variable and volatile earth: 'We cannot know exactly what to do. We stumble. We make mistakes' (2004: 191).

And mistakes have consequences. People caught up in the ongoing turbulence of earth processes do not always 'manage', and cannot be expected to do so. As Cruikshank shows in the case of the Tlingit and Athapaskan tribes, stories which convey useful lessons about living in precarious environments also deal with the trauma of stumbling and falling short. Likewise, Spivak intimates that what goes by the name of 'traditional ecological knowledge' may be as much about coping with loss and suffering as it is about transmitting practical advice. As if to awaken us from the dreams of perpetual sustainability driven by local know-how, she tells of the trials of those who inhabit the flood-prone coasts of Bangladesh: 'They build in the expectation of obliteration ... they grieve and want relief, to rebuild in the face of certain loss, yet again'. Before adding: 'This is an ecological sense of being in the world' (Spivak, 1995: 154). Massey draws out a similar point into a more general claim:

there *is* loss, as the mobile planet, human and nonhuman, continues on its way. There is *material* loss (things will disappear as they are reabsorbed into the cycles of destruction and creation); and there will also on occasions be a *sense of loss*. Moreover it is important to recognize such losses ... They require political, and ethical, attention. (2006: 40)

As physical scientists and social scientists begin to converse about the traces of environmental instability in human history and prehistory (see Davis, 2001: 279), we start to get a feeling for just how catastrophic these losses can be. Genetic mapping points to a succession of severe 'bottlenecks' in global human population as a result of episodes of abrupt climate change, as well as other perturbations such as disease outbreaks or major volcanoes. There are signs that the volcanic eruption of Indonesia's Lake Toba, which occurred some 70,000 years ago, altered global climate for at least a thousand years and levelled human numbers worldwide to perhaps as few as 15,000 individuals – odds which prompt molecular anthropologists to speak of 'survival of the luckiest' (Burroughs, 2005: 138–9).

Climatologists have identified 48 major advances and retreats of glaciation over the last 2.6 million years, together with hundreds of smaller spikes of rapidly fluctuating climatic change. When we consider that every one of these shifts would have had cataclysmic consequences for our human or hominid ancestors, there is a sense that all of us alive today are the 'improbable descendents' of a jittery line of survivors (Calvin, 2002: 3). Not only are we the beneficiaries of their ability to endure – their struggles, sacrifices or sheer luck – but they literally made us who we are: the harsh mechanisms of highly selective survival gifting us with capacities we now take to be our own.

Abyssal alterity, bodily generosity

In most cases, we cannot fully bring to light what others have endured in order to hold their ground. We do not and will not know precisely what it was like to live through the abrupt change in intensity of drought-induced fire in Australia 5,700 years ago; what risks were taken and what losses resulted from thousands of years of learning to work with new rhythms of fuel, wind and moisture. It's hard enough to get a sense of the graft and grind still going on in our own neighbourhood, let alone grasp what it would have been like to scrabble against the sudden slide into a Pleistocene glacial.

But whether we are aware of it or not, we who are 'present' – like any other enduring lineage of living beings – bear the trace of those who came before us (see Grosz, 2004: 2; Clark, 2008). We have become the selves we are by way of our embodied relationship with others: through chains of give and take, relays of encounter and inheritance that stretch back, abyssally, into the past. Most of these others are long gone, the immensity of their small daily achievements destined to go unacknowledged and immemorialized. If we humans are nothing without elephants, plants, oceans or ozone, as Latour aptly observes, so too are we unthinkable without this succession of past human lives and all *their* entwinings with landform, life forms and elemental forces.

Who and what we are now is haunted by another kind of absence, besides that of an ancestry that far outstretches cultural memory. Our bodies, our identities, our social formations, are also consequent of the non-relation we have with all those who did not make it: the ones who did not survive, the communities that were extinguished, the evolutionary lineages that flickered out. Accompanying us as negative shapes – as silent, spectral figures – are the many who did not pass safely across thresholds, who took a wrong turn at a bifurcation, whose experimental wagers did not win out. Our own flourishing may even be implicated in these falterings: for as Levinas prompts us to ponder, the 'place in the sun' claimed by our ancestors may well have visited dispossession and defeat on others. In shadowy, intangible ways, then, these others who vanished along the way form a past that did not live on to become anyone's present: 'the past (that) once was its future possibles, not those that can be realized but those that could have been realized' (Wyschogrod, 1998: 173).

This fissuring of our existence by anterior 'cataclysms' is a form of multiplicity in which the instabilities of the earth and cosmos play a constitutive part, the score of bygone upheavals ensuring that we are never – in any simple, unified sense – at one with ourselves. In the last chapter, we saw how the landscapes we traverse or settle into bear the imprint of the exertions of others – often at great cost. But the idea that warmth and light, aptitudes and potentialities are passed from one living being to another is also suggestive that our very bodies are an expression of the efforts and trials that other bodies have endured: that we are all beneficiaries of what Rosalyn Diprose refers to as 'the generosity of intercorporeal existence' (2002: 151).

As Lynn Margulis likes to remind us, all biological life encapsulates the crises it has weathered: 'life on Earth retains a memory of its past. Living bodies store in their complex chemistry memories of past environmental limitations they overcame' (2001: 18). The human species is no exception. Our cells carry the viral shards of infections that laid our forebears low, our personal distribution of bodily fat speaks of ancient tussles with climate and food availability, the tone of our skin broadcasts long conversations with the solar flux. Both Johann Goudsblom (1992: 194–5) and Stephen Pyne

(1997a: 46) have gone so far as to speculate that our use of fire may be so entrenched as to have encoded itself in our genetic make-up. Advances in the earth sciences are helping pinpoint the junctures in human evolutionary history when the selective pressures of environmental change would have been at their most acute, and already there is speculation about the specific impact of rapidly see-sawing climate on hominid brain size, tool use and patterns of sociability (Calvin, 2002). Caution is required, however, particularly when dealing with events on the scale of abrupt climate change – which may be so decisive and all-encompassing that anything and everything can be ascribed to them. In such contexts, we would do well to hang on to some of the social sciences' familiar injunctions about the range and flexibility of socio-cultural responses to external conditions.

More than this, we need to keep in mind the lessons of ethical and corporeal philosophers that the give and take between bodies resists a full accounting – not just because of the incompleteness of fossil records or other data sets, but because the 'radical passivity' that is at the core of such offerings is inherently defiant of measurement and representation. When Judith Butler proposes that 'the very bodies for which we struggle are not quite ever only our own', (2004: 26) she is not so much describing an evolutionary succession, as evoking a mode of relating in which lives can be thrown off their normal course by crossing paths with an other (as we saw in Chapter 4). Butler is writing within that philosophical tradition which conceives of 'otherness' or 'alterity' not simply in terms of someone coming from some faraway place or time, but in terms of an experience which cannot be fully absorbed, processed, comprehended. She is alluding to the ways in which we can both be made and undone by our dependence on other human beings, and by our exposure to the suffering or the allure of an other.

This sense of a constitutive vulnerability, I have been arguing, needs to take into its compass a susceptibility of bodies not only to each other but to their surrounding environment. 'We face each other as condensations of earth, light, air, and warmth', observes Alphonso Lingis (1994: 122), in an all-too-rare fusion of the thought of Deleuze and Levinas. Meaning that, in every encounter, the ones who confront each other are not only bodies composed though their exchanges with other bodies, but are also made up of the elemental flows they have learned to live with, the materials and life forms they have strained to associate with, the forces that have lured or repelled them. Beyond that, each party carries the traces of whatever their predecessors have endured, embraced, absorbed. Whether we rendezvous at the negotiating table, over the chasm rent by the disaster, or in the hubbub of daily life, we meet as beings who are deeply, unfathomably, underwritten by the earth's own eventful history.

The scientific quest to unearth the sequence of events that have shaped human and other bodies does not simply 'validate' our corporeal and environmental indebtedness to our predecessors. But nor do its illuminations of a turbulent genealogy necessarily work against the grain of an enigmatic and spectral relation to those who came before us. Earth science, however much it pursues a single, integrated and universally accepted account, inevitably generates its own forms of multiplicity, its own scintillations of presence and absence. There are, as Derrida observes, 'fantastic, ghostly … virtual happenings in the scientific domain' (1994: 63). From the time in which the fossil evidence of the extinguished creatures that so agitated Kant first came to light, through the Darwinian tale of chance-laden trajectories of life, and on into our own era of abrupt lineage-extinguishing climatic shifts, the sciences have been telling stories that resound with contingency. Their narratives speak of improbable descent and parallel possibilities, the could-have-been-otherwise, the there-by-sheer-chance and the here-but-not-for-long. As Stengers recognizes, the modern sciences have discovered a making of the earth that is utterly independent of our presence: 'even though it is a question of comprehending the history that led to us, this history interests us *in something other than what led to us*' (2000: 142, author's italics). Which means that it also interests us in what may yet lead away from us.

Cosmopolitics for a volatile planet

We are at a moment, I have been arguing, when ongoing developments in the earth sciences, some recent turns in philosophical inquiry, and a range of ethico-political issues arising out of our ecological predicament are gathering over the theme of an autonomous, dynamic, self-generating cosmos. Converging, that is, on the non-correlation of physical being with human presence or thought or enactment. If this scenario is one in which human existence is more contingent, more precarious than it might previously have seemed, it is also one that makes our eventual arrival at the current juncture all the more remarkable – should we choose to look at it like this. It is from this vantage point that I want to return to Sachs's challenge to come up with the kind of enduring social formations that are willing and able to offer a supportive terrain to the growing numbers who may need it. And to come around to the idea of a cosmopolitanism that welcomes those induced into movement across the face of the earth – but does so with an eye on the deep, tortuous journeys that brought each of us up to this 'surface'.

Kant deserves full credit for imagining a cosmopolitanism in which all human beings are deserving of 'the right of possession in common of the earth's surface' (1996 [1795]: 329). Though as Derrida notes, this inclusiveness is also exclusive, for it leaves out – or rather makes conditional – access to everything that human beings have inscribed or constructed upon our planet's uppermost strata (2001b: 20–1). Moreover, Kant's measured and regulated global hospitality makes no special provision for those 'revolutions of the earth' that haunted him career-long, the sublime machinations of planet and cosmos that he conceded 'threaten(ed) freedom with complete destruction' (1967 [1788]: 194). Though Kant supposes that the miseries visited upon our neighbours by earthquakes and other upheavals should excite empathy and generosity (1994 [1756]: 29), these early sensitivities to the 'inconstancy of the world' fail to translate into special concessions for the displaced or unworlded in his later cosmopolitical constitution.

In the resuscitation of the cosmopolitan impulse two centuries later, the earth has if anything solidified and receded still further. While Beck and others may have heeded the way debased natural or hybridized elements are increasingly impelled to cross national boundaries, the ground beneath these transgressive mobilizations remains obdurate and non-participative (see Clark, 2002). As Pheng Cheah pointedly notes, for all its renewed vigour, contemporary cosmopolitan scenarios still overwhelmingly privilege a mode of footloose, hybridized cultural agency which is defined by 'physical freedom from being tied to the earth' (1998: 301), thus leaving the physical planet itself as at best a backdrop, at worst an impediment to the real action.

Arguably, it is only in the respective 'cosmopolitics' of Isabelle Stengers and Bruno Latour that we consistently begin to see a dynamic physico-materiality – and not simply our ruffling of the stuff of the world – granted a capacity to pose meaningful questions for politics. For both Latour and Stengers, nonhumans are no more settled or stuck in their own grooves than 'we' are, and it is by way of this intrinsic motivation that 'things' constantly bring new provocations and challenges into the political arena. Just as our practical–material engagement with the world's shifting physicality calls for endless experimentation, improvisation and risk-taking, so too must we go about our politics as a kind of ceaseless experimenting with ways of manifesting and articulating the interests of the full spectrum of human and nonhuman actors.

The preeminent 'cosmopolitical' question for Latour, then, is that of how we are to assemble and administer the world we share with all these heterogeneous others (2004a, 2004b: 204). How do we compose a cosmos in which the interests and properties of all pertinent entities are accounted for – including their various tendencies to upset and derange whatever degree of order we have so far achieved? As I noted in Chapter 1, this brings Latour to a point where contest, deliberation and negotiation are the key operations in world-building. The cosmos is political through and through because it is fundamentally an 'order' which is collectively assembled by participating actors: the cosmos in his cosmopolitics is ideally a product of due political process, rather than a condition or context of actors coming together.

For all its inclusivity, however, I have been arguing that Latour's judiciously crafted realities fail to build on his own beautiful and profound idea of nonhumans composing fully autonomous worlds of their own. In this way, they circumvent any possibility of we humans being reliant on realities given to us by others. There is something strangely conventional, in a sociological sense, about Latour's conviction that any such inherited universe must by definition restrain the options open to socio-cultural agents – for this is a time when many other critical thinkers are comfortable with the idea that bio-geo-physical substrata which are not ours to recompose are nonetheless capable of providing endless provocation and potentiality for human expression (see Cheah, 1996; Ansell Pearson, 1997; Kirby, 1997; Grosz, 2005).

The challenge of thinking 'cosmopolitically', I am suggesting, is as much about how to deal constructively and compassionately with arrangements *we cannot do otherwise* as it is about devising procedures to handle those aspects of existence that are amenable to collective re-fabrication. It is the world's own becoming – and the lapses in its becoming – that generate some of the most profound problems that ethics and politics currently confront: challenges that cannot be reduced to effects of prior poorly assembled socio-natural orderings. Here, Stengers offers guidance, with her injunction to *follow* the singular and often irreversible turns delivered up by an earth that remains largely indifferent in the face of our interventions, her acknowledgement of 'the "respect" that physical theory imposes on us with regard to nature'. Our catastrophes may be mere contingencies for the earth, as she astutely notes. But nonetheless, the fallout of the planet's rumblings is for us potentially catastrophic: it has deep and troubling consequences at many different scales and across the manifold domains of our lives.

The ordinary, episodic stirrings of our earth and its many subsystems, I've been urging, are a source of estrangement for human beings and other living things. It's important to remember that the resurrection of the cosmopolitan ideal has come about largely as a response to the predicament of 'strangers' in the contemporary world. It is not simply about negotiating differences – whether these are distinct cultural practices, political beliefs or ways of composing the cosmos – though, undeniably, this soon comes into play. It is also, and perhaps primarily about being touched, swayed, perturbed by the situation in which we see others – moved to such an extent that we feel impelled to reassess our own familiar ways of acting or living. As Derrida reminds us, the ones who are most in need of a warm welcome are not so much those who have recognizably come from afar – foreigners, migrants, travellers – but those who appear before us bereft in some way, without a place to call home, disorientated or dispossessed (Derrida, 2000a: 8, 2000b: 25; Dikeç, 2002: 230). Being 'other' or 'strange', as we saw in Chapter 3, has as much to do with being estranged from one's own sense of self, from the continuity of one's time and space, as it has to do with being categorically different from others. It's about being radically 'de-worlded' as well as just finding oneself in another's world. And we live on a planet that does its own un-worlding – alongside or on top of all the other ways of unravelling worlds which we bring upon ourselves.

Global hospitality and the space–time of the other

For Derrida, hospitality – the definitive cosmopolitan gesture – is always enacted at a threshold: the threshold can be the concreteness of a front door, a wall, a border post. But it can also be a turning point in the course of a life – the kind of life-altering events visited upon us that, even when we see them coming, are inevitably more or less or different from anything we expected. And especially those situations staged around the limits of life. With regard to the story or property of 'one's own life', Derrida writes, 'the border (finis) of this property would be more essential, more originary, and more proper than those of any other territory in the world' (1993: 3). Indeed, it is the encounter with 'otherness' that helps bring the threshold into visibility: the limits of our bodies, our dwellings, our communities manifesting themselves through the event of something that pushes against or passes over them (Derrida, 1993: 33; Dikeç et al., 2009: 12). It is because they are the locus of an encounter, a transition, that Derrida counsels us not to see borders or thresholds as hindrances to free association which thereby need to be done away with, but as the junction across which relating itself becomes possible (Barnett, 2005: 16).

Such conjunctures, I am proposing, occur not only in the material space composed by human actors, not only in the life course of biological beings, but in the history of the earth and the cosmos. At every spatial and temporal scale, the physical world has its own thresholds: boundaries which separate one domain of existence from another, turning points where systems transform themselves into a different state, extremes in the ordinary rhythmical expression of variability. Living beings, ourselves included, contribute in their own ways to many of these transitions but also find themselves having to weather changes over which they have little or no leverage. Of course, creatures can experience stress and discomfort in all manner of situations. But it is the moment when crucial life support systems pass through a critical threshold – the realignment of meshing tectonic plates, the irruption of a viral epidemic, the tipping of climate into a new regime – that the tolerance levels of an individual or collective body are most likely to be pushed or breached. As we are now learning, our own ancestors had to negotiate a great many of these transitional points. And arguably with a lot less room to manoeuvre than is the case with the geo-political border crossings that have become so emblematic of social life in the contemporary globalized world.

The dynamism that inheres in material reality plays a part in the genesis of otherness. The quite ordinary eventfulness of the universe carves rifts in the continuity of life – chasms over which others meet without ever being as one. This is why, I am suggesting, we need to bring together what Derrida is saying about thresholds as the sites at which selves and others come into proximity with the understanding offered by the natural sciences (and many other forms of 'empirical' knowledge) about the discontinuous and messy trajectories of real-world physical systems. This is much more than a matter of occasionally recognizing that we or others might be thrown off course by exceptional natural forces. It is about acknowledging that the deterritorializing of the earth is the primordial condition of our existence, that the instability of the ground on which we stand precedes, accompanies and will likely succeed any material fabrications or inscriptions of our own.

The nation state may well be a machine for producing others, or manufacturing estrangement, but one of the reasons it does so is because its investment in the stability of the earth places barriers in the path of those who would move with the mobilizations of life, weather, water or rock. This wager on the solidity of the elements is one which cannot be won in the long term. Meanwhile, over shorter time spans, a world system of topographical stabilizations continues to struggle against a universe of topological shiftings: a clash in which living bodies get caught up, pinned down, pushed aside.

Then again, the time is long past for adventitious and unregulated traversal of the globe, as Kant was well aware two centuries ago. If it ever existed. The very challenges that elemental instability poses can, among other possibilities, open bodies to one another. Out of the radical asymmetry of an encounter may come the emergence of reciprocity, the securing of mutual arrangements and collective efforts to secure a terrain – communities 'allied against the rumble of the world'. It is the very circumstance of having a home, a place that is at least provisionally secured, as Derrida (2000a, 2000b: 55, 77) likes to remind us, that makes the offer of hospitality more than an empty, ineffectual gesture.

This is the condition of any unconditional welcome to others: the underpinning of the Jamaat's gift of food to their neighbours after the Tsunami, of Ville Platte's warm reception of 'company' after Katrina, and perhaps (it is as yet hard to know) of Senegal's offer of a homeland to the dispossessed people of Haiti. It is why programmes are needed – plans, norms and regulations, networks of resources and knowledge. But it is also why any programme must be prepared to be interrupted: why 'we have to leave room within the programme, at the border of the programme, for the unprogrammable, for the uncalculable, ... the unpredictable event' (Derrida, 2001c: 259).

It is essential that we come round to the informed, deliberated and judicious process of setting up appropriate procedures in response to earthly imperatives, which is always also a matter of working through our differences and commonalities. And sooner rather than later. This is what will orient us toward appropriate forms of gifting and care after a disaster like Haiti's earthquake or the Indian Ocean

Tsunami; what must be done to seek justice amid the drowning fields of Katrina, what is needed if we are to have any chance of achieving equitable and effective responses to lurching climate change. It is what is required if amends are to be made for appropriated land and stolen fire. But it is the jolting of time out of joint, the exposure to events beyond our comprehension – especially as we see them furrowing the face of an other – that tips us into the orbit of strangers. It is our radical passivity that provides charge, the rush, the shock that propels us into action: our constitutive vulnerability that kicks open the door to what Latour (2004a: 455) refers to as the 'tooth and nail' of hard, sustained, demanding negotiation.

As both Levinas and Derrida have sought to show, the time of 'conditionality' – of contestation, solidarity and exchange – is out of kilter with the temporality of an 'unconditional' opening to another (see Barnett, 2004, 2005). The pursuit of collective agreement and informed action implies a certain co-presence and contemporaneity. But to be truly receptive to an other is to enter 'a time *without me*' (Levinas, cited in Bernasconi, 1997: 258): it is to tap into a world of experience that I cannot wholly identify with, may not make present to myself, will not fully integrate into my own storyline. Such a caring or generous ceding to otherness may be far from the rare and ethereal event that critics of Levinas sometimes suppose. Fully bridging the experiential chasm that divides the province of the other from our own world might be an 'impossibility', but holding out a hand across this rift is a basic and commonplace gesture, the very condition of possibility for so much of what we know as social life. However, how to move between a 'panic of empathy' sparked by individual faces or voices to a global cosmopolitanism that is routinely required to accommodate millions of estranged others remains a task of daunting magnitude.

We should not forget the irony that animates Bataille's thought: that the best way to become attuned with the convulsions of the cosmos is by commending ourselves to 'good expenditure' in our most intimate and ordinary relations. As Allan Stoekl (2007: 142) riffs off this theme, we might have a better chance of prising the planet out of its downward ecological spiral accidentally, not as the goal of a grand, visionary project but as the unintended consequence of more joyous and generous living right here and now. But as suggested by Bataille's constant conjoining of the intemperate forces of the universe with the exuberance of inter-corporeal gifting, there is inspiration to be taken from thinking through the ethico-political in terms of its constitutive openness to a vast and turbulent exteriority.

In a similar vein, an appreciation of the strung-out, hazard-strewn journeys that have brought us into the present can serve to bind us 'to everything that has ever convulsed upon the Earth'. And might in this way incite a sense of gratitude and indebtedness to the miraculously unbroken chain of bodies to which we belong: a responsibility to the past which could in turn innervate our responsibilities in the present and to the future.

With regard to the imperatives toward new forms of hospitality and solidarity at a global scale, we need also to be mindful of the gifts of those 'other' bodies which have made the very idea and experience of globalism possible. Resonating with Levinas's prompt about the 'well-trampled paths' we follow, Stengers reminds us of 'the aid received from locals, without which the person who arrives could not have invented-improvised a means of passage' (2000: 119). This assistance, whether directly proffered or inscribed in landscapes whose jagged trajectories have been smoothed by careful dwelling, comes only by way of the embodied exertions of others: the many generations who put their bodies on the line securing a terrain that later arrivals would take for granted. Or take for themselves. Only by knitting together an array of landscapes and seascapes readied by other's habitation or transversal has our current version of the global materialized. By the same token, only by way of a pre-existing atmosphere, biosphere, lithosphere, hydrosphere – a decisively *pregiven* globality – could humans have ever gained purchase across the earth's surface.

In this way, every genuine encounter with another human being is an opaque window into a particular passage through the earth's shifting, tilting course. Without discernible origin, but not necessarily without end. So too is a brush of our own with a cyclone, a heatwave, an epidemic, an opening into processes with a temporality that stretches back into a past without me, a past without any of us. And, if we keep going, a past without life at all. For if we follow their threads and chains, our elemental exchanges soon bring us into contact with the far side of the planet, and take us quickly beyond the earth to the energy of the sun and forces of the cosmos (see Lingis, 1998b: 120, 2000b: 135). This is an asynchrony and an exorbitance that no form of reciprocity, no contract, no economy on this spherical planet will ever square up. To look this far, as John Caputo puts it, is to gaze into the very 'face of a faceless cosmos' that makes of an ethical opening to an other 'an act of hyperbolic partiality and defiance' (1993: 19; see also Clark, 2010b).

We need to remember that most gifts, most transfers of abundance and potentiality come down to us deeply incised with inequity, unevenly distributed and biased in their acknowledgement: the hard graft behind them too often overlooked or accepted ungraciously (Diprose, 2002: 9; Vaughan, 2002: 111–12).[1] There is no obligation to convert an immense indebtedness into recognition or gratefulness. There is no easy or obvious passage from gratitude to justice. And there is no direct link between proximity to the violence of physical forces and the cultivation of a generous disposition towards others. We are still a long way from the cosmopolitan thought we need, the kind that might point the way to forms of justice and hospitality fitting for a planet that rips away its support from time to time: for an earth that is not nearly as human or as homely as we tend to assume.

And yet, across the world, ordinary folk redirect their ceremonial feasts to bereft neighbours, they offer beds to complete strangers, assemble ramshackle armadas of rescue vessels, dig into their wallets or their wardrobes to make offerings to people they will never meet. A million and one obscure acts of love flare and fade away: tiny sparks of generosity that arc across the cracks which will not cease to open in the earth. Improbably, we have made it this far, across unfathomable ruptures and through innumerable thresholds. Improbably, we may make it over the next tipping point.

Note

1 If we need reminding: Mary Gilmore, to return to my opening account in the previous chapter, goes so far as to suggest that some of the worst blazes in her area were deliberately lit by European settlers to drive out or exterminate Aboriginal people (1934: 153).

References

Adam, B. (1990) *Time and Social Theory*. Cambridge: Polity Press.

Adam, B. (1993) 'Time and Environmental Crisis: An Exploration with Special Reference to Pollution', *Innovation in Social Science Research* 6 (3): 399–413.

Adam, B. (1998) *Timescapes of Modernity: The Environment and Invisible Hazards*. London: Routledge.

Adorno, T. (1973) *Negative Dialectics*. London: Routledge.

Agamben, G. (2005) *The Coming Community*. Minneapolis, MN: University of Minnesota Press.

Ahmed, S. (2000) *Strange Encounters: Embodied Others in Post-Coloniality*. London and New York: Routledge.

Alley, R. B. (2000) *The Two-Mile Time Machine: Ice Cores, Abrupt Climate Change, and Our Future*. Princeton, NJ: Princeton University Press.

Alley, R. B., Marotzke, J., Nordhaus, W. D., Overpeck, J. T., Peteet, D. M., Pielke, R. A., Pierrehumbert, R. T., Rhines, P. B., Stocker, T. F., Talley, L. D. and Wallace, J. M. (2003) 'Abrupt Climate Change', *Science* 299 (5615): 2005–10.

Ansell Pearson, K. (1997) *Viroid Life: Perspectives on Nietzsche and the Transhuman Condition*. London: Routledge.

Ayre, M. (2007) 'Metropolis Strives to Meet its Thirst', *BBC News*, 3 May. Available at: http://news.bbc.co.uk/1/hi/sci/tech/6620919.stm (accessed 13/07/2007).

Azar, C. and Lindgren, K. (2003) 'Catastrophic Events and Stochastic Cost–benefit Analysis of Climate Change', *Climatic Change* 56: 245–55.

Bachelard, G. (1987 [1938]) *The Psychoanalysis of Fire*. London: Quartet.

Badiou, A. (2000) *Deleuze: The Clamor of Being*. Minneapolis, MN: University of Minnesota Press.

Badiou, A. (2001) *Ethics: An Essay on the Understanding of Evil*. London: Verso.

Badiou, A. (2005) *Infinite Thought*. London: Continuum.

Bakker, K. (2005) 'Katrina: The Public Transcript of "Disaster"', *Environment and Planning D: Society and Space* 23: 795–802.

Bankoff, G. (2006) 'The Tale of the Three Pigs: Taking Another Look at Vulnerability in the Light of the Indian Ocean Tsunami and Hurricane Katrina', in *Understanding Katrina: Perspectives from the Social Sciences*. Available at: http://understandingkatrina. ssrc.org/Bankoff/ (accessed 23/10/2001).

Barnett, C. (2004) 'Deconstructing Radical Democracy: Articulation, Representation, and Being-with-Others', *Political Geography* 23: 503–28.

Barnett, C. (2005) 'Ways of Relating: Hospitality and the Acknowledgement of Otherness', *Progress in Human Geography* 29 (1): 5–21.

Barnett, C. and Land, D. (2007) 'Geographies of Generosity: Beyond the Moral Turn', *Geoforum* 38 (6): 1065–75.

Barry, J. M. (1997) *Rising Tide: The Great Mississippi Flood of 1927 and How it Changed America*. New York: Simon & Schuster.

Bataille, G. (1986 [1957]) *Erotism: Death and Sensuality*. San Francisco: City Lights.

Bataille, G. (1988 [1954]) *Inner Experience*. New York: State University of New York Press.

Bataille, G. (1991 [1967]) *The Accursed Share: Volume I*. New York. Zone.

Bataille, G. (1993 [1976]) *The Accursed Share: Volumes II & III*. New York. Zone.

Batha, E. (2005) 'Tsunami Response was World's Best – UN', *Reuters AlertNet*, December 19. Available at: www.alertnet.org/thefacts/reliefresources/113777913049.htm (accessed 01/08/2006).

Batty, H. and Gray, T. (1996) 'Environmental Rights and National Sovereignty', in S. Caney, D. George and P. Jones (eds) *National Rights, International Obligations*. Colorado: Westview Press.

Baudrillard, J. (1993 [1976]) *Symbolic Exchange and Death*. London: Sage.

Bauman, Z. (1991) *Modernity and Ambivalence*. Cambridge: Polity.

Bauman, Z. (1993) *Postmodern Ethics*. Oxford: Blackwell.

Bauman, Z. (2000) *Liquid Modernity*. Cambridge: Polity Press.

BBC News (2005) 'Your Experiences of Asian Disaster', *BBC News Online*, January 11. Available at: http://news.bbc.co.uk/1/hi/talking_point/4125619.stm (accessed 01/08/2006).

Beck, U. (1989) 'On the Way to the Industrial Risk-Society? Outline of an Argument', *Thesis Eleven* 23: 86–103.

Beck, U. (1992) Risk Society: *Towards a New Modernity*. London: Sage.

Beck, U. (1995) *Ecological Politics in an Age of Risk*. Cambridge: Polity Press.

Beck, U. (1999) *World Risk Society*. Cambridge: Polity Press.

Beck, U. (2000a) 'The Cosmopolitan Perspective: Sociology of the Second Age of Modernity', *British Journal of Sociology* 51 (1): 79–105.

Beck, U. (2009) *World at Risk*. Cambridge: Polity Press.

Bengtsson, L. and Hammer, C. (eds) (2001) *Geosphere–Biosphere Interactions and Climate*. Cambridge: Cambridge University Press.

Bennett, J. (2004) 'The Force of Things: Steps Toward an Ecology of Matter', *Political Theory* 32 (3): 347–72.

Bernasconi, R. (1997) 'What Goes Around Comes Around: Derrida and Levinas on the Economy of the Gift and Gift of Genealogy', in A. Schrift (ed.) *The Logic of the Gift: Toward an Ethic of Generosity*. New York: Routledge.

Black, M. P. and Mooney, S. D. (2007) 'The Response of Aboriginal Burning Practices to Population Levels and El Niño-Southern Oscillation Events during the Mid- to Late-Holocene: A Case Study from the Sydney Basin using Charcoal and Pollen Analysis', *Australian Geographer* 38 (1): 37–52.

Blanchot, M. (1995 [1980]) *The Writing of the Disaster*. Lincoln, NE and London: University of Nebraska Press.

Bonta, M. and Protevi, J. (2004) *Deleuze and Geophilosophy: A Guide and Glossary*. Edinburgh: Edinburgh University Press.

Booker, J. (2006) 'Deadly Alpine Quake Predicted', *NZ Herald.co.nz*, 24 August. Available at: www.nzherald.co.nz/nz/news/article.cfm?c_id=1&objectid=1039 7752 (accessed 06/05/2009).

Botkin, D. (1990) *Discordant Harmonies: A New Ecology for the Twenty-First Century*. New York: Oxford University Press.

Brassier, R. (2007) *Nihil Unbound: Enlightenment and Extinction*. Houndmills, Basingstoke: Palgrave Macmillan.

Braudel, F. (1980 [1969]) *On History*. London: Weidenfeld and Nicolson.

Braudel, F. (1995 [1949]) *The Mediterranean and the Mediterranean World in the Age of Philip II, Volume 1*, Berkeley CA: University of California Press.

Braun, B. (2006) 'Global Natures in the Space of Assemblage', *Progress in Human Geography*, 30 (5): 644–54.

Braun, B. (2007) 'Biopolitics and the Molecularization of Life', *Cultural Geographies* 14: 6–28.

Braun, B. (2008) 'Environmental Issues: Inventive Life', *Progress in Human Geography* 32 (5): 667–79.

Braun, B. and McCarthy, J. (2005) 'Hurricane Katrina and Abandoned Being', *Environment and Planning D: Society and Space* 23: 802–9.

British Red Cross (2005) 'Life After the Tsunami', *Lifeline*, autumn (19): 6–8.

Broecker, W. S. (1987) 'Unpleasant Surprises in the Greenhouse', *Nature* 328 (9 July): 123–6.

Brown, S. and Capdevila, R. (1999) '*Perpetuum Mobile*: Substance, Force and the Sociology of Translation', in J. Law and J. Hassard (eds) *Actor Network Theory and After*. Oxford: Blackwell.

Bryant, L. (2009) Larval Subjects Blog, 6 August. Available at: http://larvalsubjects.wordpress.com/2009/08/page/4/ (accessed 20/09/2009).

Bryant, S. and Gaza, C. L. (2005) 'School Bus Comandeered by Renegade Refugees First to Arrive at Astrodome', *Houston Chronicle*, 1 September. Available at: www.chron.com/disp/story.mpl/topstory2/3334317.html (accessed 23/01/2010).

Buck-Morss, S. (2002) 'A Global Public Sphere', *Radical Philosophy* 111: 2–10.

Burroughs, W. J. (2001) *Climate Change: A Multidisciplinary Approach*. Cambridge: Cambridge University Press.

Burroughs, W. J. (2005) *Climate Change in Prehistory: The End of the Reign of Chaos*. Cambridge: Cambridge University Press.

Butler, J. (2004) *Precarious Life: The Powers of Mourning and Violence*. London: Verso.

Calder, N. (1997) *The Manic Sun: Weather Theories Confounded*. London: Pilkington Press.

Callon, M. and Law, J. (1989) 'On the Construction of Sociotechnical Networks: Content and Context Revisited', *Knowledge and Society* 8: 57–83.

Calvin, W. H. (2002) *A Brain for all Seasons: Human Evolution and Abrupt Climate Change*. Chicago: University of Chicago Press.

Canguilhem, G. (1994) *A Vital Rationalist: Selected Writings from Georges Canguilhem* (F. Delaporte (ed.)). New York: Zone.

Caputo, J. (1993) *Against Ethics*. Bloomington, IN: Indiana University Press.

Carballo, M., Heal, B. and Horbaty, G. (2006) 'Impact of the Tsunami on Psychosocial Health and Well-being', *International Review of Psychiatry* 18 (3): 217–23.

Caviedes, C. N. (2001) *El Niño in History: Storming through the Ages*. Gainesville, FL: University Press of Florida.

Chalier, C. (2002) *What Ought I to Do? Morality in Kant and Levinas*. London: Cornell University Press.

Cheah, P. (1996) 'Mattering', *Diacritics* 26 (1): 108–39.

Cheah, P. (1998) 'Given Culture: Rethinking Cosmopolitical Freedom in Transnationalism', in P. Cheah and B. Robbins (eds) *Cosmopolitics: Thinking and Feeling Beyond the Nation*. Minneapolis, MN: University of Minnesota Press.

Cheah, P. (1999) 'Spectral Nationality: The Living-On [sur-vie] of the Postcolonial Nation in Neocolonial Globalization', in E. Grosz (ed.) *Becomings: Explorations in Time, Memory, and Futures*. Ithaca, NY and London: Cornell University Press.

Chester, D. (2001) 'The 1755 Lisbon Earthquake', *Progress in Physical Geography* 25 (3): 363–83.

Clark, N. (1997) 'Panic Ecology: Nature in the Age of Superconductivity', *Theory, Culture and Society* 14 (10): 77–96.

Clark, N. (1999) 'Wild Life: Ferality and the Frontier with Chaos', in K. Neumann, H. Ericksen and N. Thomas (eds) *Quicksands: Foundational Histories of Australia and Aotearoa New Zealand*. Sydney: University of New South Wales Press.

Clark, N. (2000) '"Botanizing on the Asphalt?" The Complex Life of Cosmopolitan Bodies', *Body and Society*, 6 (3): 12–33.

Clark, N. (2002) 'The Demon-Seed: Bioinvasion as the Unsettling of Environmental Cosmopolitanism', *Theory Culture and Society* 19 (1–2): 101–26.

Clark, N. (2003a) 'Turbulent Prospects: Sustaining Urbanism on a Dynamic Planet', in T. Hall and M. Miles (eds) *Urban Futures: Critical Commentaries on Shaping Cities*. London: Routledge.

Clark, N. (2003b) 'The Play of the World', in M. Pryke, G. Rose and S. Whatmore (eds) *Thinking Through Research*. London: Sage.

Clark, N. (2005a) 'Ex-orbitant Globality', *Theory, Culture and Society* 22 (5): 165–85.

Clark, N. (2005b) 'Disaster and Generosity', *The Geographical Journal*: 171 (4): 384–6.

Clark, N. (2005c) 'Postcolonial Natures', *Antipode* 37 (2): 364–8.

Clark, N. (2006) 'Offering', *Space and Culture* 9 (1): 100–2.

Clark, N. (2007a) 'Animal Interface: The Generosity of Domestication', in R. Cassidy and M. Mullin (eds) *Where the Wild Things Are Now: Domestication Reconsidered*, Wenner-Gren International Symposium Series. Oxford: Berg.

Clark, N. (2007b) 'Living through the Tsunami: Vulnerability and Generosity on a Volatile Earth', *Geoforum*, 38 (6): 1127–39.

Clark, N. (2008) 'Aboriginal Cosmopolitanism', *International Journal of Urban and Regional Studies* 32 (3): 737–44.

Clark, N. (2010a) 'Volatile Worlds, Vulnerable Bodies: Confronting Abrupt Climate Change', *Theory, Culture and Society* 27 (2–3): 31–53.

Clark, N. (2010b) 'Ex-orbitant Generosity: Gifts of Love in a Cold Cosmos', *Parallax* 16 (1): 80–95.

Clark, N. (2010c) 'Acquiescence: Fluid Realities and Planned Retreat', *Reading Room: A Journal of Art and Culture* 4: 42–59.

Clark, N. and Stevenson, N. (2003) 'Care in the Time of Catastrophe: Citizenship, Community and the Ecological Imagination', *Journal of Human Rights* 2 (2): 235–46.

Cline, W. (2007) *Global Warming and Agriculture: Impact Estimates by Country*. Washington, DC: Peterson Institute. Available at: http://bookstore.piie.com/book-store/4037.html (accessed 10/01/2010).

Colling, A., Dise, N., Francis, P., Harris, N. and Wilson, C. (1997) *The Dynamic Earth*. Milton Keynes: The Open University.

Committee on Abrupt Climate Change, National Research Council (2002) *Abrupt Climate Change: Inevitable Surprises*. Available at: www.nap.edu/catalog.php?record_id=10136 (accessed 10/03/2008).

Cooper, M. (2006) 'Pre-empting Emergence: The Biological Turn in the War on Terror', *Theory, Culture and Society* 23 (4): 113–35.

Cornell, D. (1992) *The Philosophy of the Limit*. New York and London: Routledge.

Craw, R. and Heads, M. (1988) 'Reading Croizat', *Rivista di Biologia Biology Forum* 81 (4): 499–532.

Crowley, S. (2006) 'Where is Home? Housing for Low-Income People after the 2005 Hurricanes', in C. Hartman and G. Squires (eds) *There is No Such Thing as a Natural Disaster: Race, Class, and Hurricane Katrina*. New York: Routledge.

Cruikshank, J. (2005) *Do Glaciers Listen? Local Knowledge, Colonial Encounters and Social Imagination*. Vancouver: University of British Columbia Press.

Crutzen, P. J. (2002) 'Geology of Mankind', *Nature* 415 (6867) 3 January: 23.

Curr, E. (1965 [1883]) *Recollections of Squatting in Victoria*. Melbourne: Melbourne University Press.

Cutter, S. (2006) 'The Geography of Social Vulnerability: Race, Class, and Catastrophe', in *Understanding Katrina: Perspectives from the Social Sciences*. Available at http://understandingkatrina.ssrc.org/Cutter/ (accessed 23/10/2001).

Davis, M. (1996) 'Cosmic Dancers on History's Stage? The Permanent Revolution in the Earth Sciences', *New Left Review* 217: 48–84.

Davis, M. (1998) *Ecology of Fear: Los Angeles and the Imagination of Disaster*. New York: Metropolitan Books.

Davis, M. (2001) *Late Victorian Holocausts: El Nino Famines and the Making of the Third World*. London: Verso.

Davis, M. (2008) 'Living on the Ice Shelf: Humanity's Meltdown', *TomDispatch. com*, 26 June. Available at: www.tomdispatch.com/post/174949 (accessed 20/11/2009).

Davis, M. and Fontenot, A. (2006) 'Hurricane Gumbo', in A. Reed, Jr (ed.) *Unnatural Disaster: The Nation on Hurricane Katrina*. New York: Nation Books.

Deffeyes, K. S. (2005) *Beyond Oil: The View from Hubbert's Peak*. New York: Hill and Wang.

De Landa, M. (1992) 'Nonorganic Life', in J. Crary and S. Kwinter (eds) *Incorporations*. New York: Zone.

De Landa, M. (1997) *A Thousand Years of Nonlinear History*. New York: Swerve.

Delay, T. (2007) 'Carbon is the New Business Currency', *Director Special Supplement: The New Economy*. Available at: www.director.co.uk/Content/pdfs/CarbonTrust_Apr07.pdf (accessed 10/01/2010).

Deleuze, G. (1990) *Bergsonism*. New York: Zone.

Deleuze, G. (1994 [1962]) *Difference and Repetition*. London: Athlone Press.

Deleuze, G. (1995) *Negotiations*. New York: Columbia University Press.

Deleuze, G. and Guattari, F. (1983 [1977]) *Anti-Oedipus: Capitalism and Schizophrenia*. Minneapolis, MN: University of Minnesota Press.

Deleuze, G. and Guattari, F. (1986) *Kafka: Toward a Minor Literature*. Minneapolis, MN: University of Minnesota Press.

Deleuze, G. and Guattari, F. (1987) *A Thousand Plateaus: Capitalism and Schizophrenia*. Minneapolis, MN: University of Minnesota Press.

Deleuze, G. and Guattari, F. (1994) *What is Philosophy?* London: Verso.

Demeritt, D. (2001) 'The Construction of Global Warming and the Politics of Science', *Annals of the Association of American Geographers* 91 (2): 307–37.

Derrida, J. (1978) *Writing and Difference*. London: Routledge.

Derrida, J. (1981) *Dissemination*. Chicago: University of Chicago Press.

Derrida, J. (1984) 'My Chances/Mes Chances: A Rendezvous with some Epicurean Stereophonies', in W. Kerrigan and J. Smith (eds) *Taking Chances: Derrida, Psychoanalysis and Literature*. Baltimore, MD: Johns Hopkins University Press.

Derrida, J. (1988) *Limited Inc*. Evanston, IL: Northwestern University Press.

Derrida, J. (1989 [1962]) *Edmund Husserl's Origins of Geometry: An Introduction*. Lincoln, NE: University of Nebraska Press.

Derrida, J. (1992a) *Given Time: 1. Counterfeit Money*. Chicago: University of Chicago Press.

Derrida, J. (1992b) 'Force of Law: The "Mystical Foundation of Authority"', in D. Cornell, M. Rosenfeld and D. G. Carlson (eds) *Deconstruction and the Possibility of Justice*. New York: Routledge.

Derrida, J. (1993) *Aporias*. Stanford, CA: Stanford University Press.

Derrida, J. (1994) *Specters of Marx: The State of the Debt, the Work of Mourning, and the New International*. New York: Routledge.

Derrida, J. (1995a) *The Gift of Death*. Chicago: University of Chicago Press.

Derrida, J. (1995b) *Points ... Interviews, 1974–1994*. Stanford, CA: Stanford University Press.

Derrida, J. (2000a) 'Hostipitality', *Angelaki* 5 (3): 3–18.

Derrida, J. (2000b) *Of Hospitality*. Stanford, CA: Stanford University Press.

Derrida, J. (2001a) 'The Future of the Profession or the Unconditional University', in L. Simmons and H. Worth (eds) *Derrida Downunder*. Palmerston North: Dunmore Press.

Derrida, J. (2001b) *On Cosmopolitanism and Forgiveness*. London: Routledge.

Derrida, J. (2001c) 'A Roundtable Discussion with Jacques Derrida', in L. Simmons and H. Worth (eds) *Derrida Downunder*. Palmerston North: Dunmore Press.

de Waal, A. (2006) 'An Imperfect Storm: Narratives of Calamity in a Liberal–Technocratic Age', in *Understanding Katrina: Perspectives from the Social Sciences*. Available at http://understandingkatrina.ssrc.org/deWaal/ (accessed 23/10/2001).

Dikeç, M. (2002) 'Pera Peras Poros: Longings for Spaces of Hospitality', *Theory Culture and Society* 19: (1–2): 227–47.

Dikeç, M., Clark, N. and Barnett, C. (2009) 'Extending Hospitality: Giving Space, Taking Time', *Paragraph* 32 (1): 1–14.

Dillon, M. (1999) 'The Scandal of the Refugee: Some Reflections on the "Inter" of International Relations and Continental Thought', in D. Campbell and M. Shapiro (eds) *Moral Spaces: Rethinking Ethics and World Politics*. Minneapolis, MN: University of Minnesota Press.

Dillon, M. (2007) 'Governing Terror: The State of Emergency of Biopolitical Emergence', *International Political Sociology* 1: 7–28.

Diprose, R. (2002) *Corporeal Generosity: On Giving with Nietzsche, Merleau-Ponty, and Levinas*. Albany, NY: State University of New York Press.

Disaster Management and Information Programme (2004) 'Portrait of a Disaster.' Available at: www.humanitarianinfo.org/srilanka/infocentre/assessments/others/doc/DMIP/DMIP_Rapid_Assess.pdf (accessed 01/08/2006).

Dyson, M. E. (2006) 'Great Migrations?', in D. D. Troutt (ed.) *After the Storm: Black Intellectuals Explore the Meaning of Hurricane Katrina*. New York: New Press.

Emmerich, R. (dir.) (2004) *The Day After Tomorrow*. 20th Century Fox.

Erikson, K. (1994) *A New Species of Trouble: Explorations in Disaster, Trauma and Community*. New York: W.W. Norton.

Fagan, B. (2004) *The Long Summer: How Climate Changed Civilization*. London: Granta.

Fejo, W. (1994) 'Welcome Address' in D. Bird Rose (ed.) *Country in Flames: Proceedings of the 1994 Symposium on Biodiversity and Fire in North Australia*. Canberra: Department of the Environment, Sport and Territories and Australian National University. Available at: www.environment.gov.au/biodiversity/publications/series/paper3/index.html (accessed 20/10/2006).

Fernández-Galiano, L. (2000) *Fire and Memory: On Architecture and Energy*. Cambridge, MA: MIT Press.

Flannery, T. (2005) *The Weather Makers: The History and Future Impact of Climate Change*. London: Allen Lane.

Fogarty, D. (2008) 'Kiribati Creates World's Largest Marine Reserve', *Reuters UK*, 14 February. Available at: http://uk.reuters.com/article/idUKSP23110320080214 (accessed 06/01/2010).

Foucault, M. (1987) 'Maurice Blanchot: The Thought from Outside', in M. Blanchot and M. Foucault *Foucault/Blanchot*. New York: Zone.

Foucault, M. (1991 [1975]) *Discipline and Punish: The Birth of the Prison*. London: Penguin.

Frank, A. (2004) *The Renewal of Generosity: Illness, Medicine, and How to Live*. Chicago: The University of Chicago Press.

Franklin, A. (2006) 'Burning Cities: A Posthumanist Account of Australians and Eucalypts', *Environment and Planning D: Society and Space* 24 (4): 555–76.

Frodeman, R. (2000) 'Preface: Shifting Plates: The New Earth Sciences', in R. Frodeman (ed.) *Earth Matters: The Earth Sciences, Philosophy, and the Claims of Community*. Upper Saddle River, NJ: Prentice-Hall.

Frodeman, R. (2003) *Geo-Logic: Breaking Ground between Philosophy and the Earth Science*. Albany, NY: State University of New York Press.

Frow, J. (2001) 'A Pebble, A Camera, A Man', *Critical Inquiry* 28: 270–85.

Funtowicz, S. and Ravetz, J. R. (1994) 'Emergent Complex Systems', *Futures* 26 (6): 568–82.

Gatens, M. and Lloyd, G. (1999) *Collective Imaginings: Spinoza, Past and Present*. London: Routledge.

Gelbspan, R. (2006) 'Scepticism, Disinformation and Obstruction in U.S. Climate Circles', *Tipping Point Conference*, Environmental Change Institute, Oxford University, September 2006. Available at: www.capefarewell.com/climate-science/comment-opinion/scepticism.html (accessed 20/06/2010).

Ghodse, H. and Galea, S. (2006) 'Tsunami: Understanding Mental Health Consequences and the Unprecedented Response', *International Review of Psychiatry* 18 (3): 289–97.

Gibson, T. (2006) 'New Orleans and the Wisdom of Lived Space', *Space and Culture* 9 (1): 45–7.

Giddens, A. (1990) *The Consequences of Modernity*. Cambridge: Polity Press.

Giddens, A. (1999) *Runaway World*. London: Profile Books.

Giddens, A. (2009) *The Politics of Climate Change*. Cambridge: Polity Press.

Gilmore, M. (1934) *Old Days: Old Ways, A Book of Recollections*. Sydney: Angus and Robertson.

Glassman, J. (2005) 'Tsunamis and Other Forces of Destruction', *Environment and Planning D: Society and Space* 23: 164–70.

Goenjian, A., Steinberg, A., Najarian, L., Fairbanks, L., Tashjian, M. and Pynoos, R. (2000) 'Prospective Study of Posttraumatic Stress, Anxiety and Depressive Reactions after Earthquake and Political Violence', *American Journal of Psychiatry* 157 (6): 911–16.

Goodchild, P. (1996) *Deleuze and Guattari: An Introduction to the Politics of Desire*. London: Sage.

Goudsblom, J. (1992) *Fire and Civilization*. London: Allen Lane, the Penguin Press.

Grant, I. H. (2000) 'Kant after Geophilosophy: The Physics of Analogy and the Metaphysics of Nature', in A. Rehberg and R. Jones (eds) *The Matter of Critique: Readings in Kant's Philosophy*. Manchester: Clinamen Press.

Grant, I. H. (2006) *Philosophies of Nature after Schelling*. London: Continuum.

Grant, I. H. (2007) 'Speculative Realism', *Collapse* III: 334–45, 360–1.

Grant, I. H. (2010) 'Introduction to Schelling's *On the World Soul*', *Collapse* VI: 58–65.

Griffiths, T. (2001) *Forests of Ash: An Environmental History*. Cambridge: Cambridge University Press.

Grosz, E. (1998) 'The Time of Violence: Deconstruction and Value', *Cultural Values* 2 (2–3): 190–205.

Grosz, E. (2004) *The Nick of Time: Politics, Evolution, and the Untimely*. Durham and London: Duke University Press.

Grosz, E. (2005) *Time Travels: Feminism, Nature, Power*. Durham and London: Duke University Press.

Gualandi, A. (2009) 'Errancies of the Human: French Philosophies of Nature and the Overturning of the Copernican Revolution', *Collapse* V: 501–48.

Guggenheim, D. (dir.) (2006) *An Inconvenient Truth*. Paramount Classics.

Guyer, P. (2005) *Kant's System of Nature and Freedom: Selected Essays*. Oxford: Clarendon Press.

Habermas, J. (1983) 'Modernity – An Incomplete Project', in H. Foster (ed.) *The Anti-Aesthetic: Essays on Postmodern Culture*: London: Pluto Press.

Habermas, J. (1987) *The Philosophical Discourse of Modernity*. Cambridge: Polity Press.

Hallam, S. (1979) *Fire and Hearth: A Study of Aboriginal Usage and European Usurpation in South-Western Australia*. Canberra: Australian Institute of Aboriginal Studies.

Hallward, P. (2003) *Badiou: A Subject to Truth*. Minneapolis, MN: University of Minnesota Press.

Hallward, P. (2010) 'Securing Disaster in Haiti', *MRZine*, 20 January. Available at: http://mrzine.monthlyreview.org/2010/hallward240110.html (accessed 21/01/2010).

Hamacher, W. (1999) *Premises: Essays on Philosophy and Literature from Kant to Celan*. Stanford, CA: Stanford University Press.

Hansen, J., Sato, M., Kharecha, P., Beerling, D., Berner, R., Masson-Delmotte, V., Pagani, M., Raymo, M., Royer, D.L. and Zachos, J. C. (2008) 'Target Atmospheric CO2: Where Should Humanity Aim?', *The Open Atmospheric Science Journal* 2: 217–31.

Hardt, M. and Negri, A. (2001) *Empire*. Cambridge, MA: Harvard University Press.

Harman, G. (2002) *Tool-Being: Heidegger and the Metaphysics of Objects*. Chicago and La Salle, IL: Open Court.

Harman, G. (2005) *Guerrilla Metaphysics: Phenomenology and the Carpentry of Things*. Chicago and La Salle', IL: Open Court.

Harman, G. (2007) 'Speculative Realism', *Collapse* III: 367–88.

Harman, G. (2009) *Prince of Networks: Bruno Latour and Metaphysics*. Melbourne: re.press.

Harman, G. (2010) 'Asymmetrical Causation: Influence without Recompense', *Parallax* 16 (1): 96–109.

Harrison, P. (2008) 'Corporeal Remains: Vulnerability, Proximity, and Living on after the End of the World', *Environment and Planning A* 40 (2): 423–45.

Hayles, N. K. (1999) *How We Became Posthuman: Virtual Bodies in Cybernetics, Literature, and Informatics*. Chicago: University of Chicago Press.

Heidegger, M. (1976) 'Interview with Rudolf Augstein and Georg Wolff, 23 September 1966', *Der Spiegel*, 31 May. Available at: http://lacan.com/heidespie.html (accessed 25/10/2009).

Hewitt, K. (1998) 'Excluded Perspectives in the Social Construction of Disaster', in E. L. Quarantelli (ed.) *What is a Disaster? Perspectives on the Question.* London: Routledge.

Himanka, J. (2005) 'Husserl's Argumentation for the Pre-Copernican View of the Earth', *Review of Metaphysics* 58: 621–44.

Hinchliffe, S. (2003) '"Inhabiting" – Landscapes and Natures', in K. Anderson, M. Domosh, S. Pile and N. Thrift (eds) *Handbook of Cultural Geography.* London: Sage.

Hinchliffe, S. and Bingham, N. (2008a) 'Securing Life: the Emergent Practices of Biosecurity', *Environment and Planning A* 40: 1534–51.

Hinchliffe, S. and Bingham, N. (2008b) 'People, Animals, and Biosecurity in and through Cities', in S. H. Ali and R. Keil (eds) *Networked Disease: Emerging Infections in the Global City.* Chichester, West Sussex: Wiley-Blackwell.

The Hindu (2005) 'Tourists Making Huge Donations to Relief Fund', *The Hindu Online*, 5 January. Available at: www.hindu.com/2005/01/05/stories/ 2005010516340300.htm (accessed 12/01/2005).

Hird, M. J. (2009) *The Origins of Sociable Life: Evolution after Science Studies.* New York: Palgrave Macmillan.

Hurlbert, J., Beggs, J. and Haines, V. (2006) 'Bridges Over Troubled Waters: What are the Optimal Networks for Katrina's Victims?', in *Understanding Katrina: Perspectives from the Social Sciences.* Available at: http://understandingkatrina.ssrc. org/Hurlbert_Beggs_Haines/ (accessed 23/01/2010).

Ingersoll, R. (2004) 'The Death of the City and the Survival of Urban Life.' Paper presented at Urban Traumas: The City and Disasters Conference, Center of Contemporary Culture of Barcelona, 7–11 July. Available at: www.cccb.org/rcs_ gene/death_city.pdf. (accessed 06/12/2009).

Jeganathan, P. (2005) 'South Paw: Philanthropy After the Tsunami', *Lines Magazine*, 5 February. Available at: www.lines-magazine.org/Art_Feb05/Pradeep.htm (accessed 01/08/2006).

Johnson, C. (1993) *System and Writing in the Philosophy of Jacques Derrida.* Cambridge, NY: Cambridge University Press.

Jones, R. (1969) 'Fire-stick Farming', *Australian Natural History* 16 (7): 224–8.

Jones, T. (2005) 'A Man-made Tsunami', *Guardian Unlimited*, 11 January. Available at: www.guardian.co.uk/comment/story/0,3604,1387399,00.html (accessed 12/01/2005).

Kaika, M. (2005) *City of Flows: Modernity, Nature and the City.* New York: Routledge.

Kant, I. (1967 [1788]) *Critique of Practical Reason.* London: Longman.

Kant, I. (1981 [1755]) *Universal Natural History and Theory of the Heavens.* Edinburgh: Scottish Academic Press.

Kant, I. (1993 [1938]) *Opus Postumum.* Cambridge: Cambridge University Press.

Kant, I. (1994 [1756]) 'History and Physiography of the Most Remarkable Cases of the Earthquake which Towards the End of the Year 1755 Shook a Great Part of the Earth' in *Four Neglected Essays.* Hong Kong: Philopschy Press.

Kant, I. (1996 [1795]) 'Toward Perpetual Peace', in M. J. Gregor (ed.) *The Cambridge Edition of the Works of Immanuel Kant: Practical Philosophy.* Cambridge: Cambridge University Press.

Kant, I. (2005 [1790]) *Critique of Judgement.* Mineola, NY: Dover Publications.

Kartik (2005) 'Update from AID Chennai-6', The South-East Asia Earthquake and Tsunami Blog. Available at: http://tsunamihelp.blogspot.com/2004_12_26_ archive.html# 110459850000796791 (accessed 20/11/2009).

Kirby, V. (1997) *Telling Flesh: The Substance of the Corporeal*. London: Routledge.

Kirby, V. (2001) 'Quantum Anthropologies', in L. Simmons, L. and H. Worth (eds) *Derrida Downunder*. Palmerston North: Dunmore Press.

Klein, N. (2008) *The Shock Doctrine: The Rise of Disaster Capitalism*. London: Penguin.

Knabb, R., Rhome, J. and Brown, D. (2005; updated 2006) 'Tropical Cyclone Report: Hurricane Katrina: 23–30 August 2005', National Hurricane Center. Available at: www.nhc.noaa.gov/pdf/TCR-AL122005_Katrina.pdf (accessed 23/01/2010).

Kohen, J. L. (1995) *Aboriginal Environmental Impacts*. Sydney: University of New South Wales Press.

Korf, B. (2005) 'Sri Lanka: The Tsunami After the Tsunami', *International Development Planning Review* 27 (3): i–vii.

Kozak, J. and James, C. (1998) 'Historical Depictions of the 1755 Lisbon Earthquake', National Information Service for Earthquake Engineering. Available at: http://nisee.berkeley.edu/lisbon/ (accessed 06/12/2009).

Kull, C. (2002) 'Madagascar Aflame: Landscape Burning as Peasant Protest, Resistance, or a Resource Management Tool?', *Political Geography* 21: 927–53.

Kwatra, A. (2005) 'The Tsunami: One Year On – "We Don't Want to Cry Anymore", *Christian Aid News* 30 (winter): 8–11.

Land, N. (1992) *The Thirst for Annihilation: Georges Bataille and Virulent Nihilism*. London: Routledge.

Langton, M. (1998) *Burning Questions: Emerging Environmental Issues for Indigenous Peoples in Northern Australia*. Darwin: Centre for Indigenous Natural and Cultural Resource Management, Northern Territory University.

Langton, M. (1999) '"The Fire that is the Centre of Each Family": Landscapes of the Ancients', in A. Hamblin (ed.) *Visions of Future Landscapes*. Canberra: Proceedings of the Australian Academy of Science. Fenner Conference on the Environment 2.5.

Laris, P. and Wardell, D. (2006) 'Good, Bad or "Necessary Evil?" Reinterpreting the Colonial Burning Experiments in the Savanna Landscapes of West Africa', *The Geographical Journal* 172 (4): 271–90.

Latour, B. (1988) *The Pasteurization of France*. Cambridge, MA: Harvard University Press.

Latour, B. (1993) *We Have Never Been Modern*. Cambridge, MA: Harvard University Press.

Latour, B. (1998) 'To Modernise or Ecologise? That is the Question', in B. Braun and N. Castree (eds) *Remaking Reality: Nature at the Millenium*. London and New York: Routledge.

Latour, B. (1999a) 'On Recalling ANT', in J. Law and J. Hassard (eds) *Actor Network Theory and After*. Oxford: Blackwell.

Latour, B. (1999b) *Pandora's Hope: Essays on the Reality of Science Studies*. Cambridge, MA: Harvard University Press.

Latour, B. (2003) 'Atmosphère, Atmosphère', in S. May (ed.) *Olafur Eliasson: The Weather Project*. London: Tate Publishing.

Latour, B. (2004a) 'Whose Cosmos, Which Cosmopolitics', *Common Knowledge* 10 (3): 450–62.

Latour, B. (2004b) *Politics of Nature*. Cambridge, MA: Harvard University Press.

Latour, B. (2005) 'From Realpolitik to Dingpolitik or How to Make Things Public', in B. Latour and P. Weibel (eds) *Making Things Public: Atmospheres of Democracy*. Karlsruhe and Cambridge, MA: ZKM Centre for Art and Media and MIT Press.

Latour, B. (2007) 'A Plea for Earthly Sciences', Annual Meeting of the British Sociological Association, London, April. Available at: www.bruno-latour.fr/articles/index.html (accessed 20/09/2009).

Latour, B. (2008) '"It's Development, Stupid !" or How to Modernize Modernization.' Available at: www.bruno-latour.fr/articles/article/107-NORDHAUS&SHELLENBERGER.pdf (accessed 20/09/2009).

Law, J. (1999) 'After ANT: Complexity, Naming and Topology', in J. Law and J. Hassard (eds) *Actor Network Theory and After*. Oxford: Blackwell.

Law, J. (2004) *After Method: Mess in Social Science Research*. London and New York: Routledge.

Law, J. and Hetherington, K. (1999) 'Materialities, Spatialities, Globalities' (draft), Department of Sociology, Lancaster University. Available at: www.comp.lancaster.ac.uk/sociology/soc029jl.html (accessed 15/05/2004).

Lefebvre, H. (1995 [1962]) *Introduction to Modernity*. London: Verso.

Lenton, T. M., Held, H., Kriegler, E., Hall, J. W., Lucht, W., Rahmstorf, S. and Schellnhuber, H. J. (2008) 'Tipping Elements in the Earth's Climate System', *Proceedings of the National Academy of Sciences USA* 105 (6): 1786–93.

Lester, B. (2006) 'Australia's Drought May Stay for Keeps', *Cosmos Online*. Available at: www.cosmosmagazine.com/node/927 (accessed 21/05/2008).

Levinas, E. (1969) *Totality and Infinity*. Pittsburgh, PA: Duquesne University Press.

Levinas, E. (1987) *Time and the Other*. Pittsburgh, PA: Duquesne University Press.

Levinas, E. (1989) *The Levinas Reader* (S. Hand (ed.)). Oxford: Blackwell.

Levinas, E. (1998a [1974]) *Otherwise Than Being or Beyond Essence*. London: Kluwer Academic Publishing.

Levinas, E. (1998b) *Entre Nous*. London: Continuum.

Levinas, E. (2001 [1978]) *Existence and Existents*. Pittsburgh, PA: Duquesne University Press.

Lingis, A. (1994) *The Community of Those Who Have Nothing in Common*. Bloomington and Indianapolis, IN: Indiana University Press.

Lingis, A. (1998a) 'Translator's Introduction', in E. Levinas, *Otherwise Than Being Or Beyond Essence*. London: Kluwer Academic Publishing.

Lingis, A. (1998b) *The Imperative*. Bloomington and Indianapolis, IN: Indiana University Press.

Lingis, A. (2000a) 'Ecological Emotions', in R. Frodeman (ed.) *Earth Matters: The Earth Sciences, Philosophy, and the Claims of Community*. Upper Saddle River, NJ: Prentice-Hall.

Lingis, A. (2000b) *Dangerous Emotions*. Berkeley, CA: University of California Press.

Lingis, A. (2001) 'Translator's Introduction', in Levinas, E., *Existence and Existents*, Pittsburgh: Duquesne University Press.

Lohmann, L. (2005) 'Marketing and Making Carbon Dumps: Commodification, Calculation and Counterfactuals in Climate Change Mitigation', *Science as Culture* 14 (3): 203–35.

Lorimer, H. (2005) 'Cultural Geography: The Busyness of Being "More-Than-Representational"', *Progress in Human Geography* 29 (1): 83–94.

Lovelock, J. (1987) *Gaia: A New Look at Life on Earth*. Oxford: Oxford University Press.

Lovelock, J. (2006) *The Revenge of Gaia*. London: Penguin.

Lynas, M. (2008) *Six Degrees: Our Future on a Hotter Planet*. London: Harper Perennial.

Lyotard, J.-F. (1988) *The Differend: Phrases in Dispute*. Manchester: Manchester University Press.

Lyotard, J.-F. (1991) *The Inhuman*. Cambridge: Polity Press.

Macdougall, D. (2004) *Frozen Earth: The Once and Future Story of Ice Ages*. Berkeley, CA: University of California Press.

McGuire, B. (2005) *Surviving Armageddon: Solutions for a Threatened Planet*. Oxford: Oxford University Press.

McGuire, B. (2006) 'Earth, Fire and Fury', *New Scientist*, 27 May, 190 (2553): 32–6.

Mackay, R. (2010) 'Editorial Introduction: Geo/Philosophy', *Collapse* VI: 3–19.

McKee, M. (2005) 'Power of Tsunami Earthquake Heavily Underestimated', New Scientist, 9 February. Available at: www.newscientist.com/article/dn6991 (accessed 20/11/2009).

Mackenzie, A. and Murphie, A. (2008) 'The Two Cultures Become Multiple? Sciences, Humanities and Everyday Experimentation', *Australian Feminist Studies* 23 (55): 87–100.

McLaughlin, C. (2005) 'Blair Must Match Words with Action', *The Big Issue*, 17–23 January, 625: 22.

McPhee, J. (1980) *Basin and Range*. New York: Farrar-Strauss Giroux.

Main, G. (2004) 'Red Steers and White Death: Fearing Nature in Rural Australia', *Australian Humanities Review* 33, August–October. Available at: www.lib.latrobe. edu.au/AHR/archive/Issue-August-2004/main.html (accessed 20/06/2008).

Margulis, L. (1998) *The Symbiotic Planet: A New Look at Evolution*. London: Phoenix.

Margulis, L. (2001) 'Bacteria in the Origins of Species', in W. J. Kress and G. W. Barrett (eds) *A New Century of Biology*. Washington, DC: Smithsonian Institution.

Margulis, L. and Sagan, D. (1995) *What is Life?* New York: Simon & Schuster.

Marks, K. (2008) 'Paradise Lost: Climate Change Forces South Sea Islanders to Seek Sanctuary Abroad', *Independent*, 6 June. Available at: www.independent.co.uk/news/world/australasia/paradise-lost-climate-change-forces-south-sea-islanders-to-seek-sanctuary-abroad-841409.html (accessed 06/01/2010).

Massey, D. (2004) 'Geographies of Responsibility', *Geografiska Annaler Series B: Human Geography* 86B (1): 5–18.

Massey, D. (2005a) 'Negotiating Nonhuman/Human Place', *Antipode* 37 (2): 353–7.

Massey, D. (2005b) *For Space*. London: Sage.

Massey, D. (2006) 'Landscape as a Provocation: Reflections on Moving Mountains', *Journal of Material Culture* 11(1/2): 33–48.

Mauss, M. (1990 [1950]) *The Gift*. London: Routledge.

Meillassoux, Q. (2008) *After Finitude: An Essay on the Necessity of Contingency*. London: Continuum.

Menard, H.W. (1986) *The Ocean of Truth: A Personal History of Global Tectonics*. Princeton, NJ : Princeton University Press.

Meyer, A. (2000) *Contraction and Convergence: The Global Solution to Climate Change*. Devon: Green Books.

Molotch, H. (2006) 'Death on the Roof: Race and Bureaucratic Failure', in *Understanding Katrina: Perspectives from the Social Sciences*. Available at: http://understandingkatrina.ssrc.org/Molotch/ (accessed 23/10/2001).

Monod, J. (1971) *Chance and Necessity*. London: Collins Fontana.

Morgan, D. (2007) 'Kant, Cosmopolitics, Multiperspectival Thinking and Technology', *Angelaki* 12 (2): 35–46.

Morris, R. (2009) 'Tiny Tuvalu Makes Big Waves at Copenhagen', *Mother Jones*, 9 December. Available at: http://motherjones.com/blue-marble/2009/12/tiny-tuvalu-makes-big-waves-copenhagen (accessed 06/01/2010).

Nah, A. M. and Bunnell, T. (2005) 'Ripples of Hope: Acehnese Refugees in Post-Tsunami Malaysia', *Singapore Journal of Tropical Geography* 26 (2): 249–56.

Nancy, J.-L. (1991) *The Inoperative Community*. Minneapolis, MN: University of Minnesota Press.

Nancy, J.-L. (2000) *Being Singular Plural*. Stanford, CA: Stanford University Press.

Nancy, J.-L. (2007) *The Creation of the World or Globalization*. Albany, NY: State University of New York Press.

Nanthikesan, S. (2005) 'Post-Tsunami Posturing', *Lines Magazine*, 5 February. Available at: www.lines-magazine.org/Art_Feb05/Editorial_Nanthi.htm (accessed 01/08/2006).

New Economics Foundation (NEF) (2009) 'The NEF/Ecologist Essay Competition: What Price Carbon?', Ruth Pots (email), NEF, 27April.

Neiman, S. (2002) *Evil in Modern Thought: An Alternative History of Philosophy*. Princeton, NJ: Princeton University Press.

Nietzsche, F. (1969 [1883]) *Thus Spake Zarathustra*. Harmondsworth: Penguin.

Nietzsche, F. (1994 [1878]) *Human, all too Human*. London. Penguin.

Nikapota, A. (2006) 'After the Tsunami: A Story from Sri Lanka', *International Review of Psychiatry* 18(3): 275–9.

NZ Herald (2008) 'Doomed Kiribati Needs Escape Plan', *NZ Herald.Co.NZ*, 6 June. Available at: www.nzherald.co.nz/population/news/article.cfm?c_id=608&objectid=10514735&pnum=1 (accessed 06/01/2010).

The Observer (2005) 'Tattenham Corner: Bailey's Tsunami Tonic', Sports Section, 16 January: 11.

Ogletree, C. J. (2006) 'Introduction', in D. D. Troutt (ed.) *After the Storm: Black Intellectuals Explore the Meaning of Katrina*. New York: New Press.

Oliver-Smith, A. (2006) 'Disasters and Forced Migration in the 21st Century', in *Understanding Katrina: Perspectives from the Social Science*. Available at: http://understandingkatrina.ssrc.org/Oliver-Smith/ (accessed 23/10/2001).

Olkowski, D. (2009) 'Political Science and the Culture of Distinction', in B. Herzogenrath (ed.) *Deleuze/Guattari and Ecology*. Houndmills, Basingstoke: Palgrave Macmillan.

Pearce, F. (2006) *The Last Generation: How Nature will Take her Revenge for Climate Change*. London: Eden Project Books.

Pefanis, J. (1991) *Heterology and the Postmodern: Bataille, Baudrillard, and Lyotard*. Durham, NC: Duke University Press.

Pels, D., Hetherington, K. and Vandenberghe, F. (2002) 'The Status of the Object: Performances, Mediations and Techniques', *Theory, Culture and Society* 19 (5–6): 1–21.

Philip, K. and Zacharias, U. (2005) 'Perfect Knowledge, Imperfect Communication', *Asia Times Online*, 2 February. Available at: www.atimes.com/atimes/South_Asia/GB02Df06.html (accessed 01/08/2006).

Philo, C. (2005) 'The Geographies that Wound', *Population, Space and Place* 11: 441–54.

Pickering, A. (2001) 'In the Thick of Things', Taking Nature Seriously, University of Oregon, 25–7 February. Available at: www.soc.uiuc.edu/CVPubs/pickerin/itt.pdf (accessed 14/01/2004).

Pilger, J. (2005) 'The Other, Man-made Tsunami', *ZNet Commentary*, 7 January. Available at: www.zmag.org/Sustainers/Content/2005–01/07pilger.cfm (accessed 12/01/2005).

Price, C. A. (2006) 'Historicizing Katrina', in D. D. Troutt (ed.) *After the Storm: Black Intellectuals Explore the Meaning of Hurricane Katrina*. New York: New Press.

Prigogine, I. and Stengers, I. (1984) *Order out of Chaos: Man's New Dialogue with Nature*. New York: Bantam Books.

Protevi, J. (2001) *Political Physics*. London: Athlone Press.

Protevi, J. (2009) 'Katrina', in B. Herzogenrath (ed.) *Deleuze/Guattari and Ecology*, Houndmills, Basingstoke: Palgrave Macmillan.

Purdue University (2006) 'North Pole's Ancient Past Holds Clues about Future Global Warming', *Physorg.com*, 31 May. Available at: www.physorg.com/news68305951.html (accessed 02/2009).

Pyne, S. (1982) *Fire in America: A Cultural History of Wildland and Rural Fire*. Princeton, NJ: Princeton University Press.

Pyne, S. (1988) *The Ice: A Journey to Antarctica*. New York: Ballantine Books.

Pyne, S. (1991) *Burning Bush: A Fire History of Australia*. New York: Henry Holt.

Pyne, S. (1997a) *World Fire: The Culture of Fire on Earth*. Seattle and London: University of Washington Press.

Pyne, S. (1997b) *Vestal Fire*. Seattle and London: University of Washington Press.

Pyne, S. (1997c) 'Frontiers of Fire', in T. Griffiths and L. Robin (eds) *Ecology and Empire: Environmental History of Settler Societies*. Carlton South, VIC: Melbourne University Press.

Pyne, S. (1998) *Burning Bush: A Fire History of Australia*. New York: Henry Holt.

Pyne, S. (2001) *Fire: A Brief History*. Seattle and London: University of Washington Press.

Pyne, S. (2004) *Tending Fire: Coping with America's Wildland Fires*. Washington, DC: Island Press.

Rabinow, P. (1994) 'Introduction', in F. Delaporte (ed.) *A Vital Rationalist: Selected writings from Georges Canguilhem*. New York: Zone.

Rabinow, P. (2008) 'Episodes or Incidents: Seeking Significance', in A. Lakoff and S. Collier (eds) *Biosecurity Interventions: Global Health and Security in Question*. New York: Columbia University Press.

Raffles, H. (2002) *In Amazonia: A Natural History*. Princeton, NJ: Princeton University Press.

Råholm, M.-B., Arman, M. and Rehnsfeldt, A. (2008) 'The Immediate Lived Experience of the 2004 Tsunami Disaster by Swedish Tourists', *Journal of Advanced Nursing* 63 (6): 597–606.

Ray, G. (2004) 'Reading the Lisbon Earthquake: Adorno, Lyotard, and the Contemporary Sublime', *Yale Journal of Criticism* 17 (1): 1–18.

Roach, J. (2005) 'Global Warming Unstoppable for 100 Years, Study Says', *National Geographic News*, 17 March. Available at: http://news.nationalgeographic.com/news/2005/03/0317_050317_warming.html (accessed 07/01/2010).

Roberts, J. T. and Parks, B. C. (2007) *A Climate of Injustice: Global Inequality, North–South Politics, and Climate Policy*. Cambridge, MA: MIT Press.

Rozner, J. (2009) 'The Genesis and the History of the "Cretto" by Alberto Burri.' Available at: www.gibellina.siciliana.it/pages/cretto.html (accessed 05/12/2009).

Rudwick, M. (2005) *Bursting the Limits of Time: The Reconstruction of Geohistory in the Age of Revolution*. Chicago: University of Chicago Press.

Russell-Brown, K. (2006) 'While Visions of Deviance Danced in Their Heads', in D. D. Troutt (ed.) *After the Storm: Black Intellectuals Explore the Meaning of Katrina*. New York: New Press.

Russell-Smith, J., Lucas, D., Gapindi, M., Gunbunuka, B., Kaparigi, N., Namingum, G., Giuliani, P. and Chaloupka, G. (1997) 'Aboriginal Resource Utilization and Fire Management Practice in Western Arnhem Land, Monsoonal Northern Australia: Notes for Prehistory, Lessons for the Future', *Human Ecology* 25 (2): 159–95.

Sachs, W. (1999) *Planet Dialectics: Explorations in Environment and Development.* London: Zed Books.

Sagan, D. and Schneider, E. (2007) 'The Pleasure of Change', in Margulis, L. and Sagan, D. (eds) *Dazzle Gradually: Reflections on the Nature of Nature.* White River Junction, VT: Chelsea Green Publishing.

Sauer, C. O. (1963) *Land and Life.* Berkeley, CA: University of California Press.

Scheffer, M., Carpenter, S., Foley, J. A., Folkes, C. and Walker, B. (2001) 'Catastrophic Shifts in Ecosystems', *Nature* 413 (11 October): 591–6.

Scheffer, M., Bascompte, J., Brock, W., Brovkin, V., Carpenter, S., Dakos, V., Held, H., van Nes, E., Rietkerk, M. and Sugihara, G. (2009) 'Early-warning Signals for Critical Transitions', *Nature* 461 (3 September): 53–9.

Schneider, S. and Boston, P. (1991) *Scientists on Gaia.* Cambridge, MA: MIT Press.

Serres, M. (1995) *The Natural Contract.* Ann Arbor, MI: University of Michigan Press.

Serres, M. (2001) *The Birth of Physics.* Manchester: Clinamen Press.

Shapiro, M. (1999) 'The Ethics of Encounter: Unreading, Unmapping the Imperium', in D. Campbell and M. Shapiro (eds) *Moral Spaces: Rethinking Ethics and World Politics.* Minneapolis, MN: University of Minnesota Press.

Sharma, D. (2005) 'Tsunami, Mangroves and Market Economy', *India Together,* 11 January. Available at: www.indiatogether.org/2005/jan/dsh-tsunami.htm (accessed 01/08/2006).

Sharp, N. (2002) *Saltwater People: The Waves of Memory.* Toronto: University of Toronto Press.

Sheppard, K. (2009) 'The 0.5 Degree Question', *Mother Jones,* 17 December. Available at: motherjones.com/blue-marble/2009/12/whats-05-degrees-between-friends (accessed 07/01/2010).

Simms, A. (2005) *Ecological Debt: The Health of the Planet and the Wealth of Nations.* London: Pluto Press.

Smart, B. (1999) *Facing Modernity: Ambivalence, Reflexivity and Morality.* London: Sage.

Smil, V. (2003) *The Earth's Biosphere: Evolution, Dynamics, and Change.* Cambridge, MA: MIT Press.

Smith, B. (1989) *European Vision in the South Pacific.* Melbourne: Oxford University Press.

Smith, N. (1984) *Uneven Development: Nature, Capital and the Production of Space.* Oxford: Basil Blackwell.

Smith, N. (2005) 'There's No Such Thing as a Natural Disaster', *Understanding Katrina: Perspectives from the Social Sciences.* Available at: http://understandingkatrina. ssrc.org/Smith/ (accessed 01/08/2006).

Solnit, R. (2005a) 'Sontag and Tsunami', Available at: www.commondreams.org/views05/0103-21.htm (accessed 25/04/2005).

Solnit, R. (2005b) 'The Uses of Disaster: Notes on Bad Weather and Good Government', *Harper's Magazine,* October. Available at: www.harpers.org/archive/2005/10/0080774 (accessed 23/01/2010).

Spivak, G. C. (1994) 'Responsibility', *Boundary* 2. 21 (3): 19–64.

Spivak, G. C. (1995) 'Acting Bits/Identity Talk', in K. Appiah and H. L. Gates, Jr (eds) *Identities*. Chicago: University of Chicago Press.

Spivak, G. C. (1999) *A Critique of Postcolonial Reason: Toward a History of the Vanishing Present*. Cambridge, MA: Harvard University Press.

Stengers, I. (1997) *Power and Invention: Situating Science*. Minneapolis, MN: University of Minnesota Press.

Stengers, I. (2000) *The Invention of Modern Science*. Minneapolis: University of Minnesota Press.

Stephenson, W. D. and Bonabeau, E. (2007) 'Expecting the Unexpected: The Need for a Networked Terrorism and Disaster Response Strategy', *Homeland Security Affairs* 3 (1): 1–9. Available at: www.hsaj.org/?fullarticle=3.1.3 (accessed 23/01/2010).

Stern, N. (2006) *Stern Review on The Economics of Climate Change (pre-publication edition)*. HM Treasury, London. Available at: www.hm-treasury.gov.uk/sternreview_index.htm (accessed 10/01/2010).

Stoekl, A. (2007) *Bataille's Peak: Energy, Religion, and Postsustainability*. Minneapolis, MN: University of Minnesota Press.

Sullivan, B. (2006) 'Impact of Katrina Exodus Felt Far and Wide', *MSNBC.com*, 8 August. Available at: www.msnbc.msn.com/id/14542913/#storyContinued (accessed 23/01/2010).

Sutton, J. (2007) 'U.S. Readying Guantanamo Base for Migrant Influx', *Reuters*, 24 October. Available at: www.reuters.com/article/idUSN2414080320071024 (accessed 27/02/2010).

Swyngedouw, E. (2007) 'Impossible "Sustainability" and the Post-Political Condition', in R. Krueger and D. Gibbs (eds) *The Sustainable Development Paradox*, pp. 13–40. New York: Guilford Press.

Tacconi, L. and Ruchiat, Y. (2006) 'Livelihoods, Fire and Policy in Eastern Indonesia', *Singapore Journal of Tropical Geography* 27 (1): 67–81.

Tarrant, B. (2005) 'A Tide of Generosity Swamps Tsunami Towns with Boats', *The Age Online*, 5 October. Available at: www.theage.com.au/news/world/a-tide-of-generosity-swamps-tsunami-towns-with-boats/2005/10/04/ 1128191716733. html (accessed 01/08/2006).

Thekaekara, M. (2005) 'Tsunami Business', *New Internationalist*, October 863: 20–1.

Thomas, A. and Ramalingam, V. (2005) 'Response Effectiveness: Views of the Affected Population', *Forced Migration Review*, July: 46–7. Available at: www.fmreview.org/FMRpdfs/Tsunami/23.pdf (accessed 01/08/2006).

Thrift, N. (2008) *Non-Representational Theory: Space, Politics, Affect*. London and New York: Routledge.

Tidwell, M. (2006) *The Ravaging Tide: Strange Weather, Future Katrinas, and the Coming Death of America's Coastal Cities*. New York: Free Press.

Tol, R. (2003) 'Is the Uncertainty about Climate Change too Large for Expected Cost Benefit Analysis?', *Climatic Change* 56: 265–89.

Troutt, D. D. (2006) 'Many Thousands Gone Again', in D. D. Troutt (ed.) *After the Storm: Black Intellectuals Explore the Meaning of Katrina*. New York: New Press.

Turnbull, N. (2006) 'The Ontological Consequences of Copernicus: Global Being in the Planetary World', *Theory, Culture and Society* 23 (1): 125–39.

Turner, B. S. (2006) *Vulnerability and Human Rights*. University Park, PA: Pennsylvania State University Press.

Urry, J. (2003) *Global Complexity*. Cambridge: Polity Press.

Urry, J. (2005) 'The Complexity Turn', *Theory, Culture and Society* 22 (5): 1–14.

Vale, T. R. (2002) 'The Pre-European Landscape of the United States: Pristine or Humanized?', in T. R. Vale (ed.) *Fire, Native Peoples, and the Natural Landscape.* Washington, DC: Island Press.

Varma, A. (2005) 'India Uncut: The Tsunami Posts.' Available at: http://indiauncut. blogspot.com/2005/01/despatches-21-marriage.html (accessed 01/08/2006).

Vaughan, G. (2002) 'Mothering, Co-muni-cation, and the Gifts of Language', in E. Wyschogrod, J.-J. Goux and E. Boynton (eds) *The Enigma of Gift and Sacrifice.* New York: Fordham University Press.

Vernadsky, V. (1998 [1926]) *The Biosphere.* New York: Copernicus.

Verran, H. (2002) 'A Postcolonial Moment in Science Studies: Alternative Firing Regimes of Environmental Scientists and Aboriginal Landowners', *Social Studies of Science* 32 (5–6): 729–62.

Victor, D. and House, J. (2004) 'A New Currency: Climate Change and Carbon Credits', *Harvard International Review* (summer): 56–9. Available at: http://fsi. stanford.edu/publications/a_new_currency_climate_change_and_carbon_credits/ (accessed 10/01/2010).

Vidal, J. (2006) 'Australia Suffers Worst Drought in 1,000 Years', *The Guardian,* 8 November. Available at: www.guardian.co.uk/world/2006/nov/08/australia.drought (accessed 21/05/2008).

Voltaire (1756) *A Poem on the Lisbon Disaster.* Available at: http://courses.essex. ac.uk/cs/cs101/VOLT/LISBON.HTM (accessed 06/12/2009).

Wachtendorf, T. and Kendra, J. M. (2006) 'Improvising Disaster in the City of Jazz: Organizational Response to Hurricane Katrina', *Understanding Katrina: Perspectives from the Social Sciences.* Available at: http://understandingkatrina.ssrc.org/ Wachtendorf_Kendra/ (accessed 23/01/2010).

Waldman, A. (2005) 'Torn from Moorings, Villagers Grasp for Past', *New York Times,* 6 March: 1, 14.

Waterfield, B. (2010) 'Haiti Earthquake: US Ships Blockade Coast to Thwart Exodus to America', *Global Research,* 21 January. Available at: www.globalresearch.ca/ index.php?context=va&aid=17116 (accessed 04/02/2010).

Weber, M. (1976 [1930]) *The Protestant Ethic and the Spirit of Capitalism.* London: George Allen & Unwin.

Westbroek, P. (1992) *Life as a Geological Force: Dynamics of the Earth.* New York: W. W. Norton.

Whatmore, S. (2002) *Hybrid Geographies: Natures, Cultures, Spaces.* London: Sage.

White, P. S. and Pickett, S. T. A. (1985) 'Natural Disturbance and Patch Dynamics: An Introduction', in S. T. A. Pickett and P. S. White (eds) *The Ecology of Natural Disturbance and Patch Dynamics.* Orlando, FL: Academic Press.

White, S. (2000) *Sustaining Affirmation: The Strengths of Weak Ontology in Political Theory.* Princeton, NJ: Princeton University Press.

Whitney, N. (2008) 'Kiribati Leader Cites Toll of Climate Change', *The Harvard Crimson,* 23 September. Available at: www.thecrimson.com/article.aspx?ref=524174 (accessed 06/01/2010).

Williams, J. (1997) 'Deleuze on J. M. W. Turner: Catastrophism in Philosophy', in K. Ansell Pearson (ed.) *Deleuze and Philosophy: The Difference Engineer.* London: Routledge.

Williams, R. (1980) *Problems in Materialism and Culture.* London: Verso.

Wilson, E. (1998) *Neural Geographies: Feminism and the Microstructure of Cognition.* New York: Routledge.

Wisner, B. (2005) 'Will Katrina Bring Winds of Change?', *AlertNet*, 8 September. Available at: www.alertnet.org/thefacts/reliefresources/112619216015.htm (accessed 23/01/2010).

Wood, D. (2004) *Five Billion Years of Global Change: A History of the Land*. New York: The Guilford Press.

Woods, R. (2005) 'Focus: Nature's Timebomb', *The Sunday Times*, 2 January. Available at: www.timesonline.co.uk/tol/news/world/article407697.ece (accessed 25/11/2009).

Wyschogrod, E. (1990) *Saints and Postmodernism: Revisioning Moral Philosophy*. Chicago: University of Chicago Press.

Wyschogrod, E. (1998) *An Ethics of Remembering: History, Heterology, and the Nameless Others*. Chicago: University of Chicago Press.

Yibarbuk, D. (1998) 'Notes on Traditional Use of Fire on Upper Cadell River', in M. Langton (ed.) *Burning Questions: Emerging Environmental Issues for Indigenous Peoples in Northern Australia*. Darwin: Centre for Indigenous Natural and Cultural Resource Management, Northern Territory University.

Yusoff, K. (2009) 'Excess, Catastrophe, and Climate Change', *Environment and Planning D: Society and Space* 27: 1010–29.

Zillman, J. (2005) 'Uncertainty in the Science of Climate Change', in J. Zillman, W. McKibben and A. Kellow (eds) *Climate Change: The Challenge for Policy*. Canberra: Academy of the Social Sciences in Australia.

Zimmerman, M. (1994) *Contesting Earth's Future: Radical Ecology and Postmodernity*. Berkeley, CA: University of California Press.

Žižek, S. (1997) *The Plague of Fantasies*. London: Verso.

Index